MUSLIM MARRIAGE IN WESTERN COURTS

Cultural Diversity and Law

Series Editor:
Prakash Shah, School of Law, Queen Mary University of London, UK

Around the world, most states are faced with difficult issues arising out of cultural diversity in their territories. Within the legal field, such issues span across matters of private law through to public and constitutional law. At international level too there is now considerable jurisprudence regarding ethnic, religious and cultural diversity. In addition, there are several layers of legal control – from communal and religious regulation to state and international regulation. This multiplicity of norm setting has been variously termed legal pluralism, inter-legality or inter-normativity and provides a fascinating lens for academic analysis that links up to cultural diversity in new and interesting ways. The umbrella of cultural diversity encompasses various population groups throughout the world ranging from national, ethnic, religious or indigenous groupings. This series particularly welcomes work that is of comparative interest, concerning various state jurisdictions as well as different population groups.

Also in the Series

Muslim Marriage in Western Courts

Lost in Transplantation

PASCALE FOURNIER
University of Ottawa, Canada

ASHGATE

Published by
Ashgate Publishing Limited
Wey Court East
Union Road
Farnham
Surrey, GU9 7PT
England

www.ashgate.com

Ashgate Publishing Company
Suite 420
101 Cherry Street
Burlington
VT 05401-4405
USA

British Library Cataloguing in Publication Data
Fournier, Pascale.
  Muslim marriage in Western courts : lost in
  transplantation. -- (Cultural diversity and law)
  1. Dowry (Islamic law)--Canada--Interpretation and
  construction. 2. Dowry (Islamic law)--United States--
  Interpretation and construction. 3. Dowry (Islamic law)--
  France--Interpretation and construction. 4. Dowry (Islamic
  law)--Germany--Interpretation and construction.
  5. Liberalism--Cross-cultural studies. 6. Muslim women--
  Legal status, laws, etc.
  I. Title II. Series
  346.1'67016-dc22

Library of Congress Cataloging-in-Publication Data
Fournier, Pascale.
  Muslim marriage in Western courts : lost in transplantation / by Pascale Fournier.
      p. cm. -- (Cultural diversity and law)
  Includes bibliographical references and index.
  ISBN 978-1-4094-0441-5 (hardback) -- ISBN 978-1-4094-0442-2 (ebook)
  1. Dowry (Islamic law) 2. Marriage (Islamic law) 3. Conflict of laws--Marriage. I. Title.
  KBP543.953.F68 2010
  392.5088'297--dc22

                                                                            2010016246

ISBN 9781409404415 (hbk)
ISBN 9781409404422 (ebk)

Reprinted 2010

Mixed Sources
Product group from well-managed
forests and other controlled sources
www.fsc.org Cert no. SA-COC-1565
© 1996 Forest Stewardship Council

Printed and bound in Great Britain by
MPG Books Group, UK

Contents

List of Abbreviations

CLS	critical legal studies
LLPA	liberal–legal pluralist approach
LFEA	liberal–formal equality approach
LSEA	liberal–substantive equality approach

List of Cases

Canada

France

Germany

United States

Foreword

This book takes up one of the most perplexing questions of our time: how should Western states receiving an influx of Muslim immigrants deal with the unfamiliar, seemingly alien rules under which their new residents and citizens formed their marriages—the Islamic rules of marriage? But in getting ready for decisions about that, Pascale Fournier here relentlessly pursues one of the highest injunctions of legal realist analysis: get to "Ought" after you've spent a long time on "Is." What do Western courts do in fact? What is the Islamic law which plaintiffs argue Western judges should transplant into their legal toolkit? What are the options open to a Western judge trying to decide whether to transplant, and if so, how so? What do the various options on the judges' actual table mean for the wives and husbands whose divorces end up in their courts? How do actual husbands and wives strategize in light of the range of possible outcomes in Western courts?

It is virtually unknown to see work on the encounter between Islamic law and Western liberal legal systems lavish so much attention as Fournier does here on the realistic possibilities as manifested by what has actually already happened. Instead, we debate women's equality versus their choices, the value of recognizing minority cultures versus the value of integrating all citizens into liberal values, the authenticity of experience and the trap of false consciousness, etc. Across all these big questions, we see theory load itself with prescription before it even begins to describe. Fournier has managed to suspend moral judgment, to defer principled determination, to avoid polemical conclusion so that she can describe the field of judicial options and marital outcomes that are *actually* within the scope of her big question.

The surprising result is that a judge's principle is rarely if ever a sure warrant of outcome. Fournier shows with pellucid clarity how Canadian, American, German and French courts pursuing the same principle can still produce a systematically broad range of diametrically opposed outcomes. And through the ingenious device of an imagined typology of Muslim wives embroiled in Western divorces from their Muslim husbands—Fournier will be famous for her wonderfully depicted Leilas and Samirs—she shows that courts inevitably transform Islamic family law rules when they attempt to recognize them, and transform Western family law rules even when they don't—in part because that's the fate of legal transplantation, in part because the Leilas and Samirs are constantly busy transforming the law in the books into the scintillating paradoxes of law in action. These Leilas and Samirs never get pure equality or pure recognition. They do, however, produce the startling effect of orderly complexity.

Fournier's initial idea was that constitutional principles would both describe and resolve the problems faced by Muslim women seeking or resisting divorce in Western states. I well remember a conversation in which she expressed her disconcerted awareness as she discovered their almost bottomless indeterminacy. A yawning void faced her then: how to proceed outside the constitutional cocoon? A leading hypothesis of legal realism stepped in to end the feeling of analytic free fall that she was then experiencing: just as Woodward and Bernstein guided themselves through the Watergate maze by heeding the maxim "Follow the Money," she could find her way forward in uncharted ground under the motto "Follow the Background Rules." This book achieves its realism by observing how the problematic rule that enjoys the spotlight—should Western courts recognize the *mahr* promised to the Muslim bride by the Muslim groom as a condition of valid Islamic marriage—*actually works* as it sits in the nest of background rules in which it operates. Islamic law itself makes the *mahr* a complex object of human contention; so does choice of law; so does translating *mahr* into Western doctrine of, say, antenuptial contact; so does the seemingly independent questions of separate or community property between the spouses, property division and alimony. If we are lawyers following Oliver Wendall Holmes's path of the law, it is only in the context of these background rules that can *mahr mean anything at all.*

Finally, Fournier gives us a new focus for work on legal pluralism within the family law of Western states. Yes, the Islamic rules and the American, Canadian, French and German rules are different if we put them on a chart and compare them, as if they operated alone. But set into the matrix of the background rules, and then contextualized into the rhetorical and material strategies available to the judges and the parties in particular divorces, myriad outcomes offer themselves for analysis and assessment. Is it fair for a poor woman to get her *mahr* and not her half-share in the marital property? Is it fair to order a poor husband to pay them both? This question is not about recognition; it is about distribution. In Fournier's capable hands, what is plural is not only normative orders or sources of law, but also *pathways to decision, strategies, and outcomes.* The hard normative work can begin afresh.

Janet Halley
Royall Professor of Law, Harvard Law School

Acknowledgements

The six chapters of the book capture six different locations and languages—borrowing from a variety of disciplinary fields and techniques that I, in turn, experienced as deliciously stimulating, profoundly disturbing and impossibly frustrating. I never thought I could one day assemble these conflicting terminologies into one dialect and read it as a whole. I could not have endured the challenge of the journey without Janet Halley's intellectual presence in my work, translated into a rigorous and enriching space that she had constructed for us to meet, every week, on Sunday night! Years have gone by ... and my project mysteriously developed out of conversations we had about desires, identities, constraints and the "spin" that we could discover in discursive encounters if only we were willing to walk through uncertainties and envision in advance disenchantment. Can I thank her enough? Because of her, I learned to cherish the joy and the pain of writing, as well as develop a surprising confidence in "my hunch"—master these sites of "unknown knowledge," organize them, pursue them in a regulatory fashion. This is no small accomplishment. Duncan Kennedy has been a precious mentor and generous friend. Through animated discussions and numerous readings, he significantly enriched my understanding of distributive analysis, identity politics and legal transplants in the context of globalization. As time goes by, your Critical Legal Studies (CLS) imprints will remain au coeur de ma paume. Merci mon très cher.

Many friends and colleagues have contributed toward shaping this book, in personal and professional ways, with trust, support and humour, locally and transnationally. Some have patiently read drafts; others have discussed concepts or provided constructive criticism. I wish to thank: my academic soul mate Gokce Yurdakul; my dear friends and colleagues at Harvard Law School, Philomila Tsoukala, Moria Paz, Ninke Mussche, Marie-Ève Sylvestre, Fernanda Nicola, Anna di Robilant, Talha Syed, Yoav Sapir, Raef Zreik, Isabel Jaramillo, Hengameh Saberi, Libby Adler and Brenda Cossman; the members of my doctoral committee, Frank Michelman and Frank Vogel; the director of the graduate program, William Alford; and my Deans at the University of Ottawa and McGill University, Sébastien Grammond, Nathalie DesRosiers and Nicholas Kasirer. Hassan El Menyawi, Havva Guney, Leila Ahmed, Hani Sayed, Lama Abu-Odeh, Margot Badran and Amr Shalakany made a significant contribution to my understanding of Islamic family law. I also wish to acknowledge the invaluable collaboration of Christina Jones-Pauly for the German section, and the Canadian Council of Muslim Women (particularly Alia Hogbens) as well the Institute for Women's Studies and Research in Iran, whose dedicated members have been an indispensable source of knowledge with real world application. As a Trudeau scholar, I benefited enormously from the friendship and rigour of the Trudeau Foundation's "family" members, in particular Robert Leckey, Jillian Boyd, Sophie Thériault, Margarida Garcia, Bettina B. Cenerelli, Josée St-Martin, Stephen Toope and Pierre-Gerlier Forest. I would like to express my gratitude to Stephen Wiles, the excellent librarian at Harvard Law School, for the overall research; Prakash Shah at Queen Mary University of London, for his enthusiasm and generous support; and Miro Kaygalak for the original book cover. Anna R. Dekker and Janet MacMillan have been absolutely magnificent in reading and editing the manuscript. I cannot thank them enough.

The writing of this book was encouraged by several institutional and financial forms of support. Research for this study was funded by generous grants from the Pierre Elliott Trudeau Foundation, McGill University (Boulton Fellowship), the Canadian Bar Association (Viscount Bennett Scholarship), the Canada–US Fulbright Program, the American Association of University Women, the Social Sciences and Humanities Research Council Canada (SHRCC) and the Fonds québécois de la recherche sur la société et la culture (F.Q.R.S.C.).

My research has considerably benefited from presentations at conferences in Egypt, Iran, the United Kingdom, Germany, Italy, the United States and Canada. In particular, I wish to express my appreciation for invitations to: the 6th International Conference of the Arab Women's Solidarity Association in Cairo (Egypt); the Institute for Women's Studies and Research in Tehran (Iran); the International Conference of the International Sociological Association in London (United Kingdom); the International Interdisciplinary Conference at the University of Edinburgh (United Kingdom); the American Law and Society Conference in Berlin (Germany); the Workshop on Pluralism in Family Law at the Institute for Advanced Study in Berlin (Germany); the Workshop on Religion, Law and Democracy at the European University Institute in Florence (Italy); the Northeastern University School of Law's Progressive Lawyering Project in Boston (United States); the American Philosophical Association conference in San Francisco (United States); the Distributive Family conference at Harvard Law School (United States); the Workshop on Comparative Family Law at the American University Washington College of Law (United States); the Harvard–Stanford International Junior Faculty Forum at Stanford Law School (United States); the International Conference on Feminist Constitutionalism in Kingston (Canada); the Pierre Elliott Trudeau Foundation 2009 Summer Institute in Gananoque (Canada); the Politics of Community and Identity conference at the University of Ottawa (Canada); the Workshop on Religion and Citizenship at the University of Windsor Law School (Canada); the McGill Faculty of Law Seminar in Montréal (Canada); the Droit et Religion conference at the Université de Montréal (Canada); and the Chaire d'étude Claire-Bonenfant sur la condition des femmes at l'Université Laval (Canada). I received extremely helpful feedback at each of theses sites.

Some of the ideas and parts of the text of this book have previously been published elsewhere, in different and shorter forms. I thank the editors of these journals and collections, and acknowledge them here. Parts of Chapter 1 were originally published in 2006 as "In the (Canadian) Shadow of Islamic Law: Translating Mahr as a Bargaining Endowment" in volume 44, number 4 of the *Osgoode Hall Law Journal*, and was also included in a collection of essays entitled *Law and Religious Pluralism in Canada* edited by Richard Moon and published by the University of British Columbia Press in 2008. Parts of Chapters 2 and 3 appeared in 2009 as "Transit and Translation: Islamic Legal Transplants in North America and Western Europe" in volume 4, number 1 of *The Journal of Comparative Law* and "Comparative Law at the Intersection of Religion and Gender" in one of the European University Institute's Robert Schuman Centre for Advanced Studies Working Paper Series. This article was selected by the Harvard–Stanford International Junior Faculty Forum 2008. Parts of Chapter 4 appeared in 2007 as "La femme musulmane au Canada: profane ou sacrée?" in volume 19, number 2 of the *Canadian Journal of Women and the Law*. Parts of Chapters 4 and 5 were published in 2010 as "Flirting with God in Western Secular Courts: Mahr in the West" in volume 24, number 1 of the *International Journal of Law, Policy and the Family*, published by Oxford University Press. This article won the Quebec Bar Foundation prize for "best law review article" in 2009 and honourable mention by the Canadian Association of law Teachers Scholarly Paper Award in 2010. Parts of Chapter 3 and 4 appeared in 2009 as "Deconstructing the East/West Binary: Substantive Equality and Islamic Marriage in a Comparative Dialogue" in *Constituting Equality: Gender Equality and Comparative Constitutional Law*, edited by Susan H. Williams and published by Cambridge University Press, and in 2008 as "L'égalité substantielle comme école buissonnière du droit? À propos du caractère indéterminé du droit comparé religieux" in *Rapports sociaux de sexe/ genre et droit: repenser le droit*, edited by Louise Langevin and published by the Éditions des archives contemporaines in Paris.

In my own trajectory, I have been exceptionally fortunate to receive so much love and encouragement from my parents, Monique and Gilles Fournier. They gave me the most precious gift of all, so beautifully illustrated by the following passage from Antigone: "La vie n'est pas ce que tu crois. C'est une eau que les jeunes gens laissent couler sans le savoir, entre leurs doigts ouverts. Ferme tes mains, ferme tes mains, vite. Retiens-la. Tu verras, cela deviendra une petite chose dure et simple qu'on grignote, assis au soleil." With a generosity that I cannot even begin to describe, they sat aux premières loges of my many confusing and unpredictable projects, departures and journeys. From as far back as I can remember, they have always been at the Montréal airport waiting for me—with pride, tears of joy and food! They have also kindly accepted to accompany me to Iran, Italy, Egypt and Costa Rica, to share some of my fascinations throughout these years of powerful work. I embarked on this adventure because of them.

My younger and only sister Rosalie has been ma complice préférée for every step along the way. In moments of discouragement, she would simply look at me with her superb green eyes and say: "N'oublie jamais de demeurer réaliste et de demander l'impossible!", one of Che Guevara's reactionary slogans that she surely had adopted for herself while dangerously and modestly living in Congo,

Uganda, Equador and the Chiapas. The quest that she has tirelessly pursued since her early adolescence, and the promising avenue that she has established for understanding refugees here and abroad, have brought light to my own project in surprising ways.

Finally, I could not have survived the road without the love, confidence and positive disposition of my husband Xavier M. Milton, who closely witnessed many "drama queen" episodes and always responded with his classic "built for life" inclination and strength. He provided me with a calm and loving bubble to embrace at times of chaotic production, like a rock against the sky. Two beautiful baby boys, Charles and Pierre, came to the world since I started this book. Xavier made it possible for me to nourish both my passion for writing and my devotion to the children, simultaneously, as part of the same commitment. On multiple occasions, he convinced me that I did not have to choose or compromise either the private or public spheres of my life. I could hold both, with pride in my movements, and it was my duty to do so. I will always remember this one night spent in a hotel away from home, presenting at a conference that I did not want to miss despite Charles's very young age. As I unpacked my luggage, thinking of mes deux amours miles away from me, I found this note from Xavier. It read: "My dearest love, you may be asking yourself why am I here in this city, in this hotel, at this conference, in this moment, when I could be with my husband and beautiful boy? The answer is that you stand as a role model for Charles, who will grow up to be a confident, intelligent, and progressive man whose contribution to society will be equally praised. We are proud of you." For this and for so many other precious moments, I thank Xavier.

Pascale Fournier
Chelsea, Québec (Canada)

To Xavier, Charles and Pierre

To my parents and Rosalie

Introduction

If liberalism is committed to the individual and individual choice, it is also conventionally taken to be committed to freedom and equality. Giving effect to such principles will often create tensions: the "free" acts of individuals will sometimes produce inequality; and state enforcement of equality will likely reduce individual freedom. Moreover, when faced with the claims of subordinated groups, liberalism typically is asked to make concessions by which these collisions intensify and multiply. In fact, even if the mandate to address the rights or interests of groups is not perfectly consistent with liberalism's commitment to individuals, it may be *necessary* if individuals *in* groups are to be treated liberally (that is, accorded freedom *or* equality). And the mandate to address the subordination of groups generates a new collision of freedom with equality: *de facto* freedom for subordinated groups may require their specific regulation; and equality of their members may require active distributions in their favour. The "politics of recognition" called upon by subordinated groups within liberalism is thus a tensely contradictory project. Nations that are consciously, sometimes constitutionally, committed to protecting the rights of individuals and groups cannot shy away from these potentially irreconcilable differences.

These contradictions operate in the specific context of the "politics of recognition" invoked by Muslim groups in Western states. I focus on Canada, the United States, France and Germany, where members of Muslim communities have claimed recognition of their religious particularity, their autonomy and their law-making capacity *vis-à-vis* the monopoly of the state. Legal terms and concepts rooted in Islamic family law have thus penetrated these Western legal systems through one of two routes: first, in accordance with international private law rules (conflict of laws), which often directly incorporate Islamic family law (as in Germany and France); second, through the interpretation of secular domestic laws (as in Canada and the United States). These various approaches clearly affect the lives of and choices available to Muslim women who find themselves in the throes of a collapsing marriage.

This book seeks to understand the politics of transnational Islamic family law through the migration of one particular legal institution: *mahr*, "the gift which the bridegroom has to give to the bride when the contract of marriage is made and which becomes the property of the wife" (Bosworth 1991: 78). *Mahr* is usually divided into two parts: that which is paid at the time of marriage is called prompt *mahr* (*muajjal*), and that which is paid only on the dissolution of the marriage by death or divorce or other agreed events is called deferred *mahr* (*muwajjal*). The issue of *mahr* typically presents itself in times of crisis: married Muslim women, engaged in religiously structured marriages and living in Western states, reach out to the secular court upon the dissolution of their marriages to claim the enforcement of *mahr*, presumably because their husbands have previously refused to allow them the amount of deferred *mahr*.

The migration of *mahr* to Western courts unfolds at the crossroads of several doctrinal fields and disciplinary boundaries—contract and family law, constitutional and Islamic law, public policy and private ordering, (majoritarian) public order and (minority-based) identity politics, and formal and substantive equality. Through an analysis of case law from four countries (Canada, the United States, France and Germany) I suggest that once *mahr* is uprooted from Islamic family law and transplanted into a Western chamber of law, it can never go back home again. It immediately becomes rooted in the soil of the country's legal, historical, political, and social backgrounds, and flourishes (or fails) in diverse and unexpected ways. In fact, as soon as *mahr* penetrates the Canadian, American, French or German forum, it is animated by a diverse and often unpredictable set of legal constructs (concepts of multiculturalism, fairness, public policy, gender equality, etc.). Now being dynamically situated elsewhere, it becomes a hybrid and transformed version of what was once described as *mahr* by classical Islamic jurists. Some of the questions that will be addressed in this endeavour include: How are the diverse and contradictory conceptual themes around Islamic law and Islamic theory received by or brought to Western courts? What are the modes of influence in the selection and imposition processes of *mahr* as a legal transplant? Does the reification of religion by courts simultaneously fragment it as rules move across borders? Does the way *mahr* travels affect subjectivity, in both productive and reactive terms? This is all the more pertinent since courts present themselves as conduits of the law completely devoid of ideological influence. Drawing on the overarching concept of liberalism, this book proposes that although liberalism is one possible way of framing emancipatory claims by minorities in Western societies, it has become the dominant approach underlying how Western legal systems deal with claims made by Muslims in general and Muslim women in particular.

Some initial assumptions and terminology require clarification. Throughout the book, one of the fundamental assumptions is that the legal texts chosen by the judiciary are not random, but ideological. Furthermore, the notion of power is envisaged in the context of globalization, as conceived of by Duncan Kennedy (2003). Globalization, as Kennedy observes, moved in waves through various principles and movements, each with its own impetus and each with its own effects. "Classical Legal Thought," he notes,

> globalized between 1850 and 1914. ... The mechanisms of globalization were direct Western imposition in the colonized world, the forced "opening" of non-Western regimes that remained independent, and the prestige of German legal science in the European and Western Hemisphere world of nation states.

Between 1900 and 1968, what globalized was The Social, again a way of thinking without an essence, but with, as an important trait, preoccupation with rethinking law as a purposive activity, as a regulatory mechanism that could and should facilitate the evolution of social life in the direction of ever greater interdependence at every level, from the family to the world of nations. The agents of globalization were reform movements of every political stripe in the developed West, nationalist movements in the periphery, and the elites of the newly independent nation states after 1945.

Between 1945 and 2000, one trend was to think about legal technique, in the aftermath of the critiques of [Classical Legal Thought] and The Social, as the pragmatic balancing of conflicting considerations in administering the system created by the social jurists. At the same time, there was a seemingly contrary trend to envisage law as the guarantor of human and property rights and of inter-governmental order through the gradual extension of the rule of law, understood as judicial supremacy. The mechanisms of globalization were American victories in World War II and the Cold War, the "opening" of nation states to the new legal consciousness through participation in the world market on the conditions set by multinational corporations and international regulatory institutions, and the prestige of American culture. (Kennedy 2003: 633–34)

Lurking in the background of the current study is the ongoing disagreement about whether legal constructs are even *capable* of migrating across borders—whether personal or national. Alan Watson (1993: 21) accepts the possibility of such migration, writing that "legal transplants refer to the moving of a rule ... from one country to another, or from one people to another," although others notably disagree (Legrand 1997).

The focus on the locus of the state, on adjudication, on case law, is not accidental. Rather, it is a purposively chosen perspective given that courts present themselves as invested in the technical enterprise of applying the law in a non-ideological manner. One of the suggestions I offer in this book is that courts demonstrably respond to the enforceability of *mahr* in ways that can be classified ideologically. The analysis of how the law captures claims based on identity within the liberal framework suggests that in adjudicating *mahr*, courts have characterized this Islamic institution in three different ways: the Liberal–Legal Pluralist Approach (LLPA), the Liberal–Formal Equality Approach (LFEA), and the Liberal–Substantive Equality Approach (LSEA). I classify these three disciplinary discourses within the wider expression of liberalism because they all share, in both their normative and descriptive dimensions, the same commitment to autonomy and liberty of the individual, although for the LLPA individuals are racialized and for the LSEA they are gendered. Along this spectrum of ideology, *mahr* has been the subject of competing aesthetic and political representations, from a form of religious family affiliation (LLPA), to a space of mere secular contract (LFEA) and finally to the projection of a fairness symbol of gender (LSEA).

The focus on the public dimension of the law is also imperative since many players in the identity politics debate developed a strong political emphasis on issues of state recognition as capable of addressing and possibly resolving the suffering of minority citizens in Western states. Charles Taylor (1994) proposes that the liberal state affirms cultural differences in the public sphere as a remedy. He defines the modern identity as characterized by an insistence on its inner voice and capacity for authenticity, that is, the ability to find a way of being that is somehow true to oneself. Proponents of the politics of recognition argue that the liberal state has betrayed its commitment to neutrality by privileging the ways of life of dominant groups. Yet, because oppressed groups have distinct cultures, experiences, and perspectives on social life, the appropriate remedies on the part of Western states consist of integrating these distinct perspectives on social life. This is a view also espoused by Will Kymlicka (1995).

Nancy Fraser (1997), moreover, has argued that harms attributable to misrecognition are often increased by economic deprivations, and, conversely, that economic injustices are compounded by persistent patterns of cultural denigration. Hence, she concludes that "justice today requires *both* redistribution *and* recognition" (Fraser 1997: 68 (emphasis added)). Although this study does not engage this debate directly, it does so indirectly by showing that it is hopelessly naïve. In fact, I will demonstrate that the Islamic institution of *mahr*, a symbol of minority citizens' particularity and religious difference, cannot travel to Western courts without carrying a very complex interaction amongst several parties whose interests are often opposed as to its recognition.

I begin by developing the Islamic legal framework within which *mahr* is conceived. Under Islamic family law, marriage establishes a reciprocity system in which each party is assigned a set of contractual rights that confer a duty toward the other party. Chapter 1 reviews each of the contractual rights and duties as isolated from one another, and then explores the motivations and effects they are expected to produce individually, as well as relationally. Islamic family law structures the economic relations of the spouses and maintains its regulatory power at the dissolution of marriage. Three types of divorce (*talaq*, *khul*, and *faskh*) determine the degree to which each party may or may not initiate divorce and the different costs associated with it. This chapter also introduces the range of approaches, from the formalist to the more functionalist. The formalist perspective includes an overview of *mahr* as interpreted by the sources of Islamic law and schools of law, as well as the internal feminist divide. The functionalist perspective addresses the relationship between *mahr* and the larger system of family law (initiation *mahr*, *talaq mahr*, *khul mahr*, *faskh mahr*, and inherited *mahr*). I will focus on the internal and external dynamics of *mahr* when it is used as a tool of relative bargaining power by both parties "in the shadow of the law."[1]

Finally, Chapter 1 acknowledges the internal pluralism of *mahr*: although Western courts purport to treat it as a unified and invariable concept drawn from

---

1   I borrow this phrase from Mnookin and Kornhauser (1979).

Islamic law, even courts that regularly interpret and apply Islamic religious law appear to espouse a conception of *mahr* shaped by geographical and socio-political contours. The examples of Egypt, Tunisia and Malaysia thus illustrate the internal plurality of *mahr* even at its point of departure. This chapter also introduces Samir and Leila, a fictional couple whose various viewpoints, strategies and outcomes represent attempts to reveal the underlying motivations, perspectives and ideologies that inform individuals' actions and decisions with regard to *mahr*. It focuses on the internal and external dynamics of *mahr* when it is used as a tool of relative bargaining power by both parties, who negotiate with each other against the backdrop of state and Islamic family law. The objective is specifically to highlight the limitations and contradictions of the formalist interpretation of Islamic family law, as well as the personal and political stakes involved in opting for a fragmental, functional *mahr*.

Chapters 2 and 3 present four Western legal systems (Canada, the United States, France and Germany), including their domestic family law, contract law and constitutional law regimes as well as their reception of and adherence to international private law. This presentation of the legal "tool box" will help illuminate how the liberal ideology—legal pluralist, formal equality and substantive equality—works within complex and constraining rules of internal legal regulations. It will thus concretely highlight, prior to the adjudication, both the legal possibilities and the legal limits within which judges navigate when they are asked to enforce *mahr*. This section forms the basis for the subsequent analysis, from a comparative perspective, of actual cases on the enforcement of *mahr* in the four different fora. In Canada and the United States, family law rules apply regardless of whether an individual is a citizen or a resident, whereas the application of family law is directly tied to citizenship in France and Germany due to the application of those countries' international private law rules and bilateral accords. This analysis continues in a descriptive vein by projecting the various consequences—both in terms of the interpretation and the enforcement of *mahr*— of applying the discourses of legal pluralism, formal equality and substantive equality. Although the legal systems mentioned above differ considerably, not only in how they incorporate Islamic law, this appears to have little effect on the unpredictable nature of legal pluralism, formal equality and substantive equality as interpretive approaches to *mahr* in all four of the countries in question.

Chapter 3 specifically analyzes actual cases on the enforcement of *mahr* and assesses the different considerations that have coloured the ways in which judges interpret, confer meaning and generate outcomes. The aim is to map out the case law in relation to the LLPA, the LFEA and the LSEA, so as to project the various kinds of consequences, both in terms of the interpretation and the enforcement of *mahr*, of applying these three disciplinary discourses.

Chapter 4 continues the analysis of the transplanting of *mahr* in Western courts, and also returns to the tensions and contradictions presented in the opening chapters. Dualisms surface, permeate and persist in the legal reasoning of Western courts, and this study seeks to elucidate these seeming contradictions: doctrine–

outcome; ends–means; church–state; disentanglement–intensification; West–East; Western–Islamic. This chapter specifically asks whether it is possible to look beyond "recognition," "equality," and "fairness" in adjudicating Islamic marriage in Western states.

In a partial and attempted answer to this question, Chapter 5 revisits the relationship between the fictitious Samir and Leila. In a series of short vignettes, some of them based on the facts of cases presented in Chapter 3, the chapter illustrates how Leila communicates, negotiates, bargains and fights using *mahr* and (sometimes) Western courts as weapons to variously protect herself or seek revenge against Samir, or anything in between. *Mahr* can be empowering or disempowering, a bonus or a penalty, depending on the circumstances; the spectrum of possibilities is wide, and encompasses myriad real and imagined possible outcomes. Sometimes *mahr* is employed as part of a wider political or religious agenda; at other times it is deployed to show distaste, incarnations of a feminist God, market considerations, interpellation, *ressentiment*, gender submission. These possibilities are explored through the fictional circumstances of the various "Leilas."

Chapter 6 offers conclusions and reiterates the goal of the book. It is an attempt not only to describe the realities of *mahr*—both as a complex legal Islamic concept and as a result of the hybridization enacted by Western courts—but also to situate this new hybrid concept within ideological (liberal) perspectives. Far from attempting to downplay or mitigate the tensions that are created in the transplantation process, this book queries whether the structural nature of the law can register this complexity, or even reproduce it.

Chapter 1

The Roots of *Mahr* and the Hybrid Transplant: Introducing *Mahr* as an Islamic Legal Conception and a Fragmented Legal Concept

One of the underlying endeavours of this study is to review English and French scholarship on Islamic family law. The current state of legal (and social and religious) thought seems to describe *mahr* as a single, separate, autonomous and historically static institution. This unitary description of *mahr* is paradoxically sustained through great polarities from within Islamic family law. For instance, while *mahr* is seen by Islamic scholars as a religious symbol of dignity, respect and love for *all* Muslim women, its fluctuating amount is understood as a reflection of the socio-economic status of *this particular* Muslim woman. In addition, while *mahr* is conceptualized from within the feminist camp as the ultimate (positive) symbol of women's empowerment through the right to property, it is simultaneously described as the (negative) patriarchal sign of the sale of her vagina.

The first part of this chapter provides methodological propositions in relation to the formalist/functionalist approaches to Islamic family law. My purpose is to contextualize the scholarship of classical Islamic law, on the one hand, and that of Ziba Mir-Hosseini (2000), on the other, as two distinct ways of understanding Islamic family law. Mir-Hosseini's work is especially valuable to my analysis as she integrates into her work a distributional analysis of Islamic legal rules. The second part of this chapter introduces the legal institution of *mahr* as it is presented in Islamic family law, and reviews the contradictory dichotomies that animate its symbolic meaning, assuming along with many others that *mahr* is monolithic, unitary, distinct and separate from everything else. In the third part of Chapter 1, I suggest an alternative critical way of understanding *mahr* as a bargaining endowment for husband and wife before, during and after the dissolution of marriage. Using Mir-Hosseini (2000), Mnookin and Kornhauser (1979), and Robert Hale (1923), I argue that in the social life of Islamic marriages, *mahr* is not unitary and autonomous, but rather a functional institution that produces a series of inconsistent characteristics which we can study.

This functionalist reading of *mahr* is intended to offer a distributional narrative concerned primarily with the social effects created by the husband and wife as they use *mahr* as a tool of relative bargaining power. By playing with the amount of *mahr* along with other factors that colour the marital relationship, I will tell the story of Samir and Leila, a fictional couple. The goal is to provide a glimpse of the contradictory, and often unexpected, effects and uses of *mahr* by both parties. In subsequent chapters, I will show that although Western courts treat *mahr* as a unitary institution of their own apparatus, a fragmented, functional *mahr* is what actually travels to Western countries.

Mahr as a Static, Autonomous Legal Institution

I begin by outlining the formal characteristics of Islamic family law in which each element of the institution stands on its own, and is presented as having its own rationale. For this formalistic reading of Islamic family law, I will offer the scholarship of Ziba Mir-Hosseini as a critical alternative which represents in many ways the rise of a sociological impulse reaching out for a more anti-formal reading of Islamic legal rules. Although Mir-Hosseini does not explicitly refer to or borrow from the work of either Mnookin and Kornhauser or Robert Hale, the theory she proposes and the methodology she uses to analyze the social effects of legal rules emerge from the same legal realist mode. First, she applies a sociological approach using bargaining theory to observe and predict how specific rules of family law might affect the contractual conduct of Muslim men and women in Iran and Morocco. Second, she suggests a methodology to analyze the costs and benefits of abstract legal rules as they are actually used by each party *in the shadow of the law* to get something from the other, make concessions or simply put an end to the relationship.

I then adopt the sociological approach of Mir-Hosseini and Mnookin and Kornhauser/Robert Hale to highlight the internal and external dynamics of *mahr* when it is used as a tool of relative bargaining power by parties involved in a marital relationship. In breaking away from the dogmatic rules of *mahr*, my hope is to make apparent the personal and political stakes involved in opting for a fragmented, functional *mahr*, as well as the limitations and contradictions of the formalist interpretation of Islamic family law.

Classical Islamic law presents the institution of *mahr* as a system which has its own distinct institutional structure sharply separated from other components of Islamic family law. Doctor Afzal Wani, well-known Islamic scholar and specialist on the legal institution of *mahr*, presents *mahr* as if it were a European code: "The law of *mahr* as it exists today is well developed like the law relating to other Muslim law institutions. It covers all the relevant matters like: subject matter of *mahr*, amount of *mahr*, mode of its payment, when it becomes due, widowed and divorced women's claims to *mahr* and so on" (Wani 1996: 27). Doctor Wani's treatise also explores the most important legal aspects of *mahr*, as drawn from the four sources of Sunni Islamic law (the Qur'an, the Sunnah, Qiyās and Ijmā), which I present as a foundation in which to root classical interpretations of *mahr*. These sources, however, no longer present the whole story: the four Islamic schools of law offer differing interpretations, and the internal feminist debate over *mahr*'s symbolic and actual meaning for Muslim women add layers of meaning and complexity.

Mahr and the Four Sources of Islamic Law

Mahr, meaning "reward" (*ajr*) or "nuptial gift" (also designated as *sadaqa* or *faridah*), is the expression used in Islamic family law to describe the "payment that the wife is entitled to receive from the husband in consideration of the marriage" (Esposito and DeLong-Bas 2001: 23). A key element is the fact that *mahr* must be paid to the wife herself and not to her guardian (Bosworth 1991: 78).

In conducting his research and developing his analysis of *mahr*, Doctor Wani respects the corpus of Islamic dogma, norms and prescriptions: the content of *mahr* is thus revealed first by the text of the Qur'an and secondly by the auxiliary sources of the Sunnah, Qiyās and Ijmā. Following Islamic orthodoxy, I present these in order.

Qur'an

The Qur'an, considered as "the central fact of the Islamic religious experience" (Esposito and DeLong-Bas 2001: 3), represents Allah's revelation through the Prophet Muhammed from approximately AD 610 to AD 632. It is comprised of chapters, known as *surahs*, which are further subdivided into verses. As the very words of God for Muslims, the Qur'an forms the primary source of Islamic law, although other sources also influence Muslims' beliefs and actions. As Azizah Al-Hibri acknowledges, "[w]hile the *Qur'an* remains the supreme source of law for Muslims, there are important secondary and tertiary sources as well" (Al-Hibri 1999: 505). It contains general as well as specific legal principles, but the "Qur'anic legislation on civil, economic, constitutional and international affairs is, on the whole, confined to an exposition of the general principles and objectives of the law" (Kamali 1991: 30). The Qur'anic law of *mahr* is contained partly in the section of marriage, partly in that of divorce.

While Verse 24:32 encourages men and women to marry, Verses 4:24, 4:25, and 5:5 specify that a Muslim man may marry a woman from among either the believers, slave or not, or People of the book, but only on condition of paying her *mahr*.[1] The only exception to the obligatory nature of *mahr* is the marriage of a Muslim man to an atheist, a "non-believer" (Verse 60:10). While *mahr* is viewed as a "right granted to the woman as a result of *Quranic* prescription" (Esposito and DeLong-Bas 2001: 23), it can be waived by the woman (Verse 4:4) or its amount can be adjusted by both parties (Verse 4:24). However, the husband can never take *mahr* back unilaterally once it has been given to the wife (Verses 4:19, 4:20, 4:21). In cases where the wife is divorced before the consummation of marriage, the

---

1   All excerpts from the Qur'an are reproduced in Appendix A.

Qur'an provides that she is entitled to one-half of *mahr* (Verse 2:237); where *mahr* has been agreed upon, an "equitable compensation" is due to her (Verse 2:236).

Sunnah

The Sunnah refers to the normative model behaviour of the Prophet Muhammed, and it forms the second source of Islamic law. As the Prophet Muhammed is God's Messenger, his sayings and practices are seen as a further expression of Allah's will regarding the way Muslims should live their lives. Where the Qur'an is silent, jurists have looked to this source for additional guidance. The Sunnah is expressed through the narrative traditions (*hadith*) transmitted, collected and recorded by narrators. *Hadith* literature typically includes the name of the individual who heard or witnessed the Prophet Muhammed's saying or conduct, as well as the names of the individuals who transmitted this Sunnah before it was recorded in *hadith*. These records are included so that the credibility and truthfulness of the *hadith* can be verified.

Reports of the Prophet's sayings and actions on *mahr* offer concrete directions on how *mahr* should be included in marriage arrangements. First and foremost, *mahr* is obligatory (Powers 1986: 81).[2] If the amount of *mahr* had not been agreed upon, such as when the husband died before the marriage had been consummated, the wife is entitled to a *mahr* similar to that of women of her same status (Doi 1984: 160; *Hadith* 31). Guidance is also available on what is an appropriate subject matter of *mahr*. While the Qur'an is extremely vague as to the content or minimal amount of *mahr*, the *hadith* literature gives concrete specifications in this regard. For instance, it is said that in the case of an extremely poor man wanting to get married, the Prophet requested him to teach his wife the Qur'an as her *mahr* (Doi 1984: 163). *Mahr* could also be comprised of a pair of shoes, as long as the woman consented (Doi 1984: 163). *Hadith* literature offers further guidance on *mahr* and *khul* divorce (Wani 1996: 45), and *mahr* and *li'an*[3] (Wani 1996: 45).

Qiyās

Qiyās, the third source of Islamic law, is a "means of applying a known command from the Qur'an or Sunnah to a new circumstance by means of analogical

---

2   Appendix B presents excerpts of each relevant *hadith*.

3   Divorce by *li'an* involves the husband accusing the wife of adultery. He makes four oaths that she has committed adultery, and a fifth oath, by which he calls down the wrath of God upon himself if he is lying. According to Jamila Hussain (2004: 111), "*Li'an* can be invoked where there is no positive evidence of adultery to put before the court, or insufficient evidence. *Li'an* is an exception to the rule in Islamic law that failure to prove adultery results in the person making the accusation being punished by 80 lashes for the crime of *qadhf*. This form of divorce is not common and the jurists disagree about whether it is revocable."

reasoning" (Brown 2004: 124). It is based on the idea that when the rationale behind a command is understood, it can be applied to novel situations not directly enumerated in either the Qur'an or Sunnah. This process of trying to "discover" the law is referred to as *ijtihad*, meaning "personal reasoning or interpretation." For instance, by using an analogy between the Qur'anic penalty for theft (amputation of the hand) and the "theft" of the wife's virginity, Qiyās was used to fix the minimum amount of *mahr* (Esposito and DeLong-Bas 2001: 7). More specifically, the amount was established according to the minimum value of stolen goods required in Kufa and Medina, two cities central to the development of Islamic civilization, for the amputation punishment to be executed.

Ijmā

Ijmā, the fourth source of Islamic law, refers to the consensus of qualified legal scholars of a given generation on a point of law (Hodkinson 1984: 4). It derives its authority from the famous *hadith* of the Prophet Mohammed who was deemed to have said: "My community will never agree on an error" (Esposito and DeLong-Bas 2001: 7). While the Qur'an and Sunnah are generally thought to be preeminent over ijmā, many Islamic scholars contend that only those interpretations of the Qur'an and Sunnah that have passed the test of ijmā are authoritative. Thus, they argue that, in practice, ijmā is the most important source of Islamic law because it infuses interpretations of Qur'an and Sunnah with authority (Hodkinson 1984). They further contend that ijmā is a crucial influence on the development of Islamic law because it determines the interpretation and application of the Qur'an and Sunnah (An-Na'im 1990: 23).

Mahr and the Four Islamic Schools of Law

From the tenth to the nineteenth centuries, the era of Taqlid was characterized, according to received wisdom, by the closing of the gates of *ijtihad* and the simultaneous emergence of the four schools of law as authoritative legal sources:

> What distinguishes it as a unique era in its own right is that during this time, Muslim jurists and judges appear to have abandoned, for the most part, the religio/legal project of coming up with new rules of law directly inspired by the sources of the religion, or *ijtihad*. Rather than pursue the project of legal innovation typical of the preceding era of Usul, these jurists/judges concentrated their legal activity on consolidating the legal doctrine of the school of law they were affiliated with and to which they had deep feelings of loyalty. (Abu-Odeh 2004: 1054)

As described by Jamal J. Nasir (2002: 20):

> The era of the great Sunni Imams was followed ... by an era of imitation (*taqleed*) in which later scholars followed the methods laid down by the founding father and built upon them, without any individual jurist even claiming the status of the earlier Imams, the only authorities entitled to interpret the Divine Law, after whom the "gate of interpretation" was declared closed.

In different centres in Mecca, Medina, Kufa and Baghdad, various religious leaders associated themselves with the different schools of Islamic law, which were subsequently named after the Imams who founded them. The four major surviving schools are the Shafi'i, Hanafi, Maliki and Hanbali, named after Muhammad al-Shafi'i, Abu Hanafi, Malik ibn Anas and Ahmad ibn Hanbal. A brief outline of the legal understanding of *mahr* in the four schools provides background for how it subsequently plays out.

The Hanafi and Maliki schools treat *mahr* as a debt (Doi 1984: 160). *Mahr* can be monetary or non-monetary (some other form of property), but it cannot be "a mere promise to do or to abstain from doing something" (Wani 1996: 69). Hence, a man cannot marry with the promise to teach his wife religion or take her on a pilgrimage (Wani 1996: 70). In other words, the Malikis "say that the *mahr* may be a definite thing like a known animal, by looking at it or by describing it like this horse or a particular kind of horse like the Arabia horse, or it may be a definite amount of money" (Doi 1984: 165).

As specified by the Islamic scholars John L. Esposito and Natana DeLong-Bas (2001: 24), "the practice of dividing the dower into two portions, prompt (*muqaddam*) and deferred (*muakhkhar*), is universal in the Hanafi School." The Maliki school similarly prohibits the postponement of the entire *mahr* to an unknown date such as death or divorce (Doi 1984: 165). In fact, half of *mahr* should be paid immediately upon marriage: "The Maliki school insists that half of the *mahr* should be given on the spot for the consummation of a valid marriage. *Mahr* can be given promptly on marriage or can be postponed until after marriage" (Doi 1984: 165). In contrast, according to the Shafi'i and Hanbali schools, the payment of *mahr* can be delayed at the time of marriage, either in part or as a whole, but "it must not be forgotten completely or the proposal for giving the *mahr* should not be made in an ambiguous way" (Doi 1984: 165). If *mahr* is not paid when it had been agreed to be paid completely, the Shafi'i school gives the wife the following options: she can refuse consummation, be patient or take action to annul the marriage before the *qadi* (Islamic court) (Doi 1984: 165). As to the amount, *mahr* is equivalent to 10 *dirhams* under Hanafi law, 3 *dirhams* under Maliki law, and no fixed minimum under both Shafi'i and Hanbali law (Doi 1984: 164, Pearl and Menski 1998: 179, Schleifer 1985).

Mahr and the Internal Feminist Divide

While Doctor Wani presents the foundations for a positive legal system the function of which is effectively to deal with different outcomes regarding *mahr*, the feminist debate confines itself to a moral vision of *mahr*: it is either good or bad for Muslim women. They either cherish or reject it as part of a feminist agenda.

An interesting debate takes place among Islamic feminist scholars over the symbolic nature of *mahr* for Muslim women: *mahr* is seen as a complex and controversial institution structured by a series of characteristics which can be described as paired opposites. On the one hand stand the vivid proponents of *mahr*, the "Islamic feminists" who claim through a historical and emancipating narrative that *mahr* came into Islam as the first symbol of women's empowerment. Opposing them are the "liberal secular feminists"[4] who condemn *mahr* as the expression, at the time of marriage, of the sale of the Muslim woman's vagina. Ironically, classical jurists have often employed a similar language to describe *mahr*. Shaykh Khalil, a Maliki jurist, conceived of "dower" (that is, *mahr*) as analogous to the cost of purchase, thus *mahr* had attached to it the same fundamental conditions as a purchase and sale transaction. That which was sold, according to Khalil, was a part of the woman herself; her vagina became merchandise (Ruxton 1916). Muúaqqiq al-Hilli (1985: 428), the most prominent Shi'a jurist, similarly states: "[M]arriage etymologically is uniting one thing with another thing; it is also said to mean coitus and to mean sexual intercourse. In shar', there have been various interpretations of it. It has been said that it is a contract whose object is that of dominion over the vagina, without the right of its possession."

Although the two feminist discourses come to opposite ethical conclusions as to whether *mahr* should be recognized and valued, they share similar ideological assumptions: that *mahr* as an institution represents a contract. For the proponents of *mahr*, the contract is one in which the Muslim woman is an independent and consenting party; for its opponents, the woman is taken to have signed the contract under duress. However contradictory, both discourses treat *mahr* formalistically, without offering a complex view of its shifting dynamic capacity as well as its possibly perverse uses by Muslim women in the context of marriage. I will address the formalist yet polarized general/particular, love/economics, dignity/social status, respect/interest, power/subordination dualistic categories that permeate the feminist understanding of *mahr*.

The Islamic feminists claim not only that Islam provides a liberating worldview for women, but also that "the Qur'an's epistemology is inherently antipatriarchal" (Barlas 2002: 2). With the revelation of Islam through the Prophet Mohammed, so the story goes, the Qur'anic scripture offered a radical departure from the patriarchal customs of pre-Islamic Arabia and ensured an authoritative basis for the emancipation of *all* Muslim women. If the status of Muslim women during

---

4   A general view of the secularization movement of Islamic law is presented in Layish (1978).

the life of the Prophet was that of highly active and independent beings—they included "business women, poets, jurists, religious leaders and even warriors" (al-Hibri 1997: 5)—Professor Azizah al-Hibri suggests that it soon declined dramatically with the influence of external patriarchal forces: "It is worth noting that the rise of patriarchy in the Muslim world was not historically an isolated event. Muslim Arab patriarchy was greatly influenced in its development by the neighboring Byzantine and Persian empires" (1997: 5). For the Islamic feminists, the imperative to challenge internally the patriarchal readings and understandings of Islam is crucial, especially given that the choice/coercion, freedom/oppression, equality/inequality, secular/religious binaries used by the Western world equate the second term in each of these binaries with the Muslim world. Yet not only is there "nothing Islamic about misogyny, inequality or patriarchy" (Barlas 2002: 2), but, further, Muslim women must find the "stubbornly egalitarian" (Ahmed 1992: 146) voice of Islam from within:

> The majority of Muslim women who are attached to their religion will not be liberated through the use of a secular approach imposed from the outside by international bodies or from above by undemocratic governments. The only way to resolve the conflicts of these women and remove their fear of pursuing rich and fruitful lives is to build a solid Muslim feminist jurisprudential basis which clearly shows that Islam not only does not deprive them of their rights, but in fact demands these rights for them. (al-Hibri 1997: 3)

The Muslim feminist jurisprudence agenda is based on the following reasoning: "if we wish to ensure Muslim women their rights, we not only need to contest readings of the Qur'an that justify the abuse and degradation of women, we also need to establish the legitimacy of liberatory readings" (Barlas 2002: 3). Such liberatory readings, anti-secular by their very definition, involve among other things *re*valuing and *re*naming *mahr* as a sign of dignity, respect and love for *all* Muslim women. Barlas (2002: 3) touches on this point, observing that "even if such readings do not succeed in effecting a radical change in Muslim societies, it is safe to say that no meaningful change can occur in these societies that does not derive its legitimacy from the Qur'an's teachings, a lesson secular Muslims everywhere are having to learn to their own detriment." As colourfully put by Sabiq al-Sayyid (1969: 155), "*Mahr* purifies the soul of the women and cultivates trust in the proctorship of man." Emphasizing that *mahr* is not the contractual sale of the Muslim woman's vagina, Neil B.E. Baillie (1965: 91) states:

> *Mahr* is the property which is incumbent on a husband, either by reason of its being named in the contract of marriage, or by virtue of the contract itself, as opposed of the usufruct of the wife's person. ... Dower (i.e. *Mahr*) is not the exchange or consideration given by the man to the woman for entering into the contract, but an effect of the contract, imposed by the law on the husband as a token of respect for its subject, the woman.

Expressions such as "mark of respect for the wife" (Pearl and Menski 1998: 179, Rahim 1911), "honour to the bride" (Wani 1995: 193), "free gift by the husband" (Doi 1984: 159) or symbol of the "prestige of the marriage contract" (Nasir 2002: 43) are indistinctly being used to describe the very *raison d'être* of *mahr*: the recognition of the dignity of Muslim women. Even more poetically, Wani (1995: 193) conceptualizes *mahr* as:

> something lovable, or things having reference to love as a bone in the upper part of the breast, or gristles of the ribs; or something presentable as a gift like a pearl; and doing of something in a right way with skill. Under Muslim law it denotes a gift spontaneous to be presented by the husband to the wife on marriage with a willing heart. This is an honour to the bride from the husband. By so doing he makes a manifestation of his love for the wife and eagerness to respect her rights to his fullest possible capacity.

Moreover, *mahr* is conceptualized in the literature as marking the shift from the "wife as an object of sale" under the pre-Islamic era to the "wife as a contracting party in her own right" (Pearl and Menski 1998: 4) under Islam. Under the former regime,

> [b]efore the revelation of the Qur'an, women in pre-Islamic Arabia had no hope of inheritance. Rarely were they allowed to control holding or disposal of their possessions. In fact, in that political and social structure, women themselves were considered as property, subject absolutely to the men of the family and tribe, as any other possession. (Chaudhry 2004: 14)

Pearl and Menski (1998: 4) articulate the change reflected in the latter development:

> The second major reform of the Qur'an is found in family law generally, changing the status of women in particular. Thus, much of the legal material in the Qur'anic verses concerns the very real attempt to enhance the legal position of women. In customary law, women were treated as an object of sale. A woman could be fully exploited by her father; she could virtually be sold in marriage to the highest bidder, as shown in the pre-Islamic form of the bride-price. The husband was entitled to terminate the contract of marriage on any occasion and for any whim. Various Qur'anic provisions transformed this position, for example the revelation directing the husband to pay a dower (*mahr*) to the wife (Qur'an, Sura IV, verse 19) …

Even in more general terms, one of the greatest empowerments given to women by Islam lies in her right to property, rather than a non-entity subject to the whims of her (male) guardian (al-Sayyid 1969: 155). As an independent legal entity in the eyes of the law, a Muslim woman was vested with proprietary rights, symbolized by *mahr*. Her position became "equitably strong in society and before law" in that she maintains her identity even after marriage, rather than having it merge into that of her husband (Wani 1995: 194). The fact that a woman is deserving of dignity, love and respect in the eyes of men is "symbolized by making *Mahr* obligatory for her and binding upon men" (al-Sayyid 1969: 155). Doctor Wani summarizes the positive effects of Islam on women, stating, "*Mahr* has been declared as the absolute property of wives. Fathers or guardians of women cannot claim it from their husbands or bride-grooms. Thus, Islam has provided measures for the amelioration and upliftment of women and for the protection of their dignity" (Wani 1995: 29).

The main idea of the "liberal secular feminists," by contrast, consists of understanding "revelation as both text and context"—that is, as "an interpretation of the spirit and broad intention behind the specific language of the texts" (Hallaq 1997: 231). The liberal secular conception of *mahr* is accompanied by images of the family, sexuality and the significance of marriage that seek to distinguish between Islam as a pure religion, and religious doctrine as a socially constructed phenomenon subject to human context (Haddad 1988). Here, marriage is often portrayed as a "fundamentally unequal social institution" (Hoodfar 1996: 124). This feminist literature further suggests that *mahr*, in valuing the existence of virginity, perpetuates the concept of "patriarchal domination remain[ing] most entrenched in the family" (Badran 1995: 124). In fact, "it was usual that the dowry of a virgin be higher than that of a divorced woman" (Abdal-Rahim 1996: 103).

According to this view, not only is *mahr* intended to serve male interest and desire, but it also reflects "the social position of the bride's father's family as well as her own qualifications, such as … age, beauty, fortune, understanding, and virtue" (Esposito and DeLong-Bas 2001: 24). Hence, *mahr* is not, as claimed by classical Islamic law and Islamic feminists, a universal and equal symbol of dignity, love and respect for *all* women despite differences of income and status: it is rather determined *as a marketplace value*, for *that* woman, daughter of *that* man, at this *particular* moment of *her* history. Moreover, if no *mahr* has been agreed or expressly stipulated by the parties, the marriage contract is still valid but "proper *mahr*" (*mahr al-mithl*) will be determined by comparing "the *mahr* paid to other female members of the wife's family, for instance sisters, paternal aunts and female cousins" (Pearl and Menski 1998: 180). Although the husband's position may have some bearing on the negotiations, this criterion is very much subordinated to such factors as the woman's age, beauty, wealth, learning and conduct (Hodkinson 1984).

Mahr as a Bargaining Endowment: A Fragmented Legal Conception

The polar opposites created by the ongoing feminist debate reflect the fact that each side gets an important part of the story partly right: *mahr* is neither wholly the sale of a vagina nor the recognition of a woman's dignity; it cannot be reduced to an abstract symbol of women's empowerment nor to a concrete sign of female subjugation. *Mahr* is multiple, complex and contradictory. Seeing it as such will not resolve the debate, but it does help delineate its incommensurability.

In studying the dynamic functions of *mahr* through a historical narrative of Egypt, Yossef Rapoport (2000: 2) noticed: "Obviously, the amount and composition of gifts given to brides as well as their control of this property directly affect the position of women in society. The transmission of property at marriage also affects the general transmission of property across generations, modifying the effect of inheritance laws and practices." Others share this view (Goody 1990; Mundy 1988; Mir-Hossini 1993), although it is not a unanimous perspective; rather, it directly contrasts with the stance reflected in classical Islamic law that *mahr* is a static legal rule. This section addresses the stakes of conceiving *mahr* as an autonomous legal system rather than as a dynamic part in a larger marital web of rights and duties. Ultimately, I claim that the stakes are the constitution of a romantic subject in the first (the husband offers a gift to the wife upon marriage to express his love for her and his respect for God) and a calculating subject in the latter, whose actions can be analyzed through an economic analysis of the law. A distributional analysis of *mahr* is crucial since *mahr* is encountered by actual parties and often used by them as a tool of relative bargaining power in the negotiation of contractual obligations related to the family.

In order to assess the economic and functional importance of *mahr* and the negotiating structure it designs for both spouses, I will present *mahr* in relation to a set of subrules regulating the rights and duties of husband and wife under Islamic family law more broadly and affecting the internalization of different costs and bargaining endowments as the spouses navigate in time—before, during and after marriage. The functional, fragmented *mahr* permeates a broad range of personal decisions, and can guide the answers to the questions it raises: Whether to marry *this* man? When to move to the marital residence? When to have sex for the first time and how? Whether and when to ask for divorce? How many children to have?

Mahr Before Marriage: The Initiation *Mahr*

An Islamic "marriage contract can only be concluded through the principles of offer (*ijab*) and acceptance (*qabul*) by the two principals or their proxies" (Nasir 2002: 45). *Mahr* is often introduced in the literature as a symbolic representation of this contract:

> *Mahr*, when presented and accepted, makes a symbolic representation of the earnestness of each spouse to live with the other a mutually cooperative and trustful life. In other words, by giving and taking *mahr*, each spouse takes the vow to stand by the other with the purpose of attaining transcendent tranquility under the chaste alliance known as *nikah* (marriage). (Wani 1995: 193)

In its legal structure, Islamic marriage is a contract of exchange with defined terms that legally affect each spouse in various ways (Abu-Odeh 2004: 1063). The concept of initiation *mahr* encompasses the *mahr* partially paid at the time of marriage (prompt *mahr*) and the *mahr* partially deferred until divorce or death, and which activates upon marriage the set of rights and duties conferred to husband and wife as a regulatory system during their marriage.

Under Islamic family law, marriage establishes a reciprocity system in which each party is assigned a set of contractual rights that will confer a duty toward the other party. Upon marriage, the husband acquires the right to the wife's obedience and sexual availability. The wife acquires the right to her *mahr* and to maintenance. I first review each of the contractual rights and duties as isolated from one another, and then explore the motivations and effects they are expected to produce individually, as well as relationally.

Him: The Right to the Wife's Obedience and Sexual Availability

Obedience is a right which the husband can demand from his wife, and it is a duty that she must fulfill at all times. It involves abiding by "the Islamic instructions regarding her behavior toward the husband" (Wani 1995: 49), obeying "all his lawful commands for the duration of marriage" (Nasir 2002: 98), and not leaving the house without his permission or for a reasonable cause (Pearl and Menski 1998: 178). This last factor solidifies the link between obedience and the wife's presence in the matrimonial home: "If a wife leaves her husband's home without his permission or refuses to reside in a house which fits her status, she shall be considered 'disobedient' and shall not be entitled to her maintenance according to all the schools" (Maghniyyah 1995: 359). The right to be sexually available requires the wife to give her husband "free access to herself at all lawful times" (Nasir 1998: 98).

Her: The Right to Maintenance (*Nafaqah*)

Maintenance is "the husband's primary obligation" (Esposito and DeLong-Bas 2001: 26) to the wife during marriage, as well as to any minor children of the marriage (Nasir 2002: 174). This contractual responsibility continues for the period of *iddah* (three months) following the dissolution of marriage. The purpose of this extension is "notionally supposed to continue so that the opportunity of reconciliation is available to the parties" (Wani 1995: 195). The requirement that *nafaqah* continues until the wife completes three menstrual cycles is also intended to protect women who may be pregnant and avoid paternity disputes (Wani 1995: 195, Esposito and DeLong-Bas 2001: 26–7). The law presumes that if the wife proves to be pregnant during the *iddah* period, the husband is the father.

The financial commitment arises regardless of the woman's wealth, and according to the husband's means. All women are entitled to food, clothing, housing, toiletries and medical attention, while the husband could also be required to provide servants to women of certain social positions (Nasir 1994: 59). Doctor Wani specifies that "the purpose of the obligation of *nafaqah* is to create a chaste social order, to strengthen family ties and to concretize the family bonds. The husband is bound to enjoy his wealth at home only and the wife has to obtain her necessities only through legitimate means, that is, through her husband" (Wani 1995: 195). Maintenance as a central duty for the husband, and as a right for the wife, constructs man as the protector.

The Islamic Marriage Contract as Reciprocity: When He Meets Her

The obedience of the wife and her sexual availability, two crucial "duties" of the wife—often referred to by Islamic jurists as "conjugal society" (Maghniyyah 1995: 316)—give rise to the right to maintenance. These are so interrelated that as soon as she unjustifiably refuses sex or is otherwise disobedient, the duty of maintenance is temporarily suspended (Esposito and DeLong-Bas 2001: 26). But it cuts both ways: where a "refractory wife" (*nashiza*) is not legally entitled to maintenance, a negligent husband similarly "loses his right to retain the wife on failure to maintain her" (Wani 1995: 195).

The Initiation *Mahr* and What It Entails

Mahr occupies a significant role in the marital relationship, to the extent that all of the wife's duties are delayed until *mahr* is paid to her. For instance, as long as *mahr* has not been received, the wife may refuse sexual intercourse and refuse to move to the marital residence upon marriage, duties that she would otherwise have to fulfill as a wife (Maghniyyah 1995: 316). She may even go on a journey without her husband's consent, an act that would otherwise constitute disobedience. This also extends to the wife justifiably refusing to go on a journey with the husband (Schleifer 1985: 205). There are subtleties of interpretation, however, in that "[i]f the whole *mahr* is stipulated in the contracts as 'deferred' (to be paid in the future), the woman is not at liberty to refuse the embraces of her husband, as she has dropped her right by agreeing to the 'deferred' dowry" (Schleifer 1985: 205). Non-payment of prompt *mahr*, however, is considered a complete answer to a man's demands that a woman extend conjugal rights to him or move to the matrimonial home (Fyzee 1974: 141). The woman's guardian is likewise bound by this and cannot send her to comply with the husband's wishes (Esposito and DeLong-Bas 2001: 25); in fact, "[i]f all or part of the *mahr* is stipulated as 'prompt,' a woman may refuse cohabitation with her husband until she receives her dowry of him, as the dowry is payment for cohabitation rights" (Schleifer 1985: 204–205).

It may be helpful to call this initial bargaining standpoint the "initiation" *mahr*. By virtue of the power structure it designs, the initiation *mahr* presupposes a give-and-take relationship in which the differentiated line of normalcy/expected behaviour has been drawn along gender lines. But whereas the wife may fail to perform *all* marital duties until payment of *mahr*, she will still enjoy the benefits of maintenance. As specified by Pearl and Menski (1998: 181):

> Problems arise in relation to the payment of the prompt dower, not least when wives refuse to have sexual relations until the prompt dower has been paid. The matter will often come to court on the basis of a suit initiated by the husband for a decree for restitution of conjugal rights. The defence raised by the wife will invariably be that she has denied sexual intercourse to the husband because the dower has not been paid. ... [R]efusal to have sexual intercourse under these circumstances does not constitute disobedience (*nashuz*), and the husband remains under a duty to continue to provide his wife with maintenance.

This conceptually gives the woman some semblance of bargaining power: she is justified in withholding certain of the man's rights of marriage until prompt *mahr* is paid, and yet continue to be maintained by him in the style to which she has become accustomed (Wani 1987: 18, Esposito and DeLong-Bas 2001: 26).

Once the wife receives her prompt *mahr*, she must immediately start *acting as a wife* (be obedient, have sex when her husband demands it and take care of the house) *in exchange for* maintenance. But since the payment of the deferred *mahr* will depend directly on the behaviour of the parties during marriage and upon divorce, it always remains in the shadow of the relationship (Mnookin and Kornhauser 1979). I will first trace the legal portrait of *mahr*'s ritualistic and exclusive place in the Islamic family law of divorce and inheritance (what I will call *talaq mahr*, *khul mahr*, *faskh mahr* and inherited *mahr*), in an attempt to understand how *mahr* can be dynamically employed and deployed for different and contradictory purposes in a series of variable scenarios.

Mahr at Divorce: *Talaq Mahr*, *Khul Mahr*, and *Faskh Mahr*

Islamic family law structures the economic relations of the spouses and maintains its regulatory power at the dissolution of marriage. Legal institutions such as *talaq* divorce, *khul* divorce and *faskh* divorce determine the degree to which each party may or may not initiate divorce and the different costs associated with it. As pointed out by Doctor Wani (1996: 183), *mahr* will play itself out differently under each institution: "The position of a divorced woman's claim to *mahr* can be determined with reference to the respective form of marriage dissolution followed in a particular case." I will review each institutional setting independently.

Talaq *Divorce/*Talaq Mahr*: Repudiation by the Husband Without the Wife's Consent*

According to classical Islamic family law, *talaq* (repudiation) is a unilateral act which dissolves the marriage contract by a declaration made only by the husband. The law recognizes the power of the husband to divorce his wife by saying "*talaq*" three times without any need for the enforcement of his declaration by the court. If the husband says "*talaq*" only once or twice, he can rescind, but if he says "*talaq, talaq, talaq,*" this formulation will bind him as well as her to a divorce. *Talaq* divorce is the most common method of dissolving a marriage in the Muslim world. The husband can act unilaterally, without cause, and without giving the wife any recourse to change the course of events (El Alami and Hinchcliff 1996: 22).

What comes with this unlimited "freedom" of the husband to divorce at will and on any grounds, is the (potentially costly) obligation to pay *mahr* in full as soon as the third *talaq* has been pronounced. *Talaq mahr* was Islam's attempt to make of *mahr* "a real settlement in favour of the wife, a provision for a rainy day and, socially, ... a check on the capricious exercise by the husband of his almost unlimited power to divorce. A husband thinks twice before divorcing a wife when he knows that upon divorce the whole of the dower would be payable immediately" (Fyzee 1974: 133). *Mahr* immediately becoming payable to the woman herself also acts as a form of compensation to the wife once the marriage has been dissolved. Many Qur'anic verses cite the conditions upon which *mahr* becomes payable, which work to alleviate some of the potential wrong to which the wife has been exposed (Esposito and DeLong-Bas 2001: 36).

Talaq mahr thus acts as a "deterrent *mahr*": the higher *mahr* is (if not in absolute terms, at least in relation to the husband's economic situation), the higher chances are that the husband will hesitate before repudiating his wife and the more effective the wife's leverage may be (Hoodfar 1996: 131). In most cases, this will be a source of security for wives who do not want a divorce. For those who do, however, high *mahr* means the opposite of security: it will only be at the price of behaving in a disgraceful manner that the wife will obtain a *talaq* from her husband. (Throughout this section, I assume that the woman does want a divorce. I am perfectly aware that the desire to divorce does not necessarily reflect reality.) Judith Tucker (1985: 55), in analyzing peasant women in nineteenth-century Egypt, affirms that "many women who wanted a divorce preferred that their husbands repudiate them" because of "the material advantages of *talaq*." The forms of disobedience used by Muslim women to push men into repudiation have of course varied, and surely depended on the historical and social context of the society in which they lived. In her study, Tucker (1985: 55) observed the following circumstances:

> Having enlisted the cooperation of the local shaykh al-bald, one woman managed
> to bully her husband into pronouncing a divorce. Another used blackmail: she
> threatened to take her husband to court and claim that he had stolen her jewelry

unless he divorced her; so she 'frightened him' and he indeed complied with a repudiation.

In this regulatory regime, there is no shortcut for a wife who wants a divorce but cannot obtain the consent of her husband. A wife may unilaterally terminate her marriage without cause only when such power has been explicitly delegated to her by her husband in the marriage contract (Zahra 1955: 140–41). Otherwise, she may apply to the courts either for a *khul* or a *faskh* divorce.

Khul *Divorce/*Khul Mahr*: Divorce by Mutual Consent—But at What Price?*

Khul divorce can be initiated by the wife with the husband's prior consent; however, the *qadi* must grant it, and divorce by this method dissolves the husband's duty to pay the deferred *mahr* (El Alami and Hinchcliffe 1996). The further risk is that, in allowing the legal separation, the *qadi* can also require the woman to repay all or part of the prompt *mahr* paid to the woman at the time of her marriage (Abdal-Rahim 1996: 105). *Khul* divorce is therefore the *exchange* of *mahr* for "freedom," a form of divorce that has "often proved very costly indeed" (Tucker 1985: 54). This reality is reflected in the old Persian saying: "I release you from my *mahr* to free my life (*mahram halal janam azad*)" (Mir-Hosseini 2000: 82). Unsurprisingly, the Arabic word *khula* means "to take off one's dress." As suggested by Mir-Hosseini (1993: 41):

> Both the types of marriage dissolution and the nature of the payments involved suggest that a man's right to divorce emanates from his paying *mahr*. He has to forfeit what he paid as *mahr* if he takes the initiative to repudiate the wife; and he regains the *mahr* if the wife initiates the termination of the contract. Consistent with the logic of marriage as a contract, his right can be relinquished only through compensation; therefore the wife must pay in order to be on an equal footing with him.

In her study of peasant women in nineteenth-century Egypt, Tucker further argues that, at times, the economic losses entailed in waiving *mahr* were so difficult that they would act as "a brake on [wives'] recourse to *khul* proceedings" (Tucker 1985: 54). Depending on the woman's level of desperation to remove herself from the marriage, she would go to great lengths and pay a high premium for her freedom—to the point of giving up child support payments and maintenance during the *iddah* period. Tucker (1985: 54) cites the example of one Bedouin who "obtained her divorce by canceling her husband's debts to her, forfeiting all claim to support during her *iddah*, and returning a *mahr* of most handsome proportions: five silver bracelets, fifteen camels, two cows, and four woolen blankets."

Faskh *Divorce/*Faskh Mahr*: Judicial Dissolution of Marriage*

If the *khul* divorce route is not desirable or available, the wife may apply for a *faskh* divorce, but only in so far as she can demonstrate to the *qadi* that her case meets the limited grounds under which such a divorce can be granted. As a *faskh* divorce is essentially a fault-based divorce initiated by the wife, it is only available in certain situations delineated by specific conditions (El Alami and Hinchcliffe 1996). In the case of termination of marriage by *faskh* divorce, the wife is entitled to *mahr*. Tucker (1985: 53) thus concludes that *faskh* "appears the most favorable to the woman insofar as she obtains a wanted divorce but yet retains her claim to the balance of the *mahr* and support during her waiting period (*iddah*)."

Although it is most favourable to Muslim women, *faskh* divorce is also the most difficult to obtain. In fact, Tucker's study (1985: 54) "did not find a single request in the Mansurah records." The situation in which a woman would petition the *qadi* for a *faskh* divorce would arise when the husband refused to consent. The wife would thus appear before the *qadi* to state her reasons for requesting a divorce. Grounds to issue a decree of *faskh* often include impotence on the part of the husband (Abdal Rahim 1996: 105); "insufficient material support and companionship" (more poetically described as "the loneliness of the marriage bed") (Tucker 1985: 54) (such as when military recruitment stole men away from their homes, leaving women married, but with nothing to show for it); non-fulfillment of the marriage contract, which she had to demonstrate through "acceptable witnesses" (Abdal-Rahim 1996: 105); mental or physical abuse (Esposito and DeLong-Bas 2001); or a husband's lack of piety (Abdal-Rahim 1996: 105).

Mahr *After Death: The Inherited* Mahr

Mahr is not extinguished by the death of the husband, wife or both. According to Islamic family law, *mahr* is an unsecured debt payable directly to the wife (Esposito and DeLong-Bas 2001: 25) and comes under the second head, after funeral expenses, in the order of application of the property. Hence, in the event of the husband's or the wife's death, and even if prior to consummation (Pearl and Menski 1998: 180), *mahr* is a claim that can be maintained by the wife against the husband's heirs, by the wife's heirs against the husband or by the wife's heirs against the husband's heirs. This "widow's right of retention" (Fyzee 1974: 142) refers to the capacity lawfully to retain the husband's whole estate until *mahr* is paid in full. Unlike a charge or a lien, this right is a personal right against all heirs and creditors. The wife can retain—although not obtain—possession of her husband's estate. She must take care, however, since "[o]nce she loses possession … she loses her special right and is in no better position than an unsecured creditor" (Fyzee 1974: 142).

Bargaining in the Shadow of *Mahr* during Marriage: Samir and Leila

Mahr has the potential to assert a continuing regulatory power over husband and wife throughout the marriage. This form of power may control or influence their decision to remain within the institution, their performance of respective marital duties and their use of power to strike a bargain. Bargaining in the shadow of *mahr* inevitably means bargaining in the shadow of divorce, because what is at stake during marriage is the (in)visible presence of its dissolution, and with it the possibility, among other things, that deferred *mahr* will be due. Throughout this part, I use the methodology of Robert Mnookin and Lewis Kornhauser (1979) in *Bargaining in the Shadow of the Law: The Case of Divorce* to demonstrate that spouses take their respective power in marriage and/or divorce in part from the Islamic family law rules that govern their conduct. I also apply Hale's (1923) *Coercion and Distribution* approach to highlight the distributive conflict between Muslim men and Muslim women from the starting point of initiation *mahr* until the possible, perhaps never actualized, point of *talaq-khul-fashk mahr* or inherited *mahr*. As will be apparent, contradictory forces may undermine or strengthen a Muslim woman's position within the family, and law in theory is rarely a depiction of law in practice.

I introduce the story of Samir and Leila living in Egypt, and try to assess the potential costs and benefits for both spouses of putting an end to the relationship when *mahr* is either extremely high or extremely low. While this story is fictional, it draws on some of the observations of Doctor Ziba Mir-Hosseini and Professor Homa Hoodfar, well-known scholars specialized in gender, family relations and Islam. Doctor Mir-Hosseini has recorded, transcribed and assembled into dossiers case studies of the ways in which "*Mahr* was used as the main bargaining strategy" (Mir-Hosseini 1993: 75) upon divorce in Iran and Morocco from 1980–2000. Professor Homa Hoodfar has similarly highlighted, in the case of Egypt, "the ways in which women have used *mahr* and marriage negotiations to circumvent some of the limitations imposed by the legal system and traditional ideology, both of which are legitimized in the name of religion" (Hoodfar 1996: 123).

Suppose that Samir and Leila are both practising Muslims. They were raised in Egypt and they married in Cairo in 1991; Samir was 28 years old and Leila was 24. Their Islamic marriage contract specifies that *mahr* is $80,000: $5,000 as prompt *mahr* (given upon marriage) and $75,000 as deferred *mahr*. Samir works as an engineer and his salary is $90,000. Leila stays at home. Their relationship is difficult and stormy. In 1996, after five unhappy years, they both want to put an end to their marriage.

Let us assume that all the Islamic family law rules presented above apply in full force. Samir may think twice before issuing *talaq*, given that such a decision will be extremely costly for him: $75,000 is a substantial sum and well beyond his means. Leila's first thought may well be to ask for a divorce from the *qadi*. She may also be inclined to be overly disobedient (go on a journey on her own without Samir's permission, spend time in the public sphere and in an intimate fashion with Ahmed, the attractive neighbour, or similar behaviour), in order to provoke Samir to issue *talaq* and trigger his obligation to pay the deferred *mahr*. Ironically enough, and precisely because *mahr* is so high, Leila may find herself in the unfortunate situation of not obtaining *talaq* from Samir no matter how "bad" a wife she tries to be. In fact, Samir might tolerate a broader spectrum of behaviour and action than he would have had *mahr* been lower.

In disobedience, however, Leila becomes vulnerable before both Samir and the community at large. Not surprisingly, the costs of illicit sexual activities for women are higher than they are for men, and "arguments about a woman's morality, honor, and virginity are one of the common causes of domestic violence in the community" (Singerman 1995: 51). She could even feel obliged to return to her parents' home to "seek protection from physical, verbal, or economic abuse" (Singerman 1995: 54). Thus, Leila might consider negotiating her exit from the marriage through a *khul* divorce, even though she recognizes that this option would require her to surrender her claim to $75,000 and is thus economically undesirable. Before embarking on a *khul* divorce, she must acknowledge the distributional conflict she faces: what are the benefits to be gained from divorce measured against the costs of freedom? Benefits may include:

- leaving an unhappy relationship,
- putting an end to obedience,
- having sex with the attractive neighbour, and
- going to an undisclosed destination without her husband's permission.

Costs may include:

- waiving *mahr*,
- possible exclusion from the extended family and the community as a divorced woman, and higher risks of economic and social problems and exploitation (Singerman 1995: 61),
- taking the blame for the dissolution of marriage, and
- being worse off economically as a result of the absence of maintenance at the end of the *iddah* period.

For the husband, the distributional script includes a different weighing exercise. His analysis could be phrased in the following manner: what are the benefits to be gained from an unwanted divorce as opposed to the costs of giving consent to the *khul* divorce? Benefits may include:

- gaining the amount of *mahr*,
- seeing the end of maintenance after the *iddah* period, and
- increasing the chances of starting a new, happy relationship.

Costs may include:

- losing the marriage itself,
- losing the obedience of the loved one,
- less sex in the short term, and
- the high cost of remarriage (since he would have to pay *mahr* to the prospective new wife, possibly in addition to child support to children he had with his former wife) (Singerman 1995: 53, El Alami and Hinchcliffe 1996: 58).

An additional dimension materializes under Islamic law: polygamy. Classical Islamic law allows the man to marry up to four wives on the condition that he can provide for and treat them equally. The shadow of polygamy as a male prerogative remains, as Tucker states, "a powerful disciplinary tool enforcing female submission" (Tucker 1985: 53). Under Article 11 of *Egyptian Law No. 100 (1985)*, a man may marry up to four wives, but he has to inform both his future and current wife/wives of the other marriage(s) (El Alami and Hinchcliffe 1996: 58). Under Article 6 of *Egyptian Law No. 100 (1985)*, the wife can request a divorce in cases of polygamy, but only if she can prove harm, material or emotional, resulting from the new marriage (El Alami and Hinchcliffe 1996: 56). Imagine that, in response to Leila's disobedience, Samir decides not to issue *talaq*, which had been Leila's preferred outcome and one that had motivated her disobedience in the first place. Instead, Samir decides to marry a second wife in Alexandria. Leila can only prove harm with great difficulty since the court is likely to see her as a "disobedient wife." In this case, not only will Leila not receive any immediate compensation, but *mahr* will remain in an identical position, that is, deferred until divorce or death. Leila will have lost considerable bargaining power as a result of this miscalculation, as polygamy will eventually bring competing claims among wives (and their children) to the relatively scarce family resources provided by Samir. In the short term, Leila's status will likely also diminish:

> In many cases, when a man marries a second wife, for whatever reasons, the first wife and family is neglected. These women, while officially married, are better characterized as permanently separated, since they receive minimal financial support for their children from their husband and no longer engage in conjugal relations. Additionally, because they are not divorced they cannot remarry. Thus, although it is legal, this latter type of polygynous relationship is universally condemned for eroding the familial ethos in the community. (Singerman 1995: 66)

Would the script have unfolded differently had Leila been in the Egyptian market labour force? In discussing the impact of labour market participation on Egyptian women's emancipation, Hoodfar notes:

On a different occasion, I visited Umm Abir. Her husband owned a tam'iya and ful shop, which sold cooked beans and a variety of traditional sandwiches. Every day she peeled over twenty kilograms of potatoes and many kilos of onions and cleaned a huge amount of beans, then carried them on her head to the shop, which was a ten-minute walk from their home. One day while I was helping Umm Abir prepare the vegetables, we discussed women and work. She told me every woman should work and earn money because men have no respect for the wife who doesn't earn. She added that if she had had an income when her husband married a second wife, she would have left him. But with four children and no income, her only option was to accept his second wife. (Hoodfar 1997: 111)

Evidently, Umm Abir participated in the family labour force without receiving an income. Furthermore, this non-market work significantly reduced her bargaining power. Homa Hoodfar (1997: 139) states,

[A]ll the men, married or not, were adamant that it was a husband's prerogative to deny his wife the right to work. None of the informants was asked to express his view on this issue, but all volunteered an opinion. Few women contested men's claim to the right to stop their wives from "working" or leaving the house. The majority said that by custom, tradition, and religion, husbands were entitled to such rights.

A wife in such a situation could thus decide, as part of her strategies, to go to work against her husband's wishes as a form of disobedience intended to encourage him to issue *talaq*. Muslim women in contemporary Egypt justify their participation in the labour market as a way to protect themselves in the event of divorce, even if such a choice is potentially very costly. Sadia, a 37-year-old mother of three children, confesses:

This is not a life, this is misery. If only I could trust my husband, I would stop working at least for a few years because I have to spend all I earn on child care and buses. But I do not trust him. One cannot trust men these days, life is getting harder and they want to get out of their family responsibility. I feel I have to work so I will have enough to survive in my old days should my marriage fail. I don't want to give up the security of my job even at the cost of divorce. Who would look after me if tomorrow something happened to him or if he divorced me? My brothers don't even come to see me, much less look after me and my three children. I need the security. These days life is difficult. Women need security. (Hoodfar 1997: 116)

Would Leila similarly experience her bargaining power erode or increase if she entered the market labour force? In our scenario, Samir refuses to issue *talaq* or agree to a *khul* divorce, despite Leila's efforts. Presented as a system of incentives rather than as a source of values, law becomes for Leila a shifting, imaginary entity whose precise outcomes she attempts to predict within narrow bounds.[5]

At the opposite extreme would be a situation in which Samir offers a minimal financial *mahr* to Leila—a ton of jasmine—in the marriage contract. Leila thought "the idea of a ton of jasmine as *Mahr* was romantic at the time of her wedding, although it [is] of no use after she was divorced by her husband."[6] In this case, the phantasmatic initiation *mahr* (a ton of jasmine) obliges Leila to waive any bargaining power she would otherwise have had during marriage because she initially refused to conceive of *mahr* as a market value. Romantic *mahr* does not pay off. Hence, Samir issues *talaq* with no hesitation—and still with no hesitation he decides to remarry immediately. Leila would later testify that "if her *Mahr* had been high enough her husband would have thought twice before divorcing her to marry another woman, or at least she could have been compensated or exacted revenge by forcing him to pay afterwards" (Mir-Hosseini 2000: 75). As Leila is economically dependent on Samir, the benefit of a ton of jasmine is lost on her if she is divorced and left without financial support.

Between these two extremes lies a continuum of bargaining possibilities in which Samir or Leila would use *mahr* directly or indirectly in all kinds of everyday life situations to gain something from the other person. These possibilities range from agreeing to better, less or more sex during marriage to entering or not entering the labour market. Custody issues can also take on various shades of meaning since, according to classical Islamic family law, men have the custody of their children beyond a certain age (seven for boys and puberty for girls). A woman can thus use her *mahr* to bargain for custody of her children or for a sort of alimony, even if these would have been denied to her under a regular divorce (Mir-Hosseini 2000: 77, Hoodfar 1996: 130). Even the decision to wear or not wear the *hijab* can have economic implications. Some women choose to veil not merely out of custom, "but as a strategy that enables them to continue to have access to some independent cash income. At the same time, they are undermining religious conservatives, for whom veiling means women's exclusion from the labor market" (Hoodfar 1996: 116).

A number of conclusions emerge from the hypothetical scenarios of Samir and Leila in relation to *mahr*. First, although Islamic family law strictly regulates family relations and the rights/obligations of each family member, the legal framework (the law in books) does not always account for the ways in which Muslim men and

---

5   I borrow here from the methodology developed by Duncan Kennedy (1992). For law and economics literature on bargaining around marriage and divorce in the United States and Canada, see Cohen (1987), Wax (1998), and Trebilcock and Keshvani (1991).

6   The example of a ton of jasmine as a *mahr* that satisfies the romantic imagination is based on a true story. Mir-Hosseini (2000: 75) reports how such a *mahr* does not fulfill the practical exigencies required of it: "Once again, the important function of a high *Mahr* as a safeguard for women in marriage was brought into relief."

women themselves deploy power in a fluid, contradictory and at times subversive fashion in diverse scenarios (the law in action).[7] Second, initiation *mahr* designs the initial bargaining power structure that *this* particular woman will enjoy as she enters marriage and love, and which will often reflect and measure her underlying socio-economic conditions and personal characteristics. Third, *mahr* may at times be used as deterrence and/or compensation, in anticipation of *talaq* in the first case and in relation to *ex post facto* religious divorce in the latter.

By placing *mahr* at the centre of contractual obligations and in the shadow of the law, I have privileged a conception of individuals as bargaining power agents, exchanging their obligations for precise purposes. I argue that there are costs to isolating and dissociating *mahr* from the marital web of rights and duties within which husband and wife love each other, fight, hope and play through the use of various strategies. The attractive dimension of the cost/benefit analysis I use, as opposed to the unchanging and predictable subjects and outcomes of classical Islamic law, lies in its acceptance of the existing and inherent conflicts of interest between men and women in relation to *mahr* and family relations. Moreover, it brings into focus what remains hidden by the normative and normalizing discourse of Islamic law: sometimes *mahr* can be a tool of considerable discipline for *this* woman, sometimes it can oppress her, sometimes it can empower her and sometimes it can exist as an ephemeral and useless value—a ton of jasmine.

The Place of Departure: *Mahr*'s Internal Pluralism

Initial discussions about *mahr* in its various forms—at divorce, upon death— implicitly assume that *mahr* can be understood uniformly. This, however, is not the case: *mahr* is internally plural. It is not, as the proponents of the formalist school would argue, a static institution derived solely from God and spiritually detached from society. Samir and Leila can use the traditional rules surrounding *mahr* in diverse, contradictory and sometimes subversive ways. One of the reasons for this is that they have different starting points: depending on which geopolitical narrative one embraces, *mahr* can be used "in the shadow of the law" (Mnookin and Kornhauser 1979) quite differently in Cairo, Tunis or Kuala Lumpur.

This analysis offers a critique of the idea of cultural or religious authenticity— that is, the belief that there is such a thing as an Islamic *mahr* that could homogeneously travel to Canada, the United States, France or Germany and be recreated or preserved by the Western judiciary. In subsequent chapters, I will identify the three liberal approaches emerging from the adjudication of *mahr* in North American and European courts. These decisions represent *mahr* traversing the host legal, cultural and sociological boundaries to arrive in new surroundings.

---

7   For a sampling of law-in-action critiques that span several decades, see Pound (1909, 1910), Cook (1927), Llewellyn (1930), Galanter (1974), Mnookin and Kornhauser (1979), Merry (1986), and Ewick and Silbey (1998).

Every voyage, however, must have a starting point; every transplant must have its native ecosystem. Therefore, before examining in more detail the (liberal) reception of *mahr*, I present as background the description of three legal regimes in which *mahr* is rooted: the representative places of departure—Egypt, Tunisia and Malaysia. My reason for doing so is simple: even states that apply Islamic law routinely, and thus have ample opportunity to adjudicate *mahr*-related issues, are far from identical in their treatment of *mahr* in either theory or practice. Such internal pluralism, not surprisingly, is bound to engender the kind of external pluralism that arises in the European and North American courts. Far from being a uniform and static legal concept or institution, *mahr* varies by location and geopolitical space.

Mahr *in Egypt*

Egypt typifies the dichotomy of dual legal systems through its retention of both Western-inspired national law and Islamic personal law. The Egyptian legal system developed from a mix of Roman, French, Ottoman and Islamic law, as well as ancient, medieval and customary Egyptian law (Venkatraman 1995; Oppermann 2006). During the nineteenth century, Islamic law was progressively replaced by European legal systems. Eventually, only family law remained within the direct application of Islamic law (Abu-Odeh 2004), and in 1956, the Islamic courts were integrated with the national court system (Hajjar 2004). Islamic law has nonetheless remained very influential and is considered the principle source of law (Lombardi 1998), especially in family law matters (Abu-Odeh 2004; Oppermann 2006).

In Egypt, divorce rates have been rising since the 1970s (An-Na'im 2002). Despite this rise, it has proven difficult for Egyptian women to obtain a divorce. For example, under *Egyptian Law No. 100 (1985)*, a wife could only obtain a *faskh* divorce if her husband habitually failed his duty to provide her maintenance, suffered from a serious disease, was absent for a lengthy period, was imprisoned for a lengthy sentence or inflicted harm on her (Abu-Odeh 2004: 1106). In response to lobbying by women's rights activists, the Egyptian legislature adopted *Egyptian Law No.1 of 2000*. Although not without controversy (Mashhour 2005), women are now allowed to apply for a somewhat modified version of the classical *khul* divorce—if she "ransoms herself and releases herself by *khul'* (*khala'at zawjaha*) by forfeiting all of her lawful financial rights, and restores to him [her husband] the dower he gave to her [upon marriage], then the court is to divorce her from him" (Article 20). In fact, a wife can go so far as to obtain a divorce without the husband's consent and without any specific ground except for stating that the continuation of the marriage may cause her to violate God's law (Welchman 2007). Whereas classical jurists have interpreted *khul* divorce as requiring the return of the deferred *mahr* only (Mashhour 2005), a wife seeking *khul* divorce under the *Egyptian Law No.1 of 2000* must not only repay any prompt *mahr*, but also renounce *all* of her post-marriage financial rights under Islamic law, which include the unpaid portions of deferred *mahr* and maintenance (Al-Hibri 2005).

By March of 2000, the Personal Status Court in Cairo alone had received over 3,000 applications for a *khul* divorce (An-Na'im 2002). Given the considerable length of time and difficulty of proving harm to obtain a *faskh* divorce, studies show that only women of means are requesting *faskh* divorces (Al-Sharmani 2007: 8). Women lacking in financial means rather opt for a *khul* divorce, which ironically also puts them at even greater risk of significant financial hardship (Abu-Odeh 2004). In fact, the return of paid prompt *mahr* and any payments made on a deferred *mahr* may act as a deterrent against divorce for poorer women (Welchman 2007: 115; Abu-Odeh 2004: 1102).

Mahr *in Tunisia*

Tunisia's legal system is based on French civil law and Islamic law. Although the Constitution states that the country is Muslim, not all laws are required to conform with Islamic law (Charrad 2001; Brand 1998). Habib Bourguiba, the first president who administered the country from 1956 to 1987, was very influential in the development of women's rights as part of his efforts toward modernization and development (Brand 1998: 177). In 1956, the *Personal Status Code* created major reforms in the legal system based on Qur'anic reasoning, including the criminalization of polygamy. In implementing this particular reform, it was reasoned that the Qur'an favours monogamy and, as with slavery, polygamy no longer constitutes a necessary or acceptable practice. Moreover, the government adopted Muslim scholarly arguments stating that it was impossible to treat multiple wives equally, and that polygamy was historically justified only due to the decrease in the male population following the particular context of war (Venkatraman 1995: 1980; Mashhour 2005: 585). Those who defy this law are subject to a fine and/or imprisonment (Brand 1998: 208).

Tunisian family laws make divorce proceedings more equitable for women, providing them with the same access as men under Islamic law (Morse and Sayeh 1995: 719). Only courts can grant a divorce, thus *talaq* pronounced outside the court has no legal effect (Brand 1998: 178; Morse and Sayeh 1995: 712). Moreover, the traditional *faskh* divorce is not applied (Welchman 2007: 128). Divorce may be obtained by mutual consent, at the request of one of the parties without specific grounds (An-Na'im 2002: 159), or because of abuse (Brand 1998: 208).

Mahr remains an integral component of a valid marriage. Without paying prompt *mahr*, a husband cannot legitimately consummate the marriage (Morse and Sayeh 1995: 709). Deferred *mahr* is payable immediately upon divorce or death, and is considered an unsecured debt against a husband's estate if unpaid (Morse and Sayeh 1995: 713; Abu-Odeh 2004: 1107–9). Unlike many other Muslim countries, a wife does not need to remit her *mahr* if she seeks a divorce (Mehdi 2005). The practical benefits of this legal rule, however, are minimal: *mahr* amounts are quite low and there is no obligatory minimum (Labidi 2001). Bourguiba used the occasion of his own marriage in 1962 to break with tradition by giving his wife a single "symbolic dinar" as *mahr* instead of a substantial amount

(Labidi 2001: 121–22). The 1993 Amendments to the *1956 Personal Status Code* further cemented the trend by removing the requirement that *mahr* not be "trifling" (Welchman 2007: 91–2).

Mahr *in Malaysia*

The Malaysian legal system is derived from three sources: English common law, Islamic law and *Adat* (Malay customary law pre-existing Islam). *Adat* has had a significant influence on Islam, mostly in ensuring greater freedom, rights and public participation for Muslim women in Malaysia (Foley 2004; Endut 2000). The official legal system incorporates common law and Islamic law, with civil courts responsible for most areas of the law, and *Adat* influencing certain areas of law. Non-Muslim family law is regulated by federal law, which allows for some level of consistency across states, whereas Islamic family law falls under state jurisdiction. However, the federal government has developed model laws such as *The Islamic Family Law (Federal Territories) Act 1984* (Malaysia Act 303.50a) that states can choose to adopt either entirely or with modifications (Endut 2000: 37). The Islamic court system governs family law, charitable endowments, bequests, inheritance and various offences, including offences committed against Islam. In these matters, civil courts are not permitted to intervene.

A Malaysian woman has a number of legal options for divorce. First, she can request a *faskh* divorce if her husband has disappeared for over one year, if he failed to maintain her for three months or if she did not consent to marriage (Samiuddin and Khanam 2002; Endut 2000). Second, she can negotiate a *khul* divorce with the consent of her husband (*cerai tebus talaq* in Bahasa Malaysia or "divorce by redemption") (Act 303.50a §49(1); An-Na'im 2002: 255). In this latter case, she must either give up her claim to any outstanding *mahr* and return whatever portion was given to her upon the solemnization of the marriage, or pay an amount agreed upon by both parties. If the parties cannot agree, Syarian Court judges may determine the amount "in accordance with *Hukum Syarak* ... having regard to the status and the means of the parties" (Act 303.50a §49(3)). Through the process of *hakam*, a woman can also ask the court to declare a *talaq* divorce (Act 303.50(a) §49(3), §47(2), §47(11)). The first step is generally a form of counselling; if this is unsuccessful, arbitration by *hakam* based on the Qur'an takes place and, as a final option, the Islamic court presides (Endut 2000: 45–6).

In Malaysia, *mahr* is known as *Mas Kahwin*, which literally means "marriage gold" (Peletz 2002). It can be given in the form of money actually paid by the husband to the wife at the time the marriage is solemnized, or in the form of something that can be valued, or acknowledged as a debt (Act 303.50(a) §2(1)). Amounts are traditionally quite low, and maximum rates—which vary considerably by region, possibly due to changeable regional economic capacity (Hussain 2004)—are set by law. Amounts as listed for each state by the Department of Islamic Development in Malaysia are contingent upon a woman's status, that is, depending on whether she is an unmarried woman or a divorcée (Hussain 2004).

One reason *mahr* is lower in Malaysia than in other Muslim nations is because of the co-existence of *Adat* practices such as *Pemberian*, which is enshrined and protected in Act 303.50(a) as "a gift whether in the form of money or things given by a husband to a wife at the time of the marriage" and offers legal guarantees identical to *Mas Kahwin* regarding its required payment to a bride. *Pemberian* involves much higher amounts at the time of marriage, and may legally serve a similar deterrent and protective purpose as *mahr* (Peletz 2002; Hassan and Cederroth 1997). With high *Pemberian* legally recoverable upon divorce, it is not surprising that most divorce disputes in Malaysia do not involve payment of *mahr*.

Conclusion

Although Western courts treat *mahr* as a unitary institution of their own apparatus, the presentation of *mahr* as it exists in only three different Islamic jurisdictions demonstrates that what travels is actually a fragmented and disjointed *mahr*. The static, autonomous *mahr* is the technical manifestation of an underlying conceptualization of *mahr* as a religiously motivated form of dignity for *all* Muslim women, as opposed to a more diffuse idea of obligation and negotiation arising in a number of contradictory ways under Islamic family law, some less and some more apparent. My approach is to make *mahr* the focus of the interwoven web of marital contractual obligations that tie man and woman together through an Islamic marriage contract: it cannot be dissected from the rest. Further, my goal in presenting both the roots of *mahr*—both legally and geographically—has been to establish the changeable and changing qualities of *mahr* not only in the places where it has traditionally been sought and used by Muslim women, but also in the interpretations of commentators and scholars, whether Muslim or otherwise. From the roots of *mahr*, the next phase of this study engages a vision of *mahr* branching out: how does the concept of liberalism enhance or detract from minority communities' ability (or even desire) to develop a cultural identity within mainstream Western culture? I propose that the answers are as diverse not only as the countries that I present next, but also as diverse as the Samirs and Leilas who travel from place to place and inject their own complex personal and cultural understandings into the mix.

Chapter 2

When *Mahr* Travels:
Adjudicating *Mahr* in Canada, the United States, France and Germany

While family law, contract law, constitutional law and private international law constitute the foreground rules directly governing the subject of *mahr*, the scope of application of each field gets defined and constrained in relation to the other fields. Holding these considerations firmly in view, this chapter outlines the legal rules involved in the discussion of the applicability and enforcement of *mahr* in Canada, the United States, France and Germany. In doing so, I embark on a comparative exercise in which I examine the general rules applicable in each country as separate and well-defined legal systems and categories. Throughout, I will ask: What legal rules can be applied and what limitations exist, given the fact that *mahr* presents itself at the crossroads of contract law, family law, constitutional law and private international law? What are the limits of freedom of religion in the applicability of foreign law in France and Germany? What role does religious freedom play in a secular American regime and in a Canadian order constitutionally attached to multiculturalism? In introducing the legal "tool box" available to judges adjudicating *mahr*, my purpose is to lay out, on the one hand, the complex and constraining legal rules within which liberal ideology may emerge (legal pluralist, formal equality and substantive equality) and, on the other, the outcome that may flow from it in the form of the enforcement or non-enforcement of *mahr*.

The Background Legal Regime in Canada

The legal regime in Canada encompasses several concepts and principles that affect the way *mahr*-related issues and claims are perceived and adjudicated. Chief among them are the Canadian constitutional protections of religious freedom and multiculturalism, the judicial enforcement of domestic contracts and the family law legislation at the federal and provincial levels (with an emphasis on the legal framework of the provinces that have adjudicated *mahr*).

Religious Freedom and Multiculturalism

The Supreme Court of Canada has stressed the importance of freedom of religion on numerous occasions. With the adoption of the Canadian *Charter of Rights and*

Freedoms in 1982, freedom of religion became "the right of every Canadian to work out for himself or herself what his or her religious obligations, if any, should be and it is not for the state to dictate otherwise" (*Big M Drug Mart* 351). The Court articulated its nascent understanding of the freedom of religion in *R v Big M Drug Mart*:

> The essence of the concept of freedom of religion is the right to entertain such religious beliefs as a person chooses, the right to declare religious beliefs openly and without fear of hindrance or reprisal, and the right to manifest religious belief by worship and practice or by teaching and dissemination. But the concept means more than that. … Freedom means that, subject to such limitations as are necessary to protect public safety, order, health, or morals or the fundamental rights and freedoms of others, no one is to be forced to act in a way contrary to his beliefs or his conscience. (*R v Big M Drug Mart* 336–37)

The *Charter*'s preamble states, "Canada is founded upon principles that recognize the supremacy of God and the rule of law." The irony of a statute that simultaneously puts one particular deity at the forefront and entrenches freedom of religion is not lost on legal commentators. As one such critic pointed out, "To mention God with a capital letter in the preamble to the Charter and then to go on to say that the Charter provides a fundamental freedom of conscience and religion, is a contradiction which even a theologian, to say nothing of all the lawyers, must surely recognize" (Klassen 1991: 95). Not surprisingly, therefore, the Supreme Court of Canada has offered subsequent clarifications.

In *Syndicat Northcrest v Amselem*, the Court again touched on the substance of the freedom of religion, which consists of

> the freedom to undertake practices and harbour beliefs, having a nexus with religion, in which an individual demonstrates he or she sincerely believes or is sincerely undertaking in order to connect with the divine or as a function of his or her spiritual faith, irrespective of whether a particular practice or belief is required by official religious dogma or is in conformity with the position of religious officials. (*Syndicat Northcrest v Amselem* para. 46)

Religious freedom is thus closely allied with the *Charter*'s commitments to religious equality in section 15 (which enumerates equality rights generally)[1] and to the preservation and enhancement of Canada's multicultural heritage in section 27. "An important feature of our constitutional democracy," the Supreme Court of Canada suggests in the opening remarks of *Amselem*, "is respect for minorities, which includes, of course, religious minorities" (para. 1). In *Amselem*,

---

1   Relevant excerpts of the *Charter of Rights and Freedoms* and all other statutes cited in this chapter and from the four countries discussed in this chapter are included in Appendix C.

the Supreme Court upheld the right of Orthodox Jewish owners of condominiums to build *succahs* (temporary shelters) on their balconies during the Jewish festival of Succot. The case, however, gave the Court the opportunity to speak to the issue of religious freedom more generally. Iacobucci J. emphasized that "respect for and tolerance of the rights and practices of religious minorities is one of the hallmarks of an enlightened democracy" (para. 1). The concept of equal religious citizenship has recently been extended beyond the traditional realms of freedom of belief to include the right to engage in religious practices without interference (Ryder 2008). Although the Supreme Court of Canada often explores and defines the role of religion in the public sphere—that is, in relationship to "a multiethnic and multicultural country like ours" (*Amselem* para. 87) or "a free society built upon a foundation of diversity of views ... that seeks to accommodate this diversity to the greatest extent possible" (*Ross* para. 91)—religion also manifests itself as a private matter through affiliation in the family. Next, I will examine the Canadian family law framework.

The Judicial Enforcement of Domestic Contracts

Family law legislation throughout Canada recognizes the importance of domestic contracts or marriage agreements in the resolution of family disputes. Domestic contracts are subject to the same basic validity rules as other contracts. The validity of a domestic contract is determined according to the facts at the time the contract was concluded.[2] To establish an apparent contract, a person must prove offer, acceptance, consideration and intention to create legal relations (*Smith v Smith*). Under general contract law, no special form of contract is required unless a contract comes within the terms of the *Statute of Frauds*. Provincial family law legislation (such as Ontario's *Statute of Frauds*) invariably provides that a domestic contract is unenforceable as a domestic contract unless it is in writing and signed by the parties.

In interpreting provincial statutory regimes, the Supreme Court of Canada has recently emphasized that people must abide by their personal choices even in situations of apparently unequal bargaining power. For example, in *Nova Scotia (Attorney General) v Walsh*, a 2002 case appealed through the courts of the province of Nova Scotia, the Court held that a woman who "chose" not to marry was not allowed to make a claim for property division. In the case of *Miglin v Miglin*, a 2003 decision from Ontario, the wife who signed a spousal support waiver in exchange for a position in the family business was held to her agreement (Bala and Chapman 2002; Shaffer and Rogerson 2003). Finally, in *Hartshorne*

---

2 Some of the most prominent principles are: conditions precedents (*Ball v Ball*), a contract subject to condition precedent is not binding until the condition occurs (*Blair v Casey*), there must be an intention to create legal relations (*M.(N.) v A.(A.T.)*), no contract is created unless there is a meeting of the minds (*Smith v Smith*), and acceptance must be communicated before the offer is withdrawn (*Beese v Beese*).

v Hartshorne, a lawyer who signed a pre-nuptial agreement on the day of her wedding after she had been told by a legal colleague that the agreement was grossly unfair compared to what she was entitled to under the statutory regime, was held to that agreement. The Court explicitly rejected an argument relying on grounds of unequal bargaining power. In all of these cases, the Supreme Court of Canada determined that the exercise of personal choice was made within the acceptable limits of contractual law, and that people making those choices had to be responsible for them.

The Family Law Regime at the Federal and Provincial Levels

In Canada, the federal and provincial governments share jurisdiction over family law. Subsection 92(13) of the *Constitution Act*, which came into effect at the time of Confederation in 1867, granted to the provinces the general constitutional power over the family as a matter of "property and civil rights." In practice, this power has been read broadly, giving the provinces authority over numerous matters such as professional trades, labour relations and consumer protection. The federal power is outlined in subsection 91(26), and is restricted to "marriage and divorce." The categories, however, are far from watertight, thus there are some constitutional grey areas. For example, the provinces retain the power over the solemnization of marriage (s. 92(12)), thus laws related to marriage and divorce overlap occasionally. In most cases, this can be solved through principles of federal paramountcy or interjurisdictional immunity. For instance, the federal *Divorce Act* is valid legislation, even though it has some incidental effects on child custody, which is usually considered to be within the provincial jurisdictions of "civil rights" (s. 92(13)) and "matters of a private nature" (s. 92(16)). The federal *Divorce Act* thus concerns married couples who want a divorce, as well as various issues related to the divorce, such as child and spousal support claims, custody and access to children. Provincial laws govern all other family law matters, such as separation (as distinct from divorce) of married or unmarried couples, custody, access, support, division of property, restraining orders and related issues of child protection and enforcement of orders. Hence, in Canada, the division of property in the event of the dissolution of marriage depends heavily on the provincial law governing the couple (Bromley 1957). In Québec, family law is located within the civil law regime of the *Québec Civil Code*,[3] whereas in all the other provinces it is regulated by common law. Because the adjudication of *mahr* in Canada has taken place only in the provinces of Ontario, British Columbia, Nova Scotia and Québec, I will briefly review each of these family law frameworks.

---

3   The 10 books of the *Québec Civil Code* are: Persons, Family, Successions, Property, Obligations, Prior Claims and Hypothecs, Evidence, Prescription, Publication of Rights and Private International Law. For an analysis of the development and background rules of the *Code*, and especially its distinctive nature in the Canadian context, see Brierley (1992) and Pineau (1992).

The Province of Ontario   In Ontario, the *Family Law Act* generally assumes a 50/50 split of the shared assets of the divorcing spouses. Net family property is determined by considering all the property a spouse owns, accounting for certain deductions and exceptions. The spouse who holds less net family property is entitled to one half of the difference between the two net family properties. Courts are able to increase or decrease either spouse's share to correct for equitable concerns such as the intentional depletion of assets or to honour a written agreement between the spouses that is not a domestic contract. The preamble to the *Act* states that the purpose of the statute is to "recognize the equal position of the spouses as individuals within marriage and to recognize marriage as a form of partnership" and therefore to insure "an equitable settlement" when the relationship dissolves.

A domestic contract may, however, supersede the distribution rules unless the contract violates one of the public policy parameters of the Act. Pursuant to subsection 52(1) of the *Family Law Act*, a marriage contract refers to agreements made by couples who "agree on their respective rights and obligations under the marriage or on separation, on the annulment or dissolution of the marriage or on death," including support obligations and other matters in the settlement of their affairs. For the purposes of section 51, a domestic contract is defined as a marriage contract, separation agreement, or cohabitation agreement. It is open to the parties to create a marriage contract that sets aside the equalization formula of the *Family Law Act*, or to exclude a particular asset, such as a matrimonial home, from the operation of the formula (s. 52). A valid and enforceable domestic contract will be determinative of property rights falling within the scope of the contract (*Lay v Lay*). Spouses can also contract regarding the education and moral training of a child, although the court can set aside such clauses if they are deemed not to be in a child's best interest (s. 56). Moreover, the Act provides that a court may override the terms of a domestic contract, in whole or in part, if a party failed to disclose significant assets or liabilities, if a party did not understand the nature or consequences of the contract or on other grounds in accordance with the law of contract (lack of consent, duress, etc.) (s. 56).

This statutory wording has received considerable judicial interpretation and refinement. In *Underwood v Underwood*, for example, the Ontario Divisional Court maintained part of a domestic agreement while varying another part. Likewise, in *Horner v Horner* the Court of Appeal set aside some provisions of the agreement, but left the remainder intact. In the event of an allegation that a party has failed to disclose assets or liabilities, parties seeking to set aside a contract on the basis of non-disclosure must prove that an omission was material and operative in the sense that if they had known the facts, they would not have entered into the contract or would only have done so at a different consideration (*Brans v Brans*). Setting aside a contract for reasons of failure to understand the nature and effect of an agreement is, in practice, difficult: individuals who have the sophistication to negotiate a domestic contract often seek independent legal advice, which minimizes the potential for them later to allege that they did not understand an agreement. To be successful, they must argue that they did not understand what they were doing and the legal effect of the agreement when they entered into it (*Desramaux v Desramaux*).

The issue of duress has been raised frequently in the context of domestic agreements. A court may rescind a contract if a party was induced to enter the contract by duress, which involves a threat of wrongful and immediate force at the time of the formation of a contract. There is a difference between entering an agreement under stress and entering an agreement under duress (*Hill v Ilnicki*). Often, what judges describe as duress borders on practical compulsion. For example, Ontario's Superior Court of Justice set aside an agreement for duress in *Campbell v Szoke* when the husband informed the wife that she could not move to Florida if she did not sign the agreement.

The Province of British Columbia   In British Columbia, the *Family Relations Act* confers the judicial branch the discretion to depart from the rule of equal division of family assets expressed in section 43 of the *Act* where, having regard to the criteria set out in section 51, equal division would be unfair. If a determination of an unequal allocation has been made, the trial judge may, by way of remedy, reapportion family assets on the basis of fairness (*Elsom v Elsom*, *Harper v Harper*). Domestic contracts are also permitted under the *Family Relation Act*'s matrimonial property regime, in which case the terms of the agreement represent the spouses' presumptive entitlement; marriage agreements themselves are defined in subsection 61(2) of the Act. To be enforceable, however, any such agreement must operate fairly at the time of distribution. If the agreement is deemed unfair, a court may reapportion assets to achieve fairness. While section 61 permits parties to avoid the statutory default regime by entering into binding contractual arrangements to govern their relationship during and upon dissolution of the marriage, section 65 limits this freedom by permitting the court to vary the contractual terms if the division of property under the agreement is unfair at the time of distribution. Specifically, subsection 65(1) provides that if the provisions for division of property between spouses either under their marriage agreement or under the statutory regime would be unfair, the court may order that the property covered by such agreement or statutory regime be divided into shares fixed by the court. In doing so, the court must have regard to the following factors: the duration of the marriage; the duration of the period during which the spouses have lived separate and apart; the date when property was acquired or disposed of; the extent to which property was acquired by one spouse through inheritance or gift; the needs of each spouse to become or remain economically independent and self-sufficient; or any other circumstances relating to the acquisition, preservation, maintenance, improvement or use of property or the capacity or liabilities of a spouse.

The Province of Nova Scotia   In Nova Scotia, the legislature expressed its intention to promote the family through marriage in the preamble to the *Matrimonial Property Act*. The Act addresses matrimonial assets acquired during the marriage by considering the effect of marriage breakdown on the assets of the spouses, and by offering married couples a legal framework of equal shares within which the division of matrimonial assets will be addressed (s. 12(1)). However, where the court is satisfied that the division of matrimonial assets in equal shares would be unfair or unconscionable, it may "make a division of matrimonial assets that is not equal or may make a division of property that is not a matrimonial asset" (s. 13). In doing so, the legislature guides the judiciary by providing a number of factors to be considered on division of property (s. 13). Pursuant to subsection 22(1) of the Act, the division of matrimonial assets is governed by the law of the place where the parties had their last common habitual residence. The law specifically provides that only matrimonial assets—as defined in the Act—are to be divided according to the statutory scheme. Section 22 leaves open the possibility of *renvoi* determining the relevant law to govern the division of matrimonial assets. As for marriage contracts—made before or during marriage or cohabitation delineating rights and obligations at any point in the relationship, including upon death (s. 23)— the threshold for judicial oversight is a finding that any term is "unconscionable, unduly harsh on one party or fraudulent" (s. 29). If the court makes such a finding, it can "make an order varying the terms of the contract or agreement as the court sees fit."

The Province of Québec   Pursuant to the *Québec Civil Code*, marital property legislation does not allow parties to opt out of the statutory regime by means of a marriage contract (Article 423). Hence, a spouse cannot contract out of the equal division of "family patrimony" (Article 414 and 415) and only the court may "make an exception to the rule of partition into equal shares" (Article 422). This highly interventionist role of the state is said to exist in order "to diminish the distance between formal and real equality" (Poirier and Boudreau 1992: 256). In 2002, Québec extended the rights and obligations of marriage to particular registered civil unions by enacting *An Act instituting civil unions and establishing new rules of filiation*, which added a registered civil union regime to the *Civil Code*. The spousal status confers benefits such as spousal support and recognition of survivor status upon intestacy. The rights may be altered by a domestic contract, and the partnership is terminated if the partners marry each other, die or make a joint declaration that the partnership is over.

In Québec, the status and capacity of a person are governed by the law of the person's domicile (Article 3083). The Code also specifies that the law governing situations involving incapacity (Articles 3085–87), marriage (Articles 3088 and 3089), separation from bed and board (Article 3090), filiation by blood or adoption (Articles 3091–93), and obligation of support (Articles 3094–96) is the law of the person's domicile. While the form of a juridical act is generally governed by the law of the place where it is concluded (Article 3109), its content is governed by the law explicitly designated in the act or by that which is designated as a clear result of provisions of that act (Article 3111). According to private international law rules, foreign law is not of obligatory application by the judge, such that it must be proved and applied only where the parties have chosen to plead it. The Code clearly indicates that application of foreign law is subject to the condition of its having been pleaded; absent pleading of foreign law, the law of the forum is applied (Article 2809). Where such law has not been pleaded or its content cannot be established, the court applies the law in force in Québec, which need not be pleaded: Article 2807 obviates pleading and proof by the parties of Québec rules of private international law by making it the proper subject of which a judge can take judicial notice.

The Background Legal Regime in the United States

This section is concerned with the First Amendment, both as an American constitutional law rule and as a guiding principle in interpreting contract law. It also outlines the legal developments, on a state law basis, regarding community property, the possibility and validity of opting out of such statutory regime by way of antenuptial agreements and the conflict of laws at play in deciding matrimonial disputes. In order to better understand the adjudication of *mahr* as part of the wider legal regulation of the family, I will present the scope and validity of antenuptial agreements in American family law generally, with a special emphasis on the laws of states that have specifically dealt with *mahr*.

The First Amendment and Contract Law

In the United States, a proper respect for both the Free Exercise and the Establishment Clauses compels the State "to pursue a course of 'neutrality' toward religion" (*Committee for Public Education & Religious Liberty v Nyquist*).

The Free Exercise Clause, which has been made applicable to the states by incorporation into the Fourteenth Amendment (*Cantwell v Connecticut*), provides that "Congress shall make no law respecting an establishment of religion, or prohibiting the free exercise thereof." It protects freedom of conscience and freedom to adhere to such religious organizations or forms of worship as the individual may choose. As the United States Supreme Court reasoned in *Cantwell v Connecticut*,

> Free exercise embraces two concepts—freedom to believe and freedom to act. The first is absolute but, in the nature of things, the second cannot be. The freedom to act must have appropriate definition to preserve the enforcement of that protection although the power to regulate must be so exercised as not, in attaining a permissible end, unduly to infringe the protected freedom.

Government action specifically directed at religion that burdens individuals' free exercise of religion could be sustained only if the action is narrowly tailored to compelling state interests. Laws that are *not* religiously neutral are those that encroach on religious belief or impose burdens on people simply because of their religious beliefs. Such laws presumptively violate the Free Exercise Clause. In divorce cases involving claims that religious norms should apply, spouses may raise a Free Exercise claim by asserting that the state cannot force them to do something they consider to be religious, usually by arguing that the state cannot enforce a religious agreement without violating the Free Exercise Clause of the First Amendment (*In re Marriage of Goldman*; Marshall 1985).

The Establishment Clause of the First Amendment, in turn, has erected a wall of separation between church and state. In *Everson v Board of Education*, Justice Black emphasized the need for absolute separation: "That wall must be kept high and impregnable. We could not approve the slightest breach" (18). This has also been expressed as "the established principle that the government must pursue a course of complete neutrality toward religion" (*Wallace v Jaffree* 2491). A statute is valid under the Establishment Clause if it has a secular purpose, if its primary or principle effect is neither to advance nor to inhibit religion and if the statute does not foster excessive government entanglement with religion. This has played out in the courts in various ways. For example, in *Lemon v Kurtzman*, the United States Supreme Court invalidated two statutes that provided financial aid to church-related schools. The field of education has provided a fertile field for litigation of the Establishment Clause. For example, in *Board of Education v Mergens*, the Court found no violation where a high school included a Christian club in its 30 recognized student groups; but, in *Lee v Weisman*, the Court ruled that the Establishment Clause had been violated where public school officials invited members of the clergy to offer invocation and benediction prayers at a high school graduation. Similarly, in *Santa Fe Independent School District v Doe*, the school district violated the Establishment Clause in authorizing a student election to determine whether to have a student deliver a "brief invocation and/ or message [at] varsity football games to solemnize the event, to promote good sportsmanship and student safety, and to establish the appropriate environment for the competition."

The First Amendment generally provides dual protections: it guarantees government neutrality toward religion and provides for the individual's liberty in choosing and practicing a religion. Though the Court has narrowed the opportunity to obtain religious exemptions from generally applicable laws, it has not completely closed this door. The Supreme Court has denied such exemptions from generally applicable laws in *Employment Div. v Smith, Lyng v Northwest Indian Cemetery Protective Ass'n* and *Reynolds v United States*. However, there have been some cases in which the Court has provided an exemption under the Free Exercise Clause, namely *Hobbie v Unemployment Appeals Comm'n of Florida, Wisconsin v Yoder*, and *Sherbert v Verner*. In matters touching upon religious concerns in the specific context of contract law and family law, courts are not precluded from resolving a dispute simply because it involves a religious organization but they cannot "prescribe what shall be orthodox in politics, nationalism [or] religion" (*Zummo v Zummo* 1144). Judicial involvement in religious disputes is constitutionally limited to the neutral principles of law: a secular interpretation entails a commitment not to "rely on religious precepts … [or] resolve a religious controversy" (*Jones v Wolf* 604).

The Judicial Enforcement of Antenuptial Agreements

Prenuptial, premarital or antenuptial agreements are contracts executed between prospective spouses in contemplation of marriage with a view to determining marital property rights and financial responsibilities. In *In re Marriage of Spiegel*, the Supreme Court of Iowa reasoned that such agreements are designed to give greater latitude to parties "to fix and determine the interest that each spouse has in the property of the other" (313). Clearly, however, property interests are not the sole subject of antenuptial agreements. Brian Bix (1998: 150) points out:

> Other possible purposes of such agreements include: (1) ensuring that children from a prior marriage retain certain family wealth, despite possible claims by the new spouse; (2) assuring the economically weaker spouse-to-be that he or she will have adequate economic protection after divorce; (3) attempting to make any eventual divorce simpler and less contentious; and (4) assuring that certain family heirlooms or family wealth stay within a family upon divorce.

Courts have routinely stated that prenuptial agreements regarding post-dissolution support are enforceable as a matter of contract (*Lashkajani v Lashkajani*, *Mabus v Mabus*, *In re Yannalfo*, *Pysell v Keck*, *Lebeck v Lebeck*) and should be construed according to the intention of the parties (*Gordon v Munn*). In order for an antenuptial agreement to be valid, it must be entered into voluntarily by both parties (*In re Marriage of Seewald*) and "be fair, equitable, and reasonable in light of the surrounding facts and circumstances" (*Rosenberg v Lipnick* 388). In *Rosenberg*, the Massachussets court left open the factors that could be considered in determining the fairness of the circumstances:

> In judging the validity of such an antenuptial agreement, other relevant factors which we may consider are whether (1) it contains a fair and reasonable provision as measured at the time of its execution for the party contesting the agreement; (2) the contesting party was fully informed of the other party's worth prior to the agreement's execution, or had, or should have had, independent knowledge of the other party's worth; and (3) a waiver by the contesting party is set forth. (388)

Historically, antenuptial agreements made in contemplation of divorce were considered void as against public policy. In *Osborne v Osborne*, the Supreme Judicial Court of Massachusetts summarized the reasons for such holdings: "(1) they are not compatible with and denigrate the status of marriage, (2) they tend to facilitate divorce by providing inducements to end the marriage, and (3) a contract waiving or minimizing alimony may turn a spouse into a ward of the

State" (810). However, in 1970, the Florida Supreme Court departed from this approach, noting:

> We know of no community or society in which the public policy that condemned a husband and wife to a lifetime of misery as an alternative to the opprobrium of divorce still exists. And a tendency to recognize this change in public policy and to give effect to the antenuptial agreements of the parties relating to divorce is clearly discernible. (*Posner v Posner* 384)

Prior to the decision in *Posner*, premarital agreements could not include any contingent divorce-planning provisions, although premarital agreements addressing the property rights of a surviving spouse at widowhood have long been upheld in many states (*Crouch v Crouch*).

Most jurisdictions have followed Florida's lead (Swisher 1979), establishing that antenuptial contracts settling alimony and property rights upon divorce are not void *ab initio* as contrary to public policy. In *Banks v Evans*, for example, an Arkansas court held that the mere fact that a prenuptial agreement becomes operative upon divorce does not render it invalid, so long as that is not its only purpose. Moreover, most of the states have adopted the *Uniform Premarital Agreement Act* of 1983, which authorizes spouses to contract with each other regarding their respective property rights and support obligations as well as "any other matter, including their personal rights and obligations, not in violation of public policy or a statute imposing criminal liability" (s. 3). Under section 6, a premarital agreement is not enforceable if the party against whom enforcement is sought proves that: (1) the party did not execute the agreement voluntarily; or (2) the agreement was unconscionable when it was executed if a party: (a) was not provided with a fair and reasonable disclosure of the property or financial obligations of the other party; (b) did not voluntarily and expressly waive, in writing, such disclosure; and (c) did not have adequate knowledge of the property or financial obligations of the other party.

Even though prenuptial agreements are nominally entitled to the same consideration and construction as other contracts, courts have nevertheless imposed additional requirements on the basis that parties to a prenuptial agreement are said to be dealing "not at arm's length" (*Griffin v Griffin*). Hence, the reasonableness of any monetary provision in an antenuptial contract will be decided by referring to "such factors as the parties' respective worth, the parties' respective ages, the parties' respective intelligence, literacy, and business acumen, and prior family ties or commitments" (*Rosenberg v Lipnick* 389). For instance, the agreement may be modified by the courts where it is determined that one spouse is or will become a public charge (*Knox v Remick*); that the agreement is unconscionable at the time of enforcement (*Edwardson v Edwardson*); or that the agreement proves fraud, concealment, or failure to disclose material information. Because of the special nature of the relationship between a prospective husband and wife, the law imposes an additional burden upon the proponent of an antenuptial agreement to show either a fair and reasonable provision made for the party opposing the contract, or a full, fair and frank disclosure of the other spouse's worth made before execution of the contract. If neither of these applies, then the party seeking to have the contract upheld must prove that the party challenging its validity in fact had a generally accurate knowledge of the other's worth (*Matter of Lewin's Estate*).

Critical responses to judicial attempts to alleviate potentially harmful effects of contract law in the family law sphere have been varied. Some argue broadly for the enforceability of premarital contracts, viewing optimistically the private ordering of marriage, in particular premarital agreements relating to economic matters (Schultz 1982; Stake 1992). Others point out historical gender inequities, arguing that these are especially dangerous when parties are negotiating their future together (Guggenheimer 1996). Gail Frommer Brod (1994: 279) even calls on the legislative arms of government to intervene: "Lawmakers should recognize premarital agreements for what they are: contracts that violate societal norms against gender discrimination."

The Family Law and Contract Law Regimes at the State Level

The courts of four American states have adjudicated *mahr*. I thus present the specific family law and contract law regimes in California, New York, New Jersey and Florida.

The State of California   Under the *California Family Code*, marriage is a "[p]ersonal relation arising out of a civil contract between a man and a woman, to which the consent of the parties capable of making that contract is necessary. Consent alone does not constitute marriage. Consent must be followed by the issuance of a license and solemnization" (§300). The parties entering marriage must each be 18 years old (§301) or have the written consent of their guardian or a court order allowing them to get married (§302). A licence must be obtained from a county commissioner of marriages, and it must state the identity of the parties, their place of residence and their ages (§351). The marriage must be solemnized in the presence of two witnesses by someone authorized to solemnize a marriage (such as a priest or a judge) (§400), who must then sign and return the marriage license to the county commissioner of marriage (§422).

In California, the marital property rights of all state residents (§2320) are fixed in accordance with California community property law, whether or not the parties were married in California (§760). According to §751, each spouse has an existing present equal interest in the community property during the continuance of the marriage, thus all property acquired during marriage is presumed to be community property. Unless the parties are able to come to a negotiated settlement, the court has the power in a dissolution proceeding to divide equally between them the community estate. The community property presumption can be rebutted, however, in one of two ways. First, a spouse can show that the property in question is really his or her separate property (§770). Second, couples may execute a written antenuptial agreement to alter the separate or community status of their property (§1500, §1612(a)(3)). In concluding their antenuptial agreements, parties may choose the law that governs their contract (§1612(6) and (7)). Consequently, the legality of a contract is determined by the law of the place where it was made, and it will be enforced by California courts unless the contract is contrary to the public policy of the forum. Premarital agreements must be in writing and signed by both parties (§1611).

In the early to mid-1900s, California courts relied heavily on the doctrine that the terms of antenuptial agreements that encourage or promote divorce are against public policy and therefore unenforceable (*Morgan v Morgan, Whiting v Whiting, McCahan v McCahan*). This changed from 1950 to 1986. During this latter period, courts recognized nuanced interpretations available to them in rendering their judgments on antenuptial agreements. For example, in *In re Marriage of Dawley*, decided in 1976, the Court reaffirmed the rule that such contracts are offensive to the public policy of California if the "terms of the contract 'facilitate,' 'encourage,' or 'promote' divorce or dissolution" (350). However, the Court further pointed out that the term "facilitate" should not be misconstrued so as to render illegal agreements that merely define the property rights of spouses, thereby simplifying the issues and reducing the costs of a dissolution proceeding: "public policy does not render property agreements unenforceable merely because such agreements simplify the division of marital property; it is only when the agreement encourages or promotes dissolution that it offends the public policy to foster and protect marriage" (350). (It is unclear whether or to what extent this public policy limitation is superseded by the provisions of §1612(a)(3) that prospective spouses may contract with respect to the "disposition of property upon separation, marital dissolution, death or the occurrence or nonoccurrence of any other event.")

In *In re Marriage of Noghrey*, the California Court of Appeals addressed the legal enforceability of a *ketubah*, a Jewish religious marriage contract which represents the obligation of the husband under the Jewish faith to provide for his wife upon divorcing her. Some have argued that the *ketubah* may not be interpreted under traditional contract law because it fails to comply with basic contract principles, mainly because it usually is not negotiated or bargained for at arm's length and does not represent an intent to be bound (Greenberg-Kobrin 1999; Kahan 1984).

In *Noghrey*, the agreement promised the wife, in the case of a divorce, "the house … [in] Sunnyvale … [a]nd $500,000.00 or one-half of my assets, whichever is greater." Since the husband could apparently divorce his wife at will, the *ketubah* was a device created to provide economic security for the wife, and discouraged divorce by making it costly and undesirable for the husband. The wife, on the other hand, was not as free to divorce and was subject to loss or reduction of her rights should she divorce her husband on certain grounds. In *Noghrey*, the Court did not even reach the issue of whether a civil court, applying neutral principles of law, could interpret a *ketubah* according to the Establishment Clauses of the federal and state constitutions; it merely stated that such a religious document encourages and promotes divorce, and as such, is contrary to the public policy of the state and unenforceable:

> This agreement ... constitutes a promise by the husband to give the wife a very substantial amount of money and property, but only upon the occurrence of a divorce. No one could reasonably contend this agreement encourages the husband to seek a dissolution. Common sense and fiscal prudence dictate the opposite. Such is not the case with the wife. She, for her part, is encouraged by the very terms of the agreement to seek a dissolution, and with all deliberate speed, lest the husband suffer an untimely demise, nullifying the contract, and the wife's right to the money and property. (*Noghrey* 331)

Noghrey predated California's adoption of the *Uniform Premarital Agreement Act*, which specifically permits premarital agreements to address the disposition of property upon dissolution or the occurrence of a future event. This effectively attenuates the public policy argument of *Noghrey* since an agreement facilitating dissolution may now be permissible—or at least force the court to deal with the Establishment clauses of state and federal legislation when faced with religious divorce cases.

The State of New York In New York, the *Divorce Reform Act* of 1966 governs the dissolution of marriage. Although New York has not enacted any statute permitting divorce on a pure "no-fault" ground (such as irreconcilable differences or incompatibility), subsequent legislation has further expanded and refined the New York statute governing divorce grounds. New York's *Domestic Relations Law* provides six statutory grounds for divorce. The first four are "fault" grounds, and the fifth (living apart on the basis of a judicial separation), implies that a separation was granted on the basis of a "fault" ground for separation. The sixth ground (living apart on the basis of a separation agreement) is the nearest New York comes to having a "no-fault" ground.

New York's *Domestic Relations Law* also determines the economic rights of former spouses. In a matrimonial action, including an action for separation and for divorce, the court may order temporary spousal maintenance or non-temporary maintenance, unless the parties have entered into a written agreement whose terms were fair and reasonable at the time of execution of the agreement and are not unconscionable at the time of entry of final judgment (§236(B)(3)). Equitable distribution is authorized in actions for divorce and for the dissolution of a marriage (§236(B)(5)(a)).

Antenuptial agreements may be used to resolve such concerns as support and custody (§236(B)(3)). New York has taken a strong position of enforcing antenuptial agreements. Barring fraud, antenuptial agreements are presumed to be valid:

[A] duly executed antenuptial agreement is given the same presumption of legality as any other contract, commercial or otherwise. It is presumed to be valid in the absence of fraud. ... A party seeking to attack the validity of the agreement has the burden of coming forward with the evidence showing fraud. (*Matter of Sunshine* 327)

This tendency to enforce antenuptial agreements includes agreements that have religious overtones. As the Court noted in *Avitzur*, "this agreement—the *Ketubah*—should ordinarily be entitled to no less dignity than any other civil contract to submit a dispute to a nonjudicial forum, so long as its enforcement violates neither the law nor the public policy of this State" (114). New York courts have recognized contracts requiring a husband to give his wife a Jewish religious divorce (a *get*) in addition to a civil divorce and have granted specific performance of such agreements. In fact, New York has gone further still in acknowledging the rightful role of religious tribunals in weddings by recognizing it in a statute. Section 253(3) of the *Domestic Relations Law* provides:

Any party to a marriage ... who commences a proceeding to annul the marriage or for a divorce must allege, in his or her verified complaint (i) that, to the best of his or her knowledge, he or she has taken or that he or she will take, prior to the entry of final judgment, all steps solely within his or her power to remove any barrier to the defendant's remarriage following the annulment or divorce; or (ii) that the defendant has waived in writing the requirements of this subdivision.

New York's legislators have thereby attempted to address the situation of the Jewish woman who would otherwise fail to obtain a *get* and would be unable to remarry religiously without being viewed as an adulterer by her religious community. The role of the civil court in such instances is to prevent "the transfer of property or money ... pending compliance" by the party seeking divorce (*Friedenberg v Friedenberg*). The nature of the problem stems from the fact that, under Jewish law, neither a secular court nor even a *beit din* (a Jewish religious court) can dissolve a valid marriage. Only the husband has the power to hand the wife (or her designated agent) the document (the *get*) written in a prescribed form that will release her from the marriage. Since the divorce process currently requires mutual consent, and has always required the husband's consent, the possibility of blackmail, extortion or recalcitrance is ever present.

The State of New Jersey In New Jersey, other than 18-month continuous separation, all grounds for divorce are based on the fault concept. Title 2A of New Jersey's *Permanent Statutes* (*Administration of Civil and Criminal Justice*) enumerates the various "faults" that will justify a judgment of divorce. Property acquired between the date of the marriage and the date of the filing of the complaint for divorce is eligible for distribution (*Painter v Painter*). The court is authorized, where a judgment of divorce is entered, to make such award "to effectuate an equitable distribution of the property both real and personal, which was legally and beneficially acquired by them or either of them during the marriage" (Title 2A: 34–23). Any property acquired by either spouse during the marriage by way of gift, devise, or intestate succession is ineligible for equitable distribution (Title 2A: 34–23), but inter-spousal gifts between husband and wife are eligible for distribution consideration (*Pascale v Pascale*). The statute provides that, absent clear and convincing evidence that the parties did not voluntarily enter into the contract with an understanding of its practical and legal effect (Title 37:2-38), a prenuptial agreement will be upheld and enforced in New Jersey providing that it is substantively fair at the time of its enforcement (Title 37:2-38(b)).

The State of Florida   In Florida, the *Marriage Preparation and Preservation Act* provides that no county court judge or clerk of the circuit court shall issue a licence for marriage unless the parties "are over the age of 18 years ... and unless one party is male and one party is female" (§741.04(1)). Upon the dissolution of marriage, the "equitable distribution of the parties' marital assets is the first order of business" (*Paul v Paul*). According to the equitable distribution statute, the court must first distribute to each spouse that spouse's non-marital assets, and thereafter divide the marital assets in accordance with the various factors enumerated in the statute (§61.075(1)). Inter-spousal gifts during the marriage are marital assets (§61.075(5)(a)3). As for prenuptial agreements, they must be in writing and executed by the parties: oral prenuptial agreements are unenforceable by application of the *Statute of Frauds* (*Kersey v Kersey*, *Posner v Posner*).

The Background Legal Regime in France

This section explores French citizenship policy and the constitutional model of *laïcité*; French rules of private international law regarding the applicability of Islamic family law (Islamic marriages and polygamy, the reunification of polygamous families, and the *talaq* divorce); and the French matrimonial property regime. This background discussion will help identify the extent to which French courts have recognized (or rejected) Islamic family law in matters of personal status.

French Citizenship Policy and the Constitutional Model of Laïcité

The most important feature of current French politics is its neo-republican discourse on French identity (Leruth 1998; Taguieff 1995), in which membership in the national community involves an absolute commitment to the Republic and to its core values of *égalité* and *laïcité*. This republican model was forged in the context of the 1789 French Revolution as a direct reaction to the historical French struggle against its own monarchy, ruling aristocracy and religious establishment.

In France, this traditional model of *laïcité* is explicitly affirmed by two legal documents. First, Article 1 of the *Constitution of October 4, 1958* provides that "France shall be an indivisible, secular, democratic and social Republic. It shall ensure the equality of all citizens before the law, without distinction of origin, race or religion. It shall respect all beliefs." Second, the *Separation of Churches and State Act 1905* states that there is no recognition and no direct public funding of any religion in France. Consequently, France does not allow the state officially to support any exemption for or special representation of immigrant or national minorities. While strategies are employed for individual integration into the French state, the formation of communities of immigrants is highly discouraged (Safran 1991). The rule against state support of immigrant or national minorities is not without its loopholes through which these groups can wiggle to receive at least indirect assistance. As Brigitte Basdevant-Gaudemet (2004: 59) suggests:

> Equally, although there is no direct funding of religions from the public budget, public communities are not prohibited from granting subsidies to cultural or social institutions of a religious nature, and religions can also benefit from major forms of indirect aid in the form of tax deductions, in the context of private denominational schools, or by other means.

Despite this official separation between state and religion, it becomes less and less plausible to define French society in culturally homogeneous terms. Population estimates from 2004 suggest that there are over 5 million Muslims in France—about 8 percent of the French population, the highest percentage of Muslims in any Western European country (Basdevant-Gaudemet 2004: 62). This religious and cultural concentration has important sociological effects. Throughout France, more and more Muslims are expressing and demanding recognition of their religious particularity (Bencheikh 1998; Balkati 1995; Blanchard et al. 2003). Danièl Hervieu-Léger (1998: 39) has astutely emphasized the novelty and urgency of the dilemma raised by the "question of Islam":

> one of the most decisive changes that has occurred since the beginning of the 1980s has been the transformation of a society in which cultural homogeneity seemed assured within the normative space defined by the great republican referents, to a multi-cultural society. ... The question of Islam, which has become the second religion in France after Catholicism—ahead of Protestantism and Judaism—constitutes the highly sensitive point of crystallization of a problem that is much more vast: the question of the relation between particularity and universality in the very definition of French identity.

In this context, the Muslim population in France is seeking public policy recognition of cultural diversity. It began the project of establishing Islamic organizations—at present, there are dozens of such organizations, the three largest of which are the Paris Mosque, The Union of Islamic Organizations in France and the National Federation of Muslims in France. After several attempts to address the "question of Islam" in France, the Minister of the Interior launched a vast consultative exercise in 1999 among the main national Islamic institutions, as well as several mosques. This process culminated in December 1999 in the ratification of a solemn declaration by the Muslim community: *The Principles and Legal Foundation Governing the Relations between Muslim Religious Practice and Public Authorities*.[4] In May 2003, a French Council of the Muslim Religion, comprised of a General Assembly, a Board of Directors and a Bureau, was set up to represent Islam in France officially, with regional councils in each of the 25 French regions. The underlying assumption on the part of the French state is that Muslims should accept the norms governing religious practices within the French tradition of *laïcité*. This commitment to secularism is so deeply entrenched that France entered a reservation with the Secretary General of the United Nations with respect to Article 27 of the International Covenant on Civil and Political Rights. Article 27 provides: "In those States in which ethnic, religious or linguistic minorities exist, persons belonging to such minorities shall not be denied the right, in community with the other members of their group, to enjoy their own culture, to profess and practise their own religion, or to use their own language." Practically speaking, this reservation means that France has not committed to fostering special cultural rights.

French Rules of Private International Law

France has made various stipulations of international private law, and has signed bilateral agreements with various other states. As a result, French courts must apply the law of an individual's country of citizenship in matters of family law to residents who do not have French citizenship, more specifically in relation to disputes over the status and capacity of persons (Abu-Sahlieh and Bonomi 1999). This is true in so far as doing so does not contravene French public order (Rude-Antoine 1992; Deprez 1988) or violate an international convention to which France is a party. Regarding this latter factor, in family law matters, France has ratified the Convention of October 24, 1956 on the law applicable to maintenance obligations towards children, the Convention of October 2, 1973 on the Law Applicable to Maintenance Obligations, as well as the Convention of March 14, 1978 on the Law Applicable to Matrimonial Property Regimes. These three Conventions originated in the Hague Conference on Private International Law.

---

4   Brigitte Basdevant-Gaudemet, specialist of the relations between Islam and the French State and director of the Research Centre of Law and Religious Societies (*Centre de recherche Droit des Sociétés Religieuses (DSR) de la Faculté Jean Monnet (Sceaux)*), has reviewed the main aspects of this declaration in Basdevant-Gaudemet (1996). For an excerpt of this review touching on some of the main points, see Appendix C.

The Applicability of Islamic Family Law in French Courts: An Overview

The international private law rules which incorporate Islamic family principles at the domestic level and apply them to non-French citizens living in France are crucial in determining individuals' rights, especially considering that only approximately 25 percent of the 4 million Muslims living in France have obtained French citizenship (Basdevant-Gaudemet 1996: 355). Hence, faced with family law matters involving Muslim parties who are living in France, but who are citizens of a state governed by Islamic law, French judges are obliged to abide by Islamic law principles. The legality of institutions such as Islamic marriages, polygamy, and the *talaq* divorce frequently arises.

Islamic Marriages and Polygamy Polygamous marriages are prohibited in France. Thus, if a religious polygamous wedding were to take place on French soil, it would have no legal effect. Two principles ensure that this interdiction is, in practice, effective. First, those practising polygamy are prevented from obtaining French citizenship. Second, Article 147 of the French *Civil Code* specifically holds that individuals cannot enter into a second marriage unless the first one has been previously dissolved; Article 184 further authorizes certain parties to attack the validity of the marriage (that is, the spouses themselves, government ministers or anyone who has a particular interest in the matter). Consequently, even between partners whose countries of origin permit polygamy, no polygamous union can be legally contracted in France (Paris Court of Appeal 1992, Cour de Cassation 1988). The second marriage will be declared absolutely null (TGI de la Seine 1967, Cour d'appel de Reims 1976, Cour d'appel de Dijon 1995). It is on this basis that courts have at times denied benefits to Muslim women living in polygamous marriages entered into in France. In 1992, for example, the Cour d'appel de Versailles refused social security benefits to the second wife of a Muslim husband, and in 1988 the Cour d'Appel d'Aix-en-Provence similarly denied a Muslim woman her alimony on the ground that she was the second wife and that polygamy was considered contrary to French public order.

However, if the Islamic ceremony resulting in a polygamous union was conducted in the country of citizenship of the spouses, the marriage is considered to have some legal validity under French law as long as it does not violate French public order. The Cour de Cassation repeatedly held polygamy not to be a *prima facie* violation of French public order under those circumstances (Rude-Antoine 1990: 138–39, Rude-Antoine 1997: 211),[5] even though the very same union would have been declared null if contracted in France. Consequently, health insurance benefits can be paid to a woman who is registered by her husband as a dependent, regardless of whether her marriage is considered legal. If the first wife has already received social security benefits, the second cannot also claim them (Cour de

---

5   French courts use the expression *ordre public à effet atténué* to express this concept.

Cassation 1973), unless the first wife no longer lives in France (Cour de Cassation 1990). Hence, Muslim husbands have been forced to pay child support even though the marriage from which the children resulted was solely a religious marriage rather than a civil ceremony (*Benali c Makhlouf, Consorts Abdallah c M.Y.*).

The Reunification of Polygamous Families   Demographically, immigrant women in polygamous marriages in France generally arrive from a relatively narrow range of countries and regions: mainly from sub-Saharan Africa and, to a lesser extent, from Algeria and Morocco. The immigrant groups with the highest rate of polygamous families are the Soninkés and the Toucouleurs, who come from the Sudan-Sahel region of Africa (de la Chapelle 1997). Until 1980, the reunification of polygamous families was prohibited in France: the French government would deny permanent residence cards to the wives and children of men who had already arrived in France with another wife and their children. In the landmark *Montcho* case in 1980, however, the Conseil d'Etat granted for the first time permanent residency status to the second wife of a man from Algeria, thus endowing the right to family reunification with substantive meaning. The Court reasoned that, for the narrow purpose of reunification, polygamy was a different—but nonetheless legitimate—form of marriage.

In 1993, the French government reacted against this expansion of the legitimacy of polygamy on French soil. According to the Loi 93-1027 du 24 août 1993 relative *à la maîtrise de l'immigration et aux conditions d'entrée et de séjour des étrangers en France*, a polygamous marriage no longer entitles the husband to bring his second (or subsequent) wife and their children to France. The children of polygamous marriages who live abroad without their father can join him in France only in the event of the death of their mother in their home country. Section 30 of the law provides: "When a polygamous foreigner resides in French territory with his first spouse, the benefit of family reunification cannot be granted to another spouse. Unless this other spouse is deceased or has lost her parental rights, her children cannot benefit from family reunification either." This legislation has been attacked by many immigrant organizations for its unfair treatment of Muslim women. Faced with the impossibility of living with their husbands legally, they often enter the country illegally and thus must try to survive in the most vulnerable of positions (FK 2000; Turpin 1994 Gillette-Frénoy 1993a, 1993b).

The Talaq *Divorce*   In a series of no less than five judgments,[6] the first civil chamber of the French Cour de Cassation (the equivalent of a supreme court) opted in early 2004 for the non-recognition of *talaq* as a legitimate form of divorce (Déprez 1996), as it is considered contrary to French public order in general and to the principle of gender equality in particular. The highest court in France also condemned repudiation (*talaq*) on the grounds that it contravenes Article 5 of the

---

6   Published as judgment numbers 01-11.549, 02-11.618, 02-15.766, 02-17.479 and 02-10.755 on February 17, 2005.

Seventh Protocol of the European Convention on Human Rights. However, due to bilateral agreements with Morocco and Algeria, courts recognized legal effects of *talaq* in the 1980s and 1990s, as long as it was pronounced abroad and both the husband and wife were present before the French court to attest to this fact (Déprez 1996: 85; El-Husseini 1999).

The French Matrimonial Property Regime

Antenuptial agreements are well established and well regulated under French law. Article 1387 of the *Civil Code* states that prospective spouses may declare that they intend to marry under any of three matrimonial regimes provided for in the *Code*: The Regime of Community (Article 1400), the Regime of Separate Property (Article 1536) or (since 1965) a modified community property regime known as the Regime of Participation in Acquests (*Participation aux acquêts*) (Article 1569). If they make no special provision, the prospective spouses will be deemed to have subjected themselves to the regime of community property (Articles 1400 and 1401), whereby all property acquired by the husband and wife during the marriage is the community property of both of them. The only exemption is "that which is acquired by gift, devise, or descent" (Stark 2005: 117).

The Background Legal Regime in Germany

This section provides an overview of the German citizenship policy and the constitutional protection of freedom of religion; German rules of private international law as they apply in the specific context of Islamic family law, including issues of Islamic marriages, polygamy and the *talaq* divorce; and the German matrimonial property regime. In Germany, the Muslim community accounts for more than three million members out of a total population of 82 million; about 89 percent of the Muslim population, in turn, is Turkish (Rohe 2004b: 83). This background discussion will help identify the extent to which German courts and public policies have recognized (or rejected) Islamic family law in matters of personal status.

German Citizenship Policy and the Constitutional Protection of Freedom of Religion

In Germany, religious issues are regulated by European and German constitutional provisions governing freedom of religion. The European Convention on Human Rights was adopted under the auspices of the Council of Europe in 1950 to protect human rights and fundamental freedoms. All Council of Europe member states are party to the Convention. Article 9 reads:

1. Everyone has the right to freedom of thought, conscience and religion; this right includes freedom to change his religion or belief, and freedom, either alone or in community with others and in public or private, to manifest his religion or belief, in worship, teaching, practice and observance.

2. Freedom to manifest one's religion or beliefs shall be subject only to such limitations as are prescribed by law and are necessary in a democratic society in the interests of public safety, for the protection of public order, health or morals, or the protection of the rights and freedoms of others.

Specifically for Germany, the Constitution guarantees the freedom to ascribe to the faith and religious practices of individuals' choosing. Article 4 provides: "Freedom of faith and conscience, and freedom to profess a religious or philosophical creed, shall be inviolable. The undisturbed practice of religion shall be guaranteed."

German nationhood is rooted in the concept of the *Volksgeist* (spirit of the people), that is, the people as an organic cultural and racial entity marked by a common language (Savigny 1975). In opposing the French view of legislation as the primary source of law, Savigny considered law to be organically connected with the mind and the spirit of the people—law as the common consciousness of the nation. For Savigny (1975: 30), law "is developed first by custom and by popular belief, then by juristic activity—everywhere, therefore, by internal, silently operating powers, not by the arbitrary will of a legislator." In line with this strong sense of national identity, Germany has historically characterized itself as a nation based on common blood descent: the *Volk*-centred idea of German nationhood thus adopted the *jus sanguinis* principle of citizenship, which emphasized the unity of the nation and the significance of ancestry (Brubaker 1992: 82). Until 1999, in fact, a citizenship applicant had to provide evidence of at least one German ancestor in order to receive German citizenship, a requirement which in practice excluded immigrants from collective incorporation. In recent years, restrictive citizenship and naturalization laws have undergone some changes. Since the introduction of the new citizenship law in 1999 (*Staatsangehörigkeitsrecht*), the importance of ancestral origin has slowly eroded, opening the door to the gradual naturalization of the migrant population. This statutory regime provides that the children of immigrants born in Germany after the year 2000 can be granted German citizenship even if the candidate retains another citizenship. In such circumstances, however, Germany requires that such children renounce the citizenship of their parents' native country sometime between the ages of 18 and 23 (Joppke and Morawska 2003).

Islamic groups in Germany have been trying to secure legal status for their religious communities since the early 1970s. Until now, however, courts have rejected their petitions. According to the *1949 Constitution*, religious denominations can acquire the status of "public law corporation" (*Körperschaftsstatus*) provided that they guarantee continuity with by their bylaws and the number of their members. This status provides far-reaching rights, such as the right to levy taxes from members of the community and to organize a parish, the right to employ people under belief-oriented labour practices, the right to nominate members to broadcast-councils, tax reductions for property placed under public property law, etc. (Rohe 2004b). If the religious denomination cannot meet the continuity requirements, they must organize themselves as mere associations under private law. In 1977, the Islamic community in Germany applied for the status of a public law corporation, asking that Islam be publicly recognized and acknowledged as an equal religion before the law (Vocking 1993). The District Court of Baden-Württemberg rejected the application (Jonker 2000: 313) and, two years later, a similarly futile attempt was launched in Cologne. At present, no Islamic religious community has the legal status of a corporation under public law, unlike Christian churches and the Jewish community; Islamic organizations are rather considered private associations without legal standing.

From the perspective of Mathias Rohe, expert on the legal treatment of Islamic minorities in Germany, the applications made by various Muslim groups to obtain such status have been rejected on the ground that insufficient guarantees of their duration and stability were provided:

> According to a decision of the conference of the state ministers of interior in 1954 the necessary stability of the community has to be proven over a period of 30 years. Up to now, the Jewish community reached this status, whereas no Muslim community succeeded in that so far. This is certainly due to the fact that there were no ideas of a long-lasting presence among larger groups of Muslims until recent times. (Rohe 2004b: 87)

Gerdien Jonker, a scholar well known for her empirical work on religious minorities in Germany, has expressed the opposite view. She believes that the verdict was based not only on the fact that judges believed the applicants to be pursuing right-wing activities, but also due to the impression that "'Islam' shaped the everyday life of its followers in a way that was not acceptable and not in accordance with the German understanding of what religion is about" (Jonker 2000: 312). Moreover, she further suggests that these court rulings were "signals toward segregation and have had a palpable effect on contemporary Islamic religious life. For those Muslims who are observant, the clash between Islamic legal concepts and German legal guidelines has resulted in social isolation" (Jonker 2000: 312).

German Rules of Private International Law

In Germany, religious issues may also come into play through the route of private international law. Private international law (called conflict of laws in the United States) has been defined as law directed to resolving controversies between private persons, natural as well as juridical, primarily in domestic litigation, arising out of situations having a significant relationship to more than one state (Restatement, Second, Conflict of Laws). In Germany, this is so because stipulations of

private international law within the German *Civil Code* (specifically the Second
Chapter on International Private Law in *Einfuehrungsgesetz zum Buergerlichen
Gesetzbuche* (EGBGB)) provides that it is not the law of domicile, but rather the
law of the parties' citizenship that is applicable in family law matters (Article
13) as well as the law of succession (Article 17). Bilateral accords buttress this
codification. A representative example of such an accord that affects non-citizens
residing in Germany is the agreement reached by Iran and Germany. These states
have ratified a treaty that assures the application of Iranian personal status law for
Iranian citizens in Germany, and vice versa for German citizens residing in Iran
(*Niederlassungsabkommen zwischen dem Deutschen Reich und dem Kaiserreich
Persien*, December 17, 1929; confirmed by the Federal Republic of Germany on
August 15, 1955). This framework, according to one view, is intended to provide
certainty to individuals who order their affairs according to one legal regime and
then move to a location governed by a completely different set of norms and
laws:

> In the area of civil law, which essentially regulates legal relations between
> private persons, the welfare of those persons is of prime importance. If someone
> has organized his/her life in accordance with a certain legal system, this should
> be protected even when the person in question changes his/her place of abode.
> Accordingly the law of the state of origin which is familiar to the person in
> question should continue to be applied when the person crosses the borders.
> (Rohe 2003: 47)

In other contractual matters, including maintenance (EGBGB Article 18, Hague
Convention on the Law Applicable to Maintenance Obligations 1973 Article 4),
contracts, torts and debts, the law of domicile (German law) applies. For example,
the law applicable in the divorce of a Syrian couple (not German citizens) whose
marriage was contracted in Syria will be that of Syrian/Islamic family law; this rule
includes post-divorce alimony claims (EGBGB Article 18). In family law matters,
the law of domicile will apply only in cases of maintenance claims for children
(EGBGB Article 18(1)) or plural citizenships of the parties (EGBGB Article 14).
In the latter case, parties will be allowed to choose which law of citizenship should
apply. The applicability of "*Shari'a* in Germany" (Rohe 2003: 48) is, however,
subject to the legal principle of German public order (EGBGB Article 6) and the
general requirement that legal transactions not offend good morals. Further, any
international conventions to which Germany is a party are also in play. For example,
in family law matters, Germany has ratified the Convention of October 24, 1956 on
the law applicable to maintenance obligations towards children, the Convention of
October 2, 1973 on maintenance obligations, as well as the Convention of March
14, 1978 on matrimonial property regimes. Hence, if the Islamic family law
provision "would lead to a result which is obviously incompatible with the main
principles of German law, including the constitutional civil rights" (Rohe 2003:
50), German law applies instead. For instance, provisions such as constitutional

and human rights as formulated in Article 3 of the constitution (equality of the sexes and of religious beliefs), Article 4 (freedom of religion including the right not to believe) and Article 6 (special protection of marriage and family) are taken into consideration.

The Applicability of Islamic Family Law in German Courts: An Overview

Mathias Rohe, who has written extensively on the application of *shari'a* rules in European legal orders (Rohe 2004a), describes the incorporation of Islamic family law in Germany as "everyday business in German courts" (Rohe 2003: 50). Scholars have pointed out that the existence of these international private law rules incorporating Islamic family law at the domestic level to non-German citizens often comes as a (possibly unpleasant) surprise to members of the Muslim community:

> Because most foreigners in Germany—and even German citizens—are not aware of the rule that a foreigner's own law continues to apply to them in Germany, it can come as a rude shock for some when they have marital disputes. For example, many Iranians who had fled to Germany under the Shah's regime, or later under Ayatollah Khomeini's regime, who have resided in Germany for as long as thirty years and want to divorce before German courts, are suddenly faced with the application of the very Islamic laws that they wished to escape. The fact that they have retained their Iranian citizenship—until recently it has not been easy to obtain German citizenship—means that they are considered "guests," who are entitled to have their own law apply in matrimonial disputes. (Jones-Pauly 2008: 300)

Apart from the *mahr* cases, German judges have had to decide upon the legality of institutions such as Islamic marriages, polygamy and the *talaq* divorce (Elwan 1999), which I will now review.

Islamic Marriages   In deciding upon the application of Islamic legal provisions regulating marriage and the custody of minor children, German courts have identified the scope and limitations of German public order. The minimum age of consent to enter marriage in Germany is generally fixed at 18 years old by §1303 of Germany's *Civil Code*. Courts have decided that a minimum age of 12 years old (as under Iranian Islamic family law) contradicts German public order (OLG Köln 1997), but the marriage in Morocco of a 16-year-old German citizen of Moroccan origin was accepted as valid (AG Tuebingen). The Islamic concept of guardianship by male relatives in matters of marriage has been held to be contrary to German public order (LG Kassel), as with the rule providing that a male chooses the husband-to-be on behalf of his daughter or sister (AG Giessen). Similarly, the Islamic family law prohibition of inter-religious marriages between Muslim females and non-Muslim males violates the equality of religions, religious freedom and the protection of marriage granted by the German constitution (OLG Oldenburg; OLG Köln 1982; OLG Koblenz).

Polygamy   Monogamy is one of the leading German constitutional principles, as made explicit by §1306 of the *Civil Code*. It is therefore legally impossible to enter into a polygamous marriage in Germany (Rohe 2003: 46–59). However, if the polygamous marriages were concluded in a country that permits polygamy, they will be considered legally valid in Germany (LG München; LG Frankfurt A.m.; LG Osnabrueck; AG Bremen; VGH Kassel). In practice, the recognition of polygamous marriages means that Muslim women who are polygamous wives can obtain social security benefits, such as inheritance, custody rights and child support payments. For example, provisions on social security systems regulate the per capita division of pensions among widows who were living in a polygamous marriage (*Syrian Paternity Case*). As to the right to family reunification, the OVG Nordrhein-Westfalen in the *Jordanian Paternity Case* held that a Jordanian Muslim woman who was a second wife was not entitled to join her husband and his first wife in Germany. In similar cases, the courts held that co-wives did not have the right to join their husbands in Germany, although once they are in the country living with their husband, no prosecution will be launched as polygamy is not considered to be against German public order (Rohe 2003).

The Talaq *Divorce*   Generally speaking, the unilateral repudiation of a Muslim wife by her husband by *talaq* is considered against German public order and, as such, is not recognized by German courts (EGBGB Article 6, Article 17(2); BayObLG; LJV Baden-Württemberg). For instance, the Frankfurt First Instance Court held *talaq* to be the man's prerogative and, therefore, contrary to German constitutional provisions of gender equality (AGFrankfurt/Main). The most recent case is a 1998 decision in which the OLG Stuttgart decided that, due to the inability of the wife to have any say in the matter, *talaq* violated German public order. German courts will, however, recognize *talaq* if the wife agrees to the dissolution of the marriage in front of a German court. This occurred in a 1992 decision in which the judge dissolved the marriage after the husband had pronounced *talaq* in front of him and the wife agreed to be divorced (AG Esslingen).

The German Matrimonial Property Regime   In Germany, the statutory matrimonial property regime is called "community of accrued gains" (*Civil Code* §1364, §1373). Upon the dissolution of the marriage by divorce, a comparison is made between the value of the assets owned by either spouse at the beginning of the marriage ("initial assets," *Civil Code* §1374) and the value of the assets owned by either spouse at the termination of the marriage ("final assets," *Civil Code* §1375). The difference in value of the assets of either spouse (including any increase in value of property owned at the time the spouses married) is called a spouse's "accrued gains." The spouse that has higher "accrued gains" will be ordered to make an equalization payment to the other spouse as compensation

(*Civil Code* §1378). Equalization payments amount, as a rule, to one half of the difference between the accrued gains of either spouse. Inheritances, legacies and donations acquired by the spouse during the duration of the marriage will not be added to the final value of assets because the acquisition of such assets is not connected with the marriage itself (*Civil Code* §1374(2)). According to §1380 of the *Civil Code*, the claimant may have to deduct from his or her claim donations received from the other spouse during the duration of the marriage if such donations exceeded the occasional donations usual under the spouses' living conditions ("set-off advancements," *Civil Code* §1380). The general rule that the difference is divided equally can be altered by the court, pursuant to §1381 of the *Civil Code*, if an equal division would result in a "gross inequity."

Conclusion

The background legal rules differ considerably among Canada, the United States, France and Germany. In Canada, the constitutional protections of religious freedom and multiculturalism, the judicial enforcement of domestic contracts and the family law legislation at the federal and provincial levels influence how *mahr* claims are approached and adjudicated. Despite federal legislations held in common, and roughly similar provincial statutes, *mahr* claims that have been pursued in the provinces of British Columbia, Ontario, Québec and Nova Scotia have not necessarily resulted in the same outcome.

In the United States, the First Amendment of the Constitution—namely the Free Exercise and the Establishment Clauses—compels the states to pursue, above all, a course of neutrality toward religion. The United States Supreme Court has often directed lower courts in this vein, and the courts of the states that have adjudicated *mahr* claims (New Jersey, New York, California and Florida) thus add this constitutional ammunition to their judicial arsenal. Their approach to *mahr* cases, often framed as disputes about the interpretation and enforcement of antenuptial agreements, also encompass state laws on contract law, such as the *Statute of Frauds*, which requires that a contract be in writing.

Whereas family law is, generally speaking, based on provincial or state law in Canada and the United States, regardless of the distinction between an individual's residence or citizenship, family law is directly related to one's citizenship in France and Germany by virtue of the application of international private law rules. As a result, French and German courts and public policies have recognized Islamic family law in matters of personal status. The only way for courts to reject the applicability of Islamic law rules is through the interpretation of the "public order" principle. French and German courts seem to have reached similar conclusions when clarifying the limits of French or German "public order": religious Islamic marriages have no enforceable legal effect if the wedding took place on French or German soil; the unilateral repudiation of a Muslim wife by her husband by the *talaq* is not recognized as a legitimate form of divorce; and polygamous marriages are legally valid only if concluded in a country that permits polygamy. My purpose in this comparative law chapter was to map out the legal regimes as distinct and coherent bodies of knowledge, so as to see in subsequent chapters whether we can understand and classify the adjudication of *mahr* through the lines of "state law," or whether "state law" is not impossibly heterogeneous.

Chapter 3
Nourishing the Transplanted Law:
Fertile Soil or Rocky Ground?

This chapter grapples with the concept of liberalism's approach to religion, and how the specific legal institution of *mahr* is understood, reconstructed or erased by the legal system and the broader spectrum of liberal ideology that permeates it. In presenting and analyzing judicial examples, I demonstrate that objective legal rules and norms very often mask an exercise of choice involving ideological predispositions. In this, I note and concur with Duncan Kennedy's (2000: 105) observation: "When choosing a legal norm to cover a case, rational decision making selects from the continuum of normative possibilities the one that best accommodates (balances, maximizes, mini-maxes, or whatever) the conflicting considerations as they play out more or less strongly in the fact situation of which the case is an instance."

In this chapter, I attempt to uncover the road to ideology and bring back into focus the numerous and often competing considerations that coloured the background legal regime under which adjudication took place (Kennedy 1997). Based on an analysis of case law emerging from Canada, the United States, France and Germany, I suggest that Western courts have captured *mahr* in three different ways: the liberal–legal pluralist approach (LLPA), the liberal–formal equality approach (LFEA), and the liberal–substantive equality approach (LSEA). The three camps seem to have opposing views on the importance of *mahr* for the legal subjects involved. The LLPA views *mahr* as central to cultural and religious recognition, the LFEA considers it as a mere secular contract and the LSEA projects fairness principles into its regulation. Despite their apparent differences, however, I argue that the three strands share a common liberal ideology.

The "Legal State of Play" in the (Liberal) Reception of *Mahr*

First, I introduce the LLPA form of adjudication, outlining the Canadian,[1] American, French and German cases that fall under this ideological strand. I have divided the LLPA decisions along the lines of recognition: courts that have manifested many

---

1 I include Québec cases, although I will specifically note distinctions when appropriate. Legal differences and interpretations inevitably arise since Québec is the only Canadian province that is governed by a civil code as opposed to the common law tradition.

different routes to *mahr* as cultural family recognition, and enforced it on that basis; and those that have refused to recognize *mahr* because this Islamic institution was deemed too "foreign" compared to the standpoint of the Western state. I then define the LFEA, and demonstrate how the secular understanding of *mahr* in the four countries has produced either the enforcement of *mahr*-as-contract (a marriage agreement, an antenuptial agreement, a legal debt or a contractual condition of marriage), or the non-enforcement of *mahr* as an exception to contract law (void for vagueness, lack of consent and/or consideration or abstractness). The final part of this chapter is dedicated to the LSEA: it offers the conditions under which this form of equality has emerged, and presents the Québec and German decisions that have enforced *mahr* while applying gender-equity standards, as well as the German, American, French, Québec and other Canadian cases that have refused to enforce *mahr* by invoking fairness principles.

Liberal–Legal Pluralism: The Multiculturalist Understanding of *Mahr*

The LLPA is a critique of the traditional idea of law as the representation of the state—consisting of law-making, adjudication, interpretation, precedents, customs, etc. For the LLPA, law is not defined as rules imposed hierarchically from the top down, but rather as rules emerging from the accommodations of human interaction (Reisman 1999). For the centrality of state law, the LLPA substitutes a variety of interacting, competing legal orders which mutually influence the emergence and operation of each other's rules, processes and institutions. According to one view,

> [w]hen scholars of legal pluralism set sail to discover new territory, unexplored legal orders within and across state boundaries, they usually plan to find and map out relatively stable orders: geographically confined groups, ethnic or religious communities, business, political, criminal or educational organizations, or even the family. While some of those exist without formal institutions or fixed membership, their relative durability facilitates the identification of permanent features and of patterns of transformation. Those features and patterns are most evident in the governance and economic aspects of community life, and the set of norms and processes that sustain them are typically the focal point in the study of small-scale legal orders. (Jutras 2001: 47)

The LLPA explores and analyzes the many diverse manifestations of non-state law *as* sites of legal regulation: the family, the child, the socio-cultural community, the religious space, the public institution, the neighbourhood, the law school, the workplace and others. The "legal dimensions of everyday life," to borrow the expression of Daniel Jutras (2001), become, for the legal pluralist, law itself.

Because law appears as a "self-contained fiction" (Jutras 2001: 45), and because identities mirror and redefine law, the legal pluralist imagines legal subjects as "law inventing" (Kleinhans and Macdonald 1997: 39), not merely law-abiding. As a result, law no longer stands as a structure, as norms, as violence; rather, it is meaning, dialogue, narrative(s). Roderick Macdonald claims that legal pluralism is "a way of characterizing an interpretive choice for citizens about how they wish to conceive law, themselves and the relationship they have to law" (Macdonald unpublished: 19). Whatever *this* particular person, at *this* time and in *this* place, experiences as law *is* law. Another way of putting it is that law itself is simply a hypothesis (Melissaris 2004). In a fragmented world, however, one marked by the redefinition of traditional state norms as applicable law, the LLPA has attempted to envision *this* particular person, at *this* time and in *this* place, through the lens of globalization (Berman 2002, 2005a, 2005b; Fischer-Lescano and Teubner 2004; Teubner 1997). Boaventura de Sousa Santos (1987: 298) has designed this phenomenon as "interlegality," that is, "the impact of legal plurality on the legal experiences, perception and consciousness of the individuals and social groups living under conditions of legal plurality, above all the fact that their everyday life crosses or is interpenetrated by different and often contrasting legal orders and legal cultures."

The conceptual apparatus of LLPA is thus closely associated with the development of identity politics as a way of framing human societies, especially in modern, Western, multicultural and multi-ethnic states (Taylor 1994). One way of looking at the study of law is that it is a manifestation of culture (Kahn 1999) or that law is a cultural manifestation, like society itself (Legrand 1999b). Not only does (official) state law need to reflect (unofficial) indigenous, customary law, but it must also be attentive to its own pluralism—the diversity of rules, processes and institutions, as well as the multiple sources of legitimacy within any given legal system. Professor Roderick Macdonald speaks of "the plurality of sites of law." Legal pluralism, he says, systematically

> invites us to imagine that there are multiple legal orders operating in the same social and geographical space. In this respect, there are at once various international regimes of human rights norms embedded within international legal regimes generally, just as there is a national regime of human rights norms (however thin it may be in certain places). … Here I mean to highlight not only the plurality of indigenous law, but also the plurality of cosmopolitan law. Notice that every time that someone makes a claim about indigenous law, it is important to note that this is the same claim that cosmopolitan law makes about itself: a norm entrepreneur asserts that law as a normative proposition – not as a raw datum of human experience – other norm entrepreneurs within that indigenous tradition may have other, often quite divergent, views. … Even within the rationalist cosmopolitan universal human rights tradition there is normative plurality: it makes no sense to consider that international criminal law, international humanitarian law, international children's law, and so on, are indistinguishably part of the same normative system – each mediates rationality and practice (logic and experience) differently and cosmopolitan jurists do

their cause a disservice by insisting that the only site for universal norms is at
a level so abstract that conceptual and field differentiations vanish. (Macdonald
unpublished: 12, 16–17)

Thus, the LLPA inquiry can be phrased in the form of Professor Macdonald's
question: "what are the internormative trajectories between *local law* – which
is said to be located in the actual practices of local culture – and *universal or
cosmopolitan law* – which is said to be grounded in the aspiration to give rational
content to the notion of human dignity?" (Macdonald unpublished: 14).

For the purposes of the current analysis, I ask: how would the LLPA envision
the internormative trajectories between Islamic law—located in the actual practice
of Muslim culture—and Canadian, American, French or German law—grounded
in the aspiration to multiculturalism and religious freedom?

The Many Different Routes to Mahr *as Cultural Recognition*

This section analyzes Canadian, French, German and American case studies that have
used the language and theoretical aspirations of the LLPA to recognize *mahr* culturally,
either through enforcement or non-enforcement. These cases throw into striking relief
the many different routes to acknowledging *mahr* as cultural recognition. *Mahr* as
a manifestation of identity, *mahr* as an Islamic custom, *mahr* as related to a *khul*
divorce: all adopt a rather formalist view of Islamic family law. They either stress
the homogeneity of *mahr* as a legal institution, or (over)emphasize the tolerant
nature of the Western legal regime while refusing to address the complexity of the
Islamic legal order to which *mahr* is connected.

The Enforcement of Mahr *as a Manifestation of Identity: Canada*   In *Nathoo v
Nathoo* and *M.(N.M.) v M.(N.S.).*, two cases of the British Columbia Supreme Court,
mahr is represented as the religious and cultural expression of the Muslim minority
group, one that Canadian society must respect in the name of multiculturalism. In
many ways, *mahr* stands precisely as the project and fantasy of legal pluralism: it
is different, differing; it speaks from the standpoint of the local, the indigenous; it
talks back to the universal, universalist Canadian family law.

Nathoo is the story of Karim, a 37-year-old commission salesman born in
Tanzania, and Fahrah, a 29-year-old teacher born in Kenya. Both were raised in
and lived within the culture and traditions of the Muslim Ismaili community in
Vancouver. At the time of their marriage in 1994, they agreed to a deferred *mahr*
of \$20,000. They separated approximately nine months later. In 1996, Karim and
Fahrah claimed an order for divorce pursuant to Canada's federal *Divorce Act*, and
a division of family assets arising from their marriage pursuant to the Province of
British Columbia's *Family Relations Act*. The enforcement of *mahr* was presented
as part of the general framework of the division of family assets.

The *Family Relations Act* addresses entitlement to family assets on the breakup
of a marriage. The rule of equal division of family assets can be set aside by

the judge if equal division would be unfair; by way of remedy, the judge may reapportion family assets on the basis of fairness. In *Nathoo*, the trial court concluded that "the statutory equality of division would be unfair" (para. 18) for the following reasons:

> In this case the parties lived together for approximately 9 months. They lived in the matrimonial home which is registered in the name of Mr. Nathoo and was acquired, clear title, by him prior to the marriage. During their marriage each party contributed to his and her financial needs and those of the family unit according to their respective resources. Mr. Nathoo had more significant earnings and paid a greater proportion of the parties' joint expenses as a consequence. Given that the matrimonial home was clear title, the monthly expenses of the household were substantially less than in cases where mortgage payments are required. Ms. Mawani paid her own personal expenses and contributed to the joint expenses of the household as she was able, given her limited income. As well, she continued to meet her monthly obligations in respect of a line of credit, the balance of which was approximately $30,000. This debt was primarily a consolidation of student loans taken during the course of her post-secondary education. (para. 19)

Given these factors, the court awarded Mrs. Nathoo $37,747.17 upon reapportionment of family assets. Instead of considering the enforcement of *mahr* as part of family assets, the Court begins the analysis of *mahr* as a "marriage agreement" under section 48 of the *Family Relations Act* (the wording of which has since changed):

> 48. (1) This section defines marriage agreement for the purposes of this Part and this definition applies to marriages entered into, marriage agreements made and to property of a spouse acquired before or after this section comes into force.
>
> (2) A marriage agreement is an agreement entered into by a man and a woman prior to or during their marriage to each other to take effect on the date of their marriage or on the execution of the agreement, whichever is later, for
>
> (a) management of family assets or other property during marriage; or
>
> (b) ownership in, or division of, family assets or other property during marriage, or on the making of an order for dissolution of marriage, judicial separation or a declaration of nullity of marriage.
>
> (3) A marriage agreement, or an amendment or rescission of a marriage agreement, must be in writing, signed by both spouses, and witnessed by one or more other persons.

(4) Except as provided in this Part, where a marriage agreement is made in compliance with subsection (3), the terms described by subsection (2)(a) and (b) are binding between the spouses whether or not there is valuable consideration for the marriage agreement.

Expressing a clear commitment to legal pluralism and multiculturalism, Justice Dorgan introduces his interpretation of section 48 of the *Act* as one that "acknowledges cultural diversity" and which is "respectful of traditions which define various groups who live in a multi-cultural community" (para. 25). He explores the manifestation of non-state law—the traditions of the Ismaili community—as a privileged site of legal regulation, one that should penetrate and colour Canadian family law. The voice of the Muslim community, it was expected, would give meaning to *mahr* as a marriage agreement: Karim and Fahrah, who "both attend Mosque regularly and adhere to the tenets of their faith" (para. 8), agreed on the sum of $20,000, says the Court, "after taking advice from elders within their community and negotiating with each other" (para. 24). Moreover, they "met and courted for approximately two years prior to their marriage" (para. 5). Their marriage agreement was therefore not simply, as would be with other (secular) litigants, "an agreement entered into by a man and a woman before or during their marriage to each other" (*Family Relations Act*, s. 48(2)). Rather, suggests the Court, it is an act performed in "the traditions of the Ismaili community, the most significant of which, for the purposes of this litigation, is the marriage contract or 'Maher' signed by the parties on November 6, 1994, the day of their marriage" (para. 8).

Having thus redefined the issue of *mahr* as a unique and autonomous domain guided by sacred religious principles, Justice Dorgan concludes that it would *not* "be unfair to uphold the provisions" (para. 25) of the agreement, given that "the parties chose to marry within the Ismaili tradition" (para. 24), knowing "full well that provision for Maher was a condition of so doing" (para. 24). The British Columbia Supreme Court, instead of evaluating the criteria of fairness set out in section 51 of the *Family Relations Act* (as it did for the division of family assets), chose to re-examine the law, and then to reform radically its content in light of the fact that the parties were Muslims. This reasoning is extremely bizarre, given that the family law rules in British Columbia provide that a marriage agreement within the meaning of section 48 is "subject to variation under s. 51 of the *Act*," according to the British Columbia Court of Appeal in *Minckler v Minckler*, a case which should have bound Justice Dorgan in *Nathoo*.

Furthermore, *Minckler* was not the only case in which the province's Court of Appeal interpreted the effect of section 51. In *Gold v Gold*, the Court concluded that section 51 gives the power to override a spousal property agreement if it is "unfair." In such a case, the court could "order that the property covered by ... the marriage agreement ... be divided into shares fixed by the court" (para. 30). This is so since "the intent of s. 51 is to permit the court to remedy unfairness, by a reapportionment of property which would be fair" (para. 38). In *Clarke v Clarke*, the British Columbia Court of Appeal showed that, under section 51 of the *Act*, fairness depends on how the agreement is likely to provide for the parties' futures based on the facts at the time and the probable future developments. Hence, the "parties who negotiate settlements of family matters on an adversarial basis must accept the risk that the court will exercise its jurisdiction to review the results of these negotiations objectively as of the date of settlement" (para. 23).

It seems obvious from the case law that the fairness of a "marriage agreement" is measured by comparing the disposition of family property in the agreement with the various factors enumerated in section 51 of the *Family Relations Act*. In fact, the Muslim husband in *Nathoo* had argued that the effect of *mahr*'s enforcement should be considered in the general division of assets—that is, subtracted from the initial amount due to Mrs. Nathoo. Rejecting his claim, the Court found that the equal division of property between Mr. and Mrs. Nathoo was not fair, but that the enforcement of an additional $20,000 in accordance with the marriage agreement was. As a result, the Court chose to view *mahr* as a penalty: it added $20,000 to the previous $37,747.17 owed by Karim to Fahrah: "Mr. Nathoo will pay to Ms. Mawani the total sum of $57,747.17 in satisfaction of the claims raised in this litigation" (para 27). The Court's insistence on the differences between the division of family assets, on the one hand, and the enforcement of *mahr*, on the other, further indicates an LLPA to religion as a separate legal entity.

If only Canadian family law had applied, a "marriage agreement" would supplant the marital equitable regime; if only Islamic family law had applied, Mrs. Nathoo would get only *mahr* besides maintenance during the *iddah* period. To reach such an unusual outcome in *Nathoo*—the enforcement of *mahr plus* the unequal division of property under the statutory regime—the Court had to frame the issue as a minority rights one: religion is an exceptional field, it generates its own conception of the good life, and fairness is only an extension of this particularized vision. Under the disciplinary effects of the LLPA, the Court held that the same contractual principles that governed other secular contracts were not to govern Muslim marriage agreements and that under such exceptional treatment the *mahr* agreement in question would be valid. From the husband's point of view, the LLPA penalized him through the enforcement of *mahr*.

This conception of *mahr* as an exceptional penalty was similarly developed in *M.(N.M.)*, a case decided eight years later by the same court. Although the judge relied extensively on *Nathoo*, the facts of the couple's marital life in *M.(N. M.)* differed considerably. This decision thus illustrates that the complexities of conceiving of *mahr* as a penalty were not unique to *Nathoo*. In 1987, the Muslim husband and wife married in a civil and, subsequently, in a religious ceremony. They separated 13 years later and accepted by consent order the joint custody of their three children. In deciding the financial consequences of the breakdown of their marriage, the trial judge examined the division of family assets, the quantum of child support and the quantum of spousal support. Moreover, in a specific action for the enforcement of a "marriage contract" under the British Columbia *Family*

Relations Act, the Muslim wife claimed that she was entitled to an additional $51,250 as deferred *mahr* upon divorce.

Although the marriage agreement clearly provided that the Muslim husband undertook to pay the amount of *mahr* "in addition and without prejudice to and not in substitution of all my obligations provided for by the laws of the land" (para. 26), he testified that for him *mahr* "was symbolic only and that the laws of the province alone would govern in the event of a divorce" (para. 26). The wife's father, whose evidence was not challenged in cross-examination, argued that the *mahr* document was presented and explained by an Islamic religious authority and that "the parties read the printed form" (para. 27) and agreed to it prior to the marriage ceremony. From the wife's perspective, it should therefore be treated as a mere contract under the *Family Relations Act*.

Echoing *Nathoo*, the LLPA in *M.(N.M.)* emerges in a reference that the British Columbia Supreme Court makes about what is "required by the tenets of the Ismaili faith" (para. 7) and what Canadian society should do about it. Specifically, Justice Joyce emphasizes that "both parties wished to marry in the Ismaili faith and they understood and accepted that a condition of doing so was to agree to the Maher" (para. 28). Seen through the lens of commitment to diversity, *mahr* is enforceable and easily enforced as a valid marriage agreement under subsection 61(2) of the *Family Relations Act*.

The Enforcement of Mahr *as an Islamic Custom: France and Germany*   In accordance with international private law rules, the French and German decisions outlined in this section applied Islamic family law in translating and enforcing *mahr*. These LLPA case studies have attempted to recreate *mahr* as a legal transplant, and thus portray its movement as the autonomous transfer of a legal institution from one (Islamic) legal milieu to another (Western-based) one. Such a translation process has produced a spectrum of possibilities: *mahr* as an integral part of the Islamic marriage contract; *mahr* as a substitute for post-divorce maintenance and division of the surplus of marital profits; and *mahr* as *mahr al-mithl* (that is, a woman's *mahr* as determined by comparison to similarly situated women).

In a one-page 1978 decision, the French Cour de Cassation upheld *mahr* as an Islamic custom. The case does not mention either the names or origins of the parties, or the amount of *mahr*. Applying international private law rules, it concluded that *mahr* was an integral part of the Islamic marriage contract, the enforcement of which did not contravene French public order. Two years later, in 1980, the German Higher Regional Court of Bremen similarly saw *mahr* as a family law matter (OLG Bremen). Therefore, since the parties were Iranian citizens, Iranian family law would apply. Since the wife "had no claim under Iranian law at the time to post-divorce alimony or to her share of the profits accruing to the marital property" (Jones-Pauly 2008: 304), *mahr* was understood as a substitute for post-divorce maintenance and division of the surplus of marital profits. Hence, the Court attempted to enforce *mahr* as if it were *in* Iran and *for* Iranians.

Interestingly, legal transplants are temporal and vulnerable to geopolitical circumstances, as suggested by Christina Jones-Pauly (2008: 305):

> [T]he new Iranian law, in place since 1992, undermines the Bremen court's view of the function of the *mahr*. Since 1992, Iranian law allows a divorced woman to make a claim in court for the increase in family wealth or her husband's business to which she contributed with her labor. The action is separate from a claim for *mahr* in the marriage contract. This new Iranian law will complicate matters further for the German case law.

Kammergericht, a 1988 decision from Berlin, similarly embarked on the exercise of transferring *mahr* from Iran to Germany, while emphasizing the unique particularity of Islamic law as an autonomous legal regime. Here, the German Family Law Chamber applied Iranian Islamic family law to the enforcement of 42,000 DM (approximately 22,000 Euros) as *mahr*. (The parties had agreed to a *mahr* of 1,500,000 rials, calculated according to the exchange rate at the time of the agreement, to be worth 42,000 DM, plus interest.) The court rejected the wife's claim that she was entitled to an additional 4 percent interest, because such result would "violate the basic Iranian sense of justice (*ordre public*)" (Jones-Pauly 2008: 310).

The next case offers interesting insights into the phenomenon of influence and borrowing between legal systems, specifically the emergence of a potential resistance of the borrowing legal system toward the transplanted rule. In *IPRax 1983*, a divorced Iranian wife living in Germany claimed the enforcement of *mahr*, but had no written contract on which to rely. She had received, upon marriage, "a symbolic *mahr* consisting of a Qur'an and a piece of sugar cane candy symbolizing the sweetness of married life" (Jones-Pauly 2008: 306). The wife claimed 150,000 DM (approximately 75,000 Euros), plus 4 percent interest, as *mahr al-mithl*—a situation in which *mahr* is determined by comparing "the *mahr* paid to other female members of the wife's family, for instance sisters, paternal aunts and female cousins" (Pearl and Menski 1998: 180). The wife argued that, given her privileged socio-economic status and in accordance with Islamic family law, she was entitled to 75,000 Euros. The husband favoured a lower *mahr* for the wife "because she was thirty-four years old at the time of marriage, thus reducing her worth as a child-bearer" (Jones-Pauly 2008: 307).

After first classifying *mahr* as a family law matter, the Hamburg Court attempted to understand the Islamic institution of *mahr al-mithl* according to the family law provisions of the Iranian *Civil Code*, which were applicable based on the German conflict of law rules. In determining the exact amount of *mahr al-mithl*, however, the German court used "criteria for an award of maintenance to the average divorced German citizen living in Hamburg, as the parties had originally planned to stay in that city" (Jones-Pauly 2008: 307). *Mahr al-mithl*, now technically integrated into the German legal order, was thus invested with a meaning specific to Germany (or even Hamburg), which could easily vary from the meaning intended in Iran. Criteria such as "the young age of the woman, the absence of children, and her good prospects for getting a job as a translator in about ten months" were taken into consideration (Jones-Pauly 2008: 307). Given her high social status, "a monthly amount of 2,000 DM (1,000 Euros) was deemed appropriate for securing her according to her social status until she got her job in ten months" (Jones-Pauly 2008: 307). Although the award of 20,000 DM as *mahr al-mithl* (that is, 2,000 DM for 10 months) was done by comparing the wife to a similarly situated German woman, the acceptance of *mahr al-mithl* as a legitimate Islamic legal institution surely represents an LLPA move.

The LLPA presents itself as being committed to recognizing minority citizens' cultural and religious differences. However coherently it might present itself as a political vision, the LLPA cannot offer the tools to predict the practical outcomes that will flow from it in the adjudicative process. The next cases adopt the same liberal framework and commitment to legal pluralism while producing an opposite outcome: the unenforceability of *mahr* as related to *khul* divorce.

The Waiver of Mahr *in Khul Divorce: Québec and the United States* As previously noted, *khul* divorce dissolves the husband's obligation to pay the deferred *mahr*. The Québec and American cases introduced in this section adopt the LLPA in adjudicating *mahr*: in all of these cases, the wife is the one asking for divorce and, in response, courts apply the internal logic of the Islamic law regime in applying the waiver of *mahr*. I argue that these cases exemplify the LLPA in that they explicitly pluralize their own legal regime.

In *M.H.D. v E.A.*, a 1991 Québec Court of Appeal decision, the marriage contract provided for a prompt *mahr* of 10 Syrian pounds and a deferred *mahr* of 25,000 Syrian pounds. The marriage was performed in Syria in April 1985, and the parties moved to Canada seven months later. In 1991, the wife filed for divorce in Montreal and claimed the enforcement of deferred *mahr*. In applying Syrian law (which is derived in part from Islamic law) according to private international law rules, the Court of Appeal concluded that the wife had waived *mahr* by initiating the divorce; essentially, she had embarked on a *khul* divorce. The Court further found that the principles established by Syrian Islamic law in general, and those applicable to *khul* divorce in particular, did not violate any provision of the *Canadian Charter of Rights and Freedoms*. The Court reasoned that there was an equitable balancing of rights and obligations between the spouses—they were placed "on the same footing"—and what the wife lost by waiving *mahr*, she gained in freedom by virtue of provisions contained within the marriage contract (para. 33).

Fifteen years later, the Québec Superior Court adopted the same basic reasoning and outcome in *I.(S.) v E.(E.)*. In this case, however, the decision did not borrow from the framework of international private law rules, but rather incorporated the LLPA into a purely Québec family law dispute. In 2005, divorce was granted on the basis that the parties lived apart for over one year, as well as on grounds of the husband's "physical cruelty" toward the wife and the harm she suffered during "the parties' 21 years of life together" (para. 53). (The husband had accused the wife of subjecting him to "mental cruelty," but the Court dismissed this allegation as "far-fetched and without substance" (para. 53).) The Court concluded that, given the peculiar and traumatic circumstances of the case, this was an exceptional situation "where injustice would result if there were to be equal shares" (para. 100) in the division of the family patrimony:

> The evidence is clear and ample as to Mr. E.'s conduct vis-à-vis Ms. I.: as soon as she arrived in Canada as his wife, he treated her as a sexual convenience, beat her regularly and took her personal documents, i.e. passport, immigration and identity papers, to control her so that she could not leave him; he took advantage of her financially ...; he deprived her of food while she was pregnant; even though they were co-owners of the coffee shop business, she did most of the work but he controlled the cash; Ms. I. was the one who established the good relationships with the customers and the other tenants in the shopping mall, while Mr. E. would, at best, keep to himself or at worst, be insulting to third parties; he took no part in bringing up their children and left it all to her; on the contrary, he would also beat them; not only was he not generous – Ms. I.'s testimony as to the very few presents he gave her over the years is particularly clear –, he was miserly: the furniture, in the Laval residence, or lack thereof, is an ample illustration of that fact. In summary, Mr. E. did little, took undue and unfair advantage of his wife, was physically and verbally violent, and kept all the money for himself while depriving his family of the necessities of life. (paras 101–102)

Having decided in the wife's favour on the partition of the family patrimony (the wife had requested unequal shares and the husband had requested equal shares), the Court turned to the issue of the Islamic religious divorce, presented to the Court as a straightforward bargaining scenario between the husband and wife:

> Ms. I. was also asking the Court to order Mr. E. to undertake, immediately after the civil judgment of divorce, to do whatever was necessary so that Ms. I. also be divorced according to their faith. On the last day of the trial, the subject came up and Mr. E. undertook to go to the Country A Consulate in Montreal and give his wife a religious divorce within seven days of a final judgment in the present case. It was clear that for Mr. E., the granting or not of a religious divorce was an important bargaining tool: he knew *a religious divorce* was important for Ms. I. not only for religious reasons, but also for civil reasons, as it *would affect her civil status in Country A*, where all her family lives, i.e. father, siblings, cousins, etc., whom she had not seen for many years. (para. 65)

Agreeing to grant Ms. I. the religious divorce immediately, before the Court, "as a sign of good faith" (para. 66), Mr. E. pronounced "*talaq*" three times "in front of two Muslim witnesses, i.e. Ms. I. and her lawyer, Mtre Elmaraghi" (para. 66), and undertook to fill in the necessary paperwork at the appropriate Consulate.

One would have expected the enforcement of *mahr* as a direct consequence of the pronouncement of *talaq*. Instead, the Court acknowledged a sworn declaration containing the following promise: in exchange for *talaq*, Ms. I. promises not to claim the enforcement of *mahr* or any alimony according to Islamic family law in her country of birth. Although the Court used the cultural and legal expression *talaq* to acknowledge the existence of a religious divorce, the waiver of *mahr* as an outcome is clearly related to the bargaining process of a *khul* divorce.

Other examples of a court adopting the LLPA to recognize *khul mahr* can be found in *Akileh v Elchahal*, a 1996 Florida decision, and in *In re Marriage of Dajani*, a 1988 California decision. In both cases, the trial judges sought to recognize the rules of *khul* divorce and thus refused to enforce *mahr*.

Akileh v Elchahal is the story of Asma Akileh, who grew up in Syria and came to the United States in February 1990, and Safwan Elchahal, who was born and lived in Lebanon until 1979, when he came to the United States at the age of 20. Both were raised Muslims. Two months before the marriage, Safwan met Asma's father, Rahi Akileh, who raised the question of *mahr*. Rahi Akileh expressed to his future son-in-law his desire that *mahr* be paid to his daughter in two parts: a prompt *mahr* of $1 to be given on the day of the wedding, and a deferred *mahr* of $50,000. Upon completion of their negotiations, Safwan and Rahi Akileh agreed to a *mahr* of $50,001. Asma also agreed and the marriage contract of the *mahr* provision was signed on December 26, 1991; the parties married the following day. The certification of marriage incorporated *mahr* (also termed as the *sadaq* in this case), and provided: "The sadaq being fifty thousand and one dollars of which one U.S. dollar advanced and fifty thousand dollars postponed" (*Akileh* Appeal: 247).

Approximately one year after the wedding, Asma contracted genital warts from her husband and the marriage slowly deteriorated from that time on. She filed for divorce on August 24, 1993. At trial, Asma testified that her right to receive deferred *mahr* was not affected by the cause of the divorce. An Imam, who appeared as an expert witness on Asma's behalf, testified that a wife's right to receive *mahr* was not negated by her filing for divorce. On the contrary: a wife's right to the *sadaq* is absolute, and applies even if she brought the divorce action. The only exception, according to the witness, is if the wife was unfaithful. Safwan claimed that *mahr* was forfeited because it was the Muslim wife who initiated the divorce, a line of reasoning that aligns with the *khul* divorce scenario. He testified that his understanding of *mahr* stemmed from his sister's experience: she, too, had sought a divorce and pursued the postponed *mahr*, only to be told by an Islamic court that she was not entitled to receive *mahr* since she had initiated the divorce. (The *Akileh* decision does not specify where Safwan's sister's divorce took place.) Safwan also testified that a woman who seeks a divorce is entitled to *mahr* only if she is abused (that is, the Islamic principle of *darar*).

In an *obiter dictum* reproduced by the Court of Appeals, the trial judge is said to have described the enforcement of *mahr* as directly related to *khul* divorce:

> The court stated that even if the parties attached sufficiently similar meanings to the *sadaq* to show that there was a meeting of the minds, the court would find that the *sadaq* was meant to protect the wife from an unwanted divorce. As such, the trial court would not order the husband to pay the wife the postponed *sadaq* since the wife was "the one that chose to pursue the divorce." (*Akileh* Appeal: 248)

In the final judgment of dissolution of marriage, the trial court further denied the "Wife's claim for rehabilitative alimony" and "permanent alimony," but reserved jurisdiction over the issues "in the event Wife contracts cervical cancer and is unable to work, provided she can prove that the cervical cancer was caused by the genital warts and that she is unable to work because of the cancer" (*Akileh* Trial: 3). If *khul mahr* had survived the journey from Syrian Islamic law to Florida law, its culture-specific meaning did not penetrate the deep structures of American family law. In fact, the division of marital assets in *Akileh* does not follow the Islamic rule of separate property at the dissolution of marriage, but the trial court rather proceeds to identify which items are marital property (VCR, kitchen appliances, jewellery, Safwan's retirement savings, and two cars) and divides them according to the rule of equal share of the marital funds. Furthermore, the court does not fully appreciate the concept of *darar*, meaning cruelty or harm. This point of Islamic law, according to Azizah al-Hibri (2000: para. 14), could have made all the difference:

> There is an exception to the rule; a woman can seek judicial divorce for harm ... without losing her delayed *mahr*. The husband need not physically torture her; under Jordanian law, under Kuwaiti law, just verbal abuse is sufficient. ... In this case the husband transmitted venereal disease to the woman, and therefore the harm was clearly established.

In re Marriage of Dajani similarly incorporates the Islamic family law rule of *khul mahr*. In 1982, a religious marriage took place in Jordan by proxy between the two parties: Nabil resided in the United States and Awatef in Jordan. Under the terms of the foreign marriage contact, Nabil paid Awatef a prompt *mahr* of one dinar (approximately 33 cents) by proxy at the time of marriage, and agreed to deferred *mahr* of 3,000 Jordanian dinars (at the time of the trial, this was equivalent to approximately $1,700 US), plus an additional 2,000 dinars in cash or household furniture upon the dissolution of the marriage or death. Awatef joined Nabil in Orange County, California, a year later, and the couple married in a civil ceremony in California.

In 1985, Awatef initiated the divorce proceeding and sought to enforce the *mahr* provision against Nabil according to terms of the foreign proxy marriage contract. There was no dispute that the agreement was authorized by the parties—neither the original contract, written in Arabic, nor an English translation of the document was admitted in evidence. The parties disagreed only as to the amount of *mahr* and its legal effect under Islamic law. Whereas Awatef claimed that she was entitled to 3,000 Jordanian dinars and to an additional 2,000 dinars in cash or household furniture, Nabil argued that she "misrepresented the sum he would be obliged to pay if the marriage was dissolved" (*Dajani*: 1389).

At the trial court level, the significance of the Imam as the expert witness was crucial. Awatef's expert was an attorney admitted to practice in California and Egypt who testified that *mahr* provided for a cash payment to the wife in the event of death or the dissolution of the marriage, no matter which party initiated the dissolution proceedings. Nabil's expert, an Imam who taught local college courses in Islamic customs, stated that *mahr* was intended to provide security for the wife in the event of death or dissolution of the marriage, but only if the husband himself initiated the dissolution proceedings. In his opinion, a wife forfeited her right to *mahr* if she asked for or initiated a divorce.

In an *obiter dictum* reproduced by the Court of Appeal, the trial judge is said to have described the enforcement of *mahr* as directly related to *khul* divorce:

> [There] is a valid dowry in existence; ... both parties are obligated to perform the conditions of the dowry. ... The court also finds that, based upon the testimony, the law in existence would be that of the Jordanian or Moslem law and finds that if the wife initiates a termination of the relationship, she foregoes the dowry and the court so finds that in this case the wife initiated the termination of the marriage and common sense and wisdom of Mohamed [*sic*] would dictate that she forego the dowry, unless the parties agree otherwise, and here they do not agree otherwise. (*Dajani*: 1389)[2]

Mahr *as Utterly Foreign: Not Recognized and Not Enforced*

By contrast, and at the opposite extreme of the LLPA spectrum, *Kaddoura v Hammoud*, a 1998 Ontario decision, refuses to recognize *mahr* culturally on the basis of the authenticity and purity of Islamic law. Consequently, the Court fails to enforce it as a domestic contract under the *Family Law Act*. Far from being an expression of religious freedom that should be accommodated and regulated through an interpretation of Canadian family law, in this case—also following the LLPA—the Court portrays *mahr* as a threat and a danger.

Kaddoura is the story of Sam and Manira. They were 19 and 20 years old, respectively, when they became engaged. At the wedding, Sam, Manira and their official witnesses signed two sets of documents: those necessary pursuant to the province of Ontario's requirements and a Muslim marriage certificate, written

---

2   This excerpt reproduces a ruling announced from the bench, but otherwise unpublished, as quoted on appeal.

in Arabic. *Mahr* had been comprised of $5,000 Sam paid before the marriage, and an additional $30,000 deferred payment (*Kaddoura*: 6, 15). The couple's relationship was stormy, and Manira moved back to her parents' home several times; the parties were married only 18 months. Shortly after the last in a series of incidents, Sam served Manira with a divorce petition. Judgment for divorce was granted. In Manira's counter-petition, she claimed the payment of a deferred *mahr* of $30,000 due to her under a marriage contract entered into according to the Islamic religion.

In his testimony, Sam said he knew that $30,000 was the amount of the deferred portion of the *mahr*, but he thought he would not be compelled to pay it (*Kaddoura*: 16). In an argument that seems to have been borrowed from *Akileh*, Sam testified that his sister had divorced and that she had been unable to collect the deferred portion of *mahr*; he assumed his situation would follow the same analytical path. Moreover, Sam claimed that the *mahr* contract outlines purely religious obligations that should not be adjudicated in the Ontario civil courts. Manira, on the other hand, argued that the $30,000 deferred *mahr* constituted a marriage contract pursuant to subsection 52(1) of the *Family Law Act*.

In resolving the issue, Justice Rutherford of the trial court considered religious evidence in order to define the content of Muslim marriages solemnized in Canada. Two expert witnesses, the Imam of a mosque in Ottawa and the director of Ontario's Institute of Islamic Learning, expounded in their testimony on the nature of *mahr*. According to the evidence relied upon by the Court, *mahr* consists of "a gift or contribution made by the husband-to-be to his wife-to-be, for her exclusive property. It is not, however, a gift in the sense that a gift is given by the grace of the giver, but in fact 'Mahr' is obligatory and the wife-to-be receives it as of right" (para. 13). Despite the obligatory nature of *mahr* under Islamic family law, the judge held that the agreement was not enforceable by Canadian civil courts. The judge's reasoning reveals that it is the religious dimension of *mahr* that rendered the agreement unenforceable:

> The *Mahr* and the extent to which it obligates a husband to make payment to his wife is essentially and fundamentally an Islamic religious matter. Because *Mahr* is a religious matter, the resolution of any dispute relating to it or the consequences of failing to honour the obligation are also religious in their content and context. While not, perhaps, an ideal comparison, I cannot help but think that the obligation of the *Mahr* is as unsuitable for adjudication in the civil courts as is an obligation in a Christian religious marriage such as to love, honour and cherish, or to remain faithful, or to maintain the marriage in sickness or other adversity so long as both parties live, or to raise children according to specified religious doctrine. Many such promises go well beyond the basic legal commitment to marriage required by our civil law, and are essentially matters of chosen religion and morality. They are derived from and are dependent upon doctrine and faith. They bind the conscience as a matter of religious principle but not necessarily as a matter of enforceable civil law. (para. 25)

This passage reveals an assumption that social life is sharply divided into separate and untouchable spheres of religion and civil courts, on the one hand, and morality and law, on the other. The Court states that transcending this divide would almost certainly entail going "constitutionally beyond its proper territory" (para. 26). Consequently, Justice Rutherford seems to suggest that he has no authority or legitimacy, as a (Western, non-Muslim) judge dealing with the status of a foreign (Islamic) custom in a Canadian constitutional order, to speak *for, on behalf of,* or *in the name of* the Muslim population of Canada:

> I don't think, even if I had received clear and complete Islamic doctrine from these experts, that I could, *as if applying foreign law,* apply such religious doctrine to a civil resolution of this dispute. Mufti Khan in particular said that only an Islamic religious authority could resolve such a dispute ... [through] proper application of principles derived from the Holy Qur'an, the words of the Prophet and from the religious jurisprudence. (para. 28, emphasis added)

Such a conclusion is, ironically, faithful to the LLPA: religion is law's other, and *mahr* belongs to this non-state entity.

It is interesting to note that Justice Rutherford did grant the application for divorce—though not Manira's claim for deferred *mahr*—even though the marriage was concluded pursuant to the Muslim faith, and had its roots in the Holy Qur'an. Following the Court's reasoning to its logical alter-conclusion, had Manira and Sam made the same agreement in the absence of a Muslim ethos, the Court would likely have confirmed the will of the parties with regard to the $30,000 as well. In fact, for an agreement to be enforced according to subsection 52(1) of Ontario's *Family Law Act*, the court determines whether the parties entered freely and willingly into the agreement. In *Kaddoura*, both Sam and Manira acknowledged the agreement as to *mahr*. Further, no evidence showed that the provision requiring the payment of $30,000 was vague or that the agreement was signed under circumstances suggestive of inequality, improvidence or duress. In his judgment for costs of the action, Judge Rutherford acknowledged the unfairness of such legal reasoning:

> While I drew a boundary between a debt enforceable in civil law and the obligation of the *Mahr*, it nonetheless seems to me somewhat offensive and dishonourable on the part of Mr. Kaddoura, to knowingly participate in the wedding customs and practices of his Muslim community, including the *Mahr* which he clearly knew included a "written" or deferred amount of $30,000, and then eschew those customs and practices when they worked to his financial detriment. (para. 6)

By so openly holding an agreement made between Muslims unenforceable because of its rootedness in Islamic rules, the Court presents its LLPA predilections rather openly: *mahr* represents the Otherness of Muslim citizens, and such (incommensurable) difference must be adjudicated solely through an Islamic lens.

It can therefore not be a marriage contract under subsection 52(1) of the *Family Law Act*. In *Kaddoura*, we are left with anxious gazes directed at Muslim subjects, inhabitants of the "'religious thicket' ... a place that the courts cannot safely and should not go" (para. 28).[3] The irony lies in the fact that the LLPA is often praised as "embracing diversity," not rejecting it on the very basis of identity politics.

The LLPA: Differing Camps on Common Ground

The cases discussed in this section emphasized both the particularity of *mahr* as a "legal pluralist" manifestation and the ethical imperative to treat such particularity with (respectful) deference to the minority group. However, the LLPA cases, as a group, adopted contradictory assessments as to the outcome of *mahr*. The first camp, those that occupy the space reserved for the perspective labelled the "many different routes to *mahr* as cultural recognition," held *mahr* as culturally and religiously "legitimate" from the standpoint of the multicultural state, yet differed as to its enforcement in cases related to *khul* divorce. The second camp, "*mahr* as utterly foreign, therefore not recognized and not enforced," found the Islamic institution too different for the Western judge invested in the very complex mission of translating the Otherness of Muslim particularity. Despite the immediate differences these two discourses exhibit, the two are much more similar than one might expect. First, they are both committed to legal pluralism as a mode of governing identity, one in which "law" is employed to speak cultures in a diverse and multiple fashion and where legal subjects are invited

> to imagine themselves as legal agents – to discover the constitutive potential of their own actions. The pluralist hypothesis offers a hypothesis about how human rights entrepreneurs should conceive their endeavour and how they should spend their energies. The pluralist hypothesis means that we can no longer excuse ourselves by deferring to questions as formulated by others, and to agendas that are framed exclusively in a universalizing language apart from human experience. (Macdonald unpublished: 19)

Second, the two have used the "Imam as the expert witness" to represent the minority group, its culture, its religion and its legal system. Third, both view *mahr* as a non-state legal order located in the actual practices of local culture; as such, it qualifies as "law."

---

3   Interestingly, in *Khan v Khan*, a 2005 decision, the same court distanced itself from this reasoning and stated that it could consider the enforceability of a *nikah* (Islamic marriage contract): "The court is prepared to enter the 'thicket' and find that this document represented more than mere religious significance to the parties and that it did bind them civilly" (para. 32).

Liberal–Formal Equality: The Secular Understanding of *Mahr*

The LFEA supposes that law exists as an identifiable and autonomous entity detached from society and morality, a view which permeates the equally familiar tension between objectivity/subjectivity, facts/values, and science/politics, among others (Hart 1958; Fuller 1958). The specificity of the LFEA lies not only in the conception of law as determinate, but also in the principles of objectivity and neutrality as the starting point of legal language. The basic point of departure of the LFEA is the very definition of law as rules of formal logic: the legislature and legislation, courts and adjudication, government and procedures, and so on.

Manifestations of positivistic doctrine, produced by the apparatus of the state, tend to present legal knowledge as a truth claim, something that one can easily access or touch. Describing in a rather ironic fashion what he calls "the heaven of legal concepts," one which he subtitles as a fantasy, legal realist Felix Cohen suggests:

> In the world of concepts which you have before you there is no life in your sense. This is the realm of abstract thoughts and concepts which are independent of the real world, and procreate themselves by way of logical equivocal generation and they must accordingly avoid every contact with the earthly universe. ... The unfaltering belief in the supremacy of concepts and abstract principles is common to all those whom you will meet here. By this, they are protected against the temptation to worry about the practical consequences of the principles, which, as a rule, do not happen to them, anyway, but to others. (quoted in Von Jhering 1951: 691)

For the LFEA, the way to go about understanding law is thus to deduce legal rules and to correctly apply them to the facts in any given situation. I use the word "deduction" to describe the process of deducing decisions from predetermined conceptions and general propositions. I acknowledge that this definition is not without its flaws and criticisms. At the end of the nineteenth century, critiques of the traditional school of the *Exégèse*—those who believed that the civil code was complete and coherent—arose: François Gény (1919) claimed that the civil code under-determines the outcome in a given case because the supposedly objective method of finding the legislator's will through deduction is abusive—it hides the gaps, conflicts or ambiguities hidden behind the written rules. At the same time in the United States, a similar process of critique developed against American classical legal thought. Oliver Wendell Holmes (1920) criticized the *abus de la déduction* at the hands of American conceptualism. He demonstrated that deductive techniques produced arbitrariness, as they provided a vehicle for the judge to expound his own political and social views (Holmes 1920; Grey 1989).

The fundamental concept of "the individual" finds prominence in the disciplinary techniques and architecture shared by the proponents of the LFEA. This ultimate value of individuality—individual freedom, individual autonomy, individual responsibility, individual development—is directly connected to a vision of the state as interfering minimally with free choice. Individuals can best achieve their happiness, the LFEA believes, in a society where they are left free to pursue their own interests. The ideal of formal equality of opportunity is associated with the liberation of economic practices and institutions from guild privileges and restrictions and with the development of competitive market economies. For John Stuart Mill, for example, the basic principle of liberty was that the government refrains from interfering with the expressive thought and actions of the individual.

The LFEA pervades all branches of the law. In constitutional law matters, the notion of a "color blind" constitution (*Plessy v Ferguson*, per Harlan J., dissenting (United States case)), one that should be uniformly applied without reference to a person's race, religion, sex, or any other personal characteristic, is depicted as a typical LFEA assumption. What I will call the LFEA thus insists on the equal treatment principle: legislation must be neutral on its face and the state is entitled to treat people differently only if they are differently situated (Tussman and tenBrock 1949). On this view, affirmative action programs are forbidden. The basic LFEA argument goes as follows: Affirmative action programs would unfairly stigmatize minorities by creating the impression that "people of color cannot at present compete on the same playing field with people who are white" (Carter 1991: 69). In sum, the LFEA is prepared to devote special attention to equal opportunities, not to equal outcomes.

In contract law matters, LFEA adherents similarly present themselves as "technical" facilitators who simply intervene after the fact: contracts result from a "private ordering" which represents the will of the parties and, as such, the state must enforce them without regard to the social/emotional circumstances in which the negotiation took place (Pound 1954). Because it is the consent of the contracting parties that justifies their contractual obligations,[4] the state only acknowledges, through enforcement, the individual freedom used by the parties to bargain and choose which rule corresponds best to their personal preferences (Fuller and Perdue 1936). The conceptual apparatus of the LFEA doctrine thus portrays the role of the judge as a scientific inquiry aimed at discovering, through an inquisitorial gaze, "the will of the parties." This back-and-forth movement between the judge and the parties unfolds through techniques of knowledge that help produce the objective "reality" and "truth" of the pre-existing agreement— cross-examination, questioning, interpretations, expert testimony, etc. In contract and anti-discrimination matters, the LFEA is blind to outcomes; it presents itself as libertarian and legally minimalist in both settings.

---

4   For example, in *Lochner v New York* (1905), freedom of contract was used by the United States Supreme Court to strike down a law that regulated the number of hours worked by bakers. For the Court, it did not matter that the terms of the service contracts signed by the bakers were largely dictated by the employers.

Mahr-*as-Enforceable-Contract*

I will introduce seven cases to depict how courts from various jurisdictions—one from Canada, three from the United States, two from Germany and one from France—have enforced *mahr* as contracts. All insist on the irrelevance of Islam in deciding upon the validity of *mahr*. As a secular contract, *mahr* is entitled to no more and no less legal treatment and relevance than any other civil contract. In approaching the adjudication of *mahr* in this subsection, I will simultaneously explore the politics of contract law as a secular domain and argue that there are political stakes in treating contract law as merely the convergence of the will of the parties, and (religious) *mahr* as yet just another (secular) contract.

The Enforcement of Mahr *as a Marriage Agreement: Canada*   In the 2000 case of *Amlani v Hirani*, the British Columbia Supreme Court dissociated itself from *Nathoo* in reviewing *mahr* as a secular contract. The Court decided that in analyzing the validity of *mahr*, it no longer should inquire into whether the terms of the marriage agreement reflected a religious intention.

Mr. Amlani, a Canadian citizen, and Ms. Hirani, an American citizen, celebrated civil and religious wedding ceremonies in 1997 and 1998, respectively. A *mahr* of $51,000 had been negotiated. The marriage agreement stated that Mr. Amlani was obliged to "pay the agreed sum of money by way of Maher to my said wife (which) shall be in addition and without prejudice to and not in substitution of all of my obligations provided for by the laws of the land." Two years later, Mr. Amlani sought an order for divorce and a declaration that *mahr* does not constitute a marriage agreement under section 61 of British Columbia's *Family Relations Act*. Furthermore, he claimed the authority of religious law, in that "the Mehr amount is a traditional custom of Muslim law that was intended to provide financial compensation for a wife and children in the event of a marriage break-up. Muslim religious law did not allow a wife to pursue support for herself and any children, nor any rights to property" (para. 28). Ms. Hirani held a contrary view: "The Mehr Amount is the amount that must be paid to me by the Plaintiff either upon the marriage or the marriage breakdown, including a divorce. It is security for the wife and children, if any" (para. 27).

In deciding whether *mahr* met the requirements of a marriage agreement as described in paragraph 61(2)(b) of the *Family Relations Act*, Justice Sinclair-Prowse reviewed each legal element separately and concluded that four necessary conditions were met: (1) the marriage contract was made between a man and a woman, Mr. Amlani and Ms. Hirani (para. 17); (2) it was entered into during their marriage (para. 18); (3) it was to take effect upon execution of the agreement, as evidenced by the wording of the contract itself (para. 19); (4) and it provides "for ownership ... in other property" (paras 20, 23). Therefore, *mahr* is a marriage agreement for the purposes of section 61 of the *Family Relations Act*.

In examination for discovery of Mr. Amlani during preparation for trial, Mr. Amlani claimed that *mahr* can only be enforced if other civil remedies are not available to Ms. Hirani upon the dissolution of marriage. To this claim, the Court responded by categorically refusing to enter the internal logic of Islamic family law. If the parties have decided to live in a country where family law remedies are available to men and women upon divorce, they cannot pretend to be bound by another site of legal regulation simply because they are Muslims. Moreover, if Mr. Amlani willingly accepted that *mahr* "be in addition and without prejudice to and not in substitution of all of [his] obligations provided for by the laws of the land" (para. 30), the Court would not approve his request to ignore his contractual obligations in the name of religion: "If the payment of the Maher/Mehr Amount only applied in the absence of civil remedies, as suggested by Mr. Amlani in his Examination for Discovery, there would have been no reason for these parties to have entered into the Marriage Contract" (para. 31).

Clearly, the British Columbia Superior Court closes the door to the judicial exploration of *mahr* as culture: *mahr* is *a contract*—it requires an offer and its acceptance, and it names an owner in whom property is vested. Under the LFEA rhetoric, *mahr*-as-contract does not involve the question of whether it is deemed essential or merely incidental to the (Islamic) marriage contract, or whether it was understood by the (Muslim) parties as financially providing for the wife in the event of divorce (as opposed to alimony) under Islamic family law. In *Amlani*, *mahr* is an agreement which merely corresponds to the legal definition found in the *Family Relations Act*.

The Enforcement of Mahr *as an Antenuptial Agreement: The United States*   In *Aziz*, *Odatalla*, and *Akileh*, three American cases from New York, New Jersey and Florida, respectively, *mahr* is portrayed and enforced on the basis of an antenuptial agreement. Religious evidence has no bearing on the interpretation of *mahr*.

Aziz v Aziz, a very short 1985 decision from the New York Superior Court, begins with sharp distinctions between religious and secular matters, and Islamic law and Western contract law. In an action for divorce, Justice Miller described the parties "as husband and wife, against a *mahr* of $5,032 ($5,000 deferred payment and $32 prompt payment) under Islamic law" (1013), and concluded that "[t]he document at issue conforms to the requirements of the General Obligations Law ... and its secular terms are enforceable as a contractual obligation, notwithstanding that it was entered into as part of a religious ceremony" (1013). Although the Court enforced the *mahr* provisions of the marriage contract, the judge made no attempt to gain an internal appreciation of the functional role of *mahr* in a Muslim couple's wedding and subsequent relationship. Rather, the legal question is thought of as one in which Person A, after discussions and bargaining with Person B, fixes the price of *mahr* as a condition of marriage. What has to be decided from the perspective of the LFEA judge is, quite simply, whether this agreement respects the conditions of contract law in New York, in which case *mahr*—or, rather, the contract—is enforced.

In *Aziz*, Justice Miller conceived *mahr*-as-contract without incorporating the religious shape that first gives it existence, and then substance. Marooned from any particular type of private ordering, *mahr* becomes merely a contractual, monetary obligation: "As a secular document it calls for the payment of $5,000 now," concluded Justice Miller (1014). Interestingly, the judgment in *Aziz* was based on a 1983 decision of the New York Court of Appeals concerning a Jewish marriage contract, or *ketubah*.[5] In that case, *Avitzur v Avitzur*, four of seven judges applied what they called "neutral principles of contract law" (115) to avoid the religious thicket feared by the three dissenters, who refused to engage questions that, in their view, implicated "Jewish religious law and tradition" (119). The dissent considered that the religious character of the *ketubah* presented a constitutional barrier to the Court's ability to grant the relief requested.

In *Odatalla v Odatalla*, a 2002 New Jersey case, *mahr* was similarly translated as an enforceable secular contract. On June 15, 1996, Houida and Zuhair Odatalla married in the presence of an Imam at the home of Houida's parents in Linden, New Jersey. Prior to the marriage ceremony, Houida and Zuhair had signed an Islamic Marriage License containing a *mahr* provision: "According to Islamic Law Dower is: Prompt One golden pound coin/Postponed Ten Thousand U.S. Dollars" (95). The evidence presented to the Court included a videotape which showed the families negotiating the terms and conditions of the marriage licence, including those of the *mahr* agreement. It also showed the parties signing the agreement "freely and voluntarily" and Zuhair handing Houida one golden pound coin as part of the wedding ceremony (95). Six years later, Houida brought an action for divorce based upon grounds of extreme cruelty, to which the husband filed a counter-complaint for divorce on identical grounds. The decision hinges solely, however, on "the novel issue of whether a civil court can specifically enforce the terms of an Islamic *Mahr* Agreement" (94).

While Houida sought enforcement of the *mahr* agreement contained in the Islamic marriage licence, Zuhair opposed the Court ordering specific performance on two grounds: (1) the First Amendment to the Constitution precluded the Court from reviewing the *mahr* agreement under the doctrine of the separation of church and state, and (2) the agreement was not a valid contract under New Jersey law. Moreover, Zuhair requested alimony and equitable distribution of certain jewellery, furniture, wedding gifts and marital debt, demands that he could not make under Islamic family law (94).

In response to Zuhair's first argument, Justice Selser categorically asserted: "Clearly, this court can enforce a contract which is not in contravention of established law or public policy. … Why should a contract for the promise to pay money be less of a contract just because it was entered into at the time of an Islamic marriage ceremony?" (95). Furthermore, the Court affirmed that the validity of *mahr* as a contract did not involve a "doctrinal issue" (96) related to religious policy or theories; consequently, there was "no constitutional infringement" at stake in enforcing *mahr* (96). Not only was the enforcement "not void simply because it

---

5   The California of *In re Marriage of Dajani* also drew on a precedent addressing a *ketubah* dispute (*In re Marriage of Noghrey*, also out of the California Court of Appeals).

was entered into during an Islamic ceremony of marriage" (96), but to embrace "the secular parts of a written agreement is consistent with the constitutional mandate for a 'free exercise' of religious beliefs" (97). In *Odatalla*, the LFEA judge claimed merely to acknowledge a pre-existing secular agreement, "though religious in appearance" (97), and explicitly (and repeatedly) remarked on the irrelevance of recognizing Muslim subjectivity in contractual relations.

Explicitly resisting Zuhair's claim that *mahr* be considered a sacred domain of Islam impenetrable by a secular court, the Superior Court of New Jersey held that "[a]greements, though arrived at as part of a religious ceremony of any particular faith," are enforceable if they are (1) "capable of specific performance under 'neutral principles of law'" and (2) if "the agreement in question meets the state's standards for those 'neutral principles of law'" (98).

In applying the "neutral principles" of contract law in *Odatalla*, Justice Selser reviewed the definition of contract from the Restatement the law of contracts ("a set of promises for the breach of which the law gives a remedy, or performance of which the law in some way recognizes as a duty") and applied it to the *mahr* agreement. The videotape in evidence demonstrated an offer of $10,000 on the part of Zuhair Odatalla and acceptance from Houida Odatalla in the form of a signature. Insisting on the facts that each party "read the entire license and Mahr Agreement," "signed the same freely and voluntarily," "(t)he signatures were witnessed" and "the Imam continued performing the remaining parts of the Islamic ceremony of marriage" (95), the Superior Court of New Jersey found that "all of the essential elements of a contract [were] present" (98).

Moreover, Justice Selser reviewed the constitutive exceptions to the enforcement of contracts and rejected the positions that the *mahr* agreement was "too vague to comply with contract law," that it constituted a gift or that it was "unenforceable and void as being against public policy" (98). Rather, he described *mahr* as indicating a relationship of property between two contracting parties, "nothing more and nothing less than a simple contract between two consenting adults" (98). Zuhair was thus ordered to pay "to the plaintiff the sum of $10,000" (98). It is worth noting that the *Odatalla* decision, unlike most LLPA cases, does not rely on the Imam as the expert witness speaking on behalf of Muslim subjects. Rather, the Court preferred "the benefit of testimonial evidence from both plaintiff and defendant. In addition, the Court had an actual copy of the Islamic marriage license, a videotape of the entire marriage ceremony and documents relating to the alimony and equitable distribution issues in this case" (95).

In *Akileh v Elchahal*, a 1996 decision from Florida's Court of Appeals, the wife challenged the lower court's ruling that the premarital agreement was unenforceable for lack of consideration. The parties contracted their marriage in Florida and agreed upon one dollar in prompt *mahr* and $50,000 in deferred *mahr*. The trial court held that *mahr* was unenforceable for lack of consideration and because there was no meeting of the minds. The Florida Court of Appeals reviewed the contradictory evidence put before the trial court, in order to establish that "*sadaq*" is an alternative form of "*mahr*":

At trial, four witnesses testified as to the meaning of the Islamic [*sic*] word '*sadaq*.' The wife's Islamic expert, Mazi Najjar, testified that generally a *sadaq* is similar to the concept of a dowry. He stated that only the wife could waive her right to receive the postponed portion of the *sadaq*. Najjar said that the wife's right to receive the *sadaq* was not negated if the wife filed for divorce.

The wife testified that a wife's right to receive the postponed portion of the *sadaq* was absolute and not affected by the cause of a divorce. The wife stated that the exception was that a wife would forfeit the dowry if she cheated on her husband. The wife was unaware of any other instances in which the *sadaq* would be forfeited. Raju Akileh, the wife's father, also testified that the postponed portion of the *sadaq* is an absolute right of a wife to request from the husband whenever she wished and especially in the event of divorce.

The husband testified that he believed the postponed portion of the *sadaq* was forfeited if the wife chose to divorce her husband. The husband's understanding of the *sadaq* stemmed from his sister's experience. His sister had previously sought a divorce and then pursued the postponed *sadaq*. An Islamic court ruled that she was not entitled to receive the *sadaq* since she had wanted the divorce. However, the husband testified that a woman seeking a divorce is entitled to her *sadaq* if she is abused. The husband admitted that he had never discussed the meaning of *sadaq* with the wife or her father. (*Akileh* Appeal: 247–48)

Closing the door to the religious evidence, Justice Patterson followed the *Aziz* decision and held that "Florida contract law applies to the secular terms of the *sadaq*" (247). In rejecting the determination that the contract was unenforceable *de novo*, the appellate court held that marriage is sufficient consideration to uphold a prenuptial agreement: "the agreement was an antenuptial contract, executed in contemplation of a forthcoming marriage" (248). Furthermore, the Court relied on Florida contract law in concluding that there *was* a meeting of the minds—in which case the subsequent difference as to the construction of the contract does not affect the validity or indicate the minds of the parties did not meet. The husband's subjective intent at the time he entered into the agreement is not material in construing the contract. The Court also suggested that the husband did not make his unique understanding of *mahr* known to the wife prior to signing the certificate of marriage. In holding that *mahr* was valid and enforceable, the Court in *Akileh* found that the parties had agreed on the essential terms of the contract.

The Enforcement of Mahr *as a Legal Debt: Germany*   In Germany, the determination of whether *mahr* is a family alimony or a contractual debt claim has a direct impact on which law—the law of citizenship or the law of domicile— will apply to the parties and their dispute. As demonstrated in Chapter 2, German international private law rules specify that family law matters are regulated by the law of the parties' country of citizenship in the Family Law Chamber, whereas contract law matters fall under the law of domicile and follow the jurisdiction of the Civil Law Chamber. In *Hamm FamRZ*, a 1988 decision involving a Tunisian citizen married to a German citizen, the Civil Law Chamber interpreted *mahr* as a legal debt and a contractual institution in itself, rather than a post-divorce alimony. The parties had specified that "if the marriage ended in divorce, the husband was obliged to pay the wife DM 5,000 (2,500 Euros) as settlement/compensation and as dower (which seems to refer to not only *mahr* but also the classical Islamic gift on divorce, or *mut'a*)" (Jones-Pauly 2008: 313). Further, the parties had expressed their wish not to "have community property, but rather keep their fortunes separate (which also conforms to the Qur'anic injunction that the wife has control over her own property and earnings)" (Jones-Pauly 2008: 313). Because the parties had clearly distinguished in the marriage contract between "*mahr* and maintenance," on the one hand, and "community property," on the other, the Higher Regional Court (OLG) respected the intention of the parties and enforced *mahr* as separate from family law matters.

Similarly, the Court in *Amtsgericht Buende* attempted to determine the intention of the parties with regard to *mahr*. The *mahr* contract stipulated that the husband would give to the wife a Qur'an, cooking salt, green silk and 140 Azadi gold coins. After six years of marriage, the Iranian parties divorced and the wife claimed enforcement of 140 gold coins as *mahr* (the exact value of this in Euros was not determined by the Court). The husband argued that "he had already given the wife valuable gifts, like clothes, and expensive gold jewels. He wanted the value of these gifts to be calculated against the claim for the *mahr*" (Jones-Pauly 2008: 18). The Court accepted the argument that *mahr* has the nature of a gift and therefore is a matter of civil law. Consequently, it held that *mahr* was enforceable as a contractual matter if the intention of the parties was to view it as a gift. In this case, the husband had obliged himself to such a gift, and the amount of *mahr* was intended to be separate from a Qur'an, cooking salt and green silk. He was thus ordered to pay the 140 Azadi gold coins.

The Enforcement of Mahr *as a Contractual Condition of Marriage: France*   In a December 1997 Cour de Cassation decision, the French court considered *mahr* as a contractual condition of marriage under Islamic family law and enforced it on that basis. Ms. Kubicka, a Polish citizen, and Mr. Tohme, a Lebanese citizen, married in Lebanon according to Islamic law. The matrimonial regime was that of "separate property with the consideration of *Mahr*" (Cour de Cassation, Chambre Civile, December 2, 1997: 1, translated by the author). Upon divorce, Ms. Kubicka claimed that she did not consent to the family law regime described in the marriage contract, due to the fact that she neither spoke nor understood Arabic and was not aware of the mandatory regime applicable to married couples in Lebanon. The Cour de Cassation concluded that both parties expressed in French their intentions to adopt the regime of "separate property with the consideration of *Mahr*." In fact, it concluded that the trial court correctly inferred, from the "legal formulation of a reciprocal offer and acceptance" the "existence of an express will of the spouses regarding the determination of their matrimonial regime" (translated by the author).

Mahr-*as-Unenforceable-Contract*

The LFEA found in *mahr*-as-enforceable-contract can just as easily lead to an opposite outcome, as was the case in several decisions in the United States and Germany, where *mahr* was deemed unenforceable according to the contractual exceptions of vagueness, lack of consent and consideration, and abstractness.

The Unenforceability of Mahr *on Grounds of Vagueness: The United States*   In *Habibi-Fahnrich v Fahnrich*, a 1995 decision of one of New York's supreme courts, the *mahr* document read "a ring advanced and half of husband's possessions postponed" (1). The parties married in a civil ceremony in Brooklyn, and subsequently in a religious ceremony in Washington, DC, in August 1992. *Mahr* was signed by both parties. Less than one year after the parties were married, the Muslim wife brought an action for divorce against her husband and requested the enforcement of *mahr*. At trial, the wife withdrew her original request for maintenance and both parties conceded that no marital assets had been acquired during the course of the marriage. Hence, the issue of equitable distribution did not need to be discussed. The only issue remaining was that of the enforcement of *mahr* or, in the words of the Court, whether the "Islamic marriage contract signed by the parties is valid" (1). The husband argued that he agreed to *mahr* only "to appease plaintiff's family at plaintiff's urging" and did not intend to bind himself (1).

     Relying upon *Aziz* and *Avitzur*, the Court stated that *mahr* generally may be enforceable as a contractual obligation which formed the basis of the marriage. However, the enforceability of *mahr* in this case turned on whether the requirements for a contract under the *General Obligations Law* were met. Specifically, section 5-701(1) requires "the writing to contain all material terms and conditions so that one reading it can understand what the parties have agreed upon." Justice Rigler defined *mahr* (or *sadaq*) as "a document which defines the precepts of the Moslem marriage by providing for financial compensation to a woman for the loss of her status and value in the community if the marriage ends in a divorce" (1), and went on to determine that the terms of *mahr* asking for the distribution of "half of the husband's possessions" were too vague to be enforced under principles of contract law:

> In the case at bar, the material terms of the SADAQ are not specific enough that a person reading it would be able to grasp the gist of the agreement. Areas of the SADAQ which do not appear to be specific enough include the meaning of "possession" and the definition of "one half of the possessions." The SADAQ itself does not illustrate what a possession is or how an asset would even become a possession. The SADAQ also fails to display how one half of the possessions should be determined or measured or when the determination should even take place. (2)

Throughout the discussion on the enforceability of *mahr*, the Court refrained from exploring the religious structure that permeates *mahr* as an Islamic institution. *Mahr*, to the Court, simply referred to the market, to ownership—it was a contract, though not precise enough in this case. First, the Court determined that the parties did not agree to the material terms of the contract, namely "one half interest." Second, because the terms "postponed" and "one half of the possessions" were not defined, the material terms of the contract were not specific enough and, hence, the contract failed the test "that anyone reading the contract should be able to understand the dictates of the agreement" (1). Finally, the agreement was "insufficient on its face" because there was no evidence of any agreement by the parties to its terms.

Shaban v Shaban similarly concluded the unenforceability of *mahr* based on the uncertainty of the terms used by the parties in their premarital agreement. In this 2001 California Court of Appeal decision, the parties to a premarital agreement had contracted with respect to the choice of law governing the construction of the agreement, pursuant to section 1612 of the *California Family Code*. The document was a one-page piece of paper written in Arabic and signed by the husband and his future father-in-law. Providing for an immediate *mahr* of approximately 25 *piasters* (approximately one dollar), and a deferred *mahr* equal to about $30, it specified that the marriage was made in accordance with Islamic law, more specifically that "the above legal marriage has been concluded in Accordance with his Almighty God's Holy Book and the Rules of his Prophet to whom all God's prayers and blessings be, by legal offer and acceptance from the two contracting parties" (402). Mr. and Mrs. Shaban married in Egypt in 1974 and divorced in 1998 in the Superior Court of Orange County, having lived in the United States for about 17 years.

In *Shaban*, the wife claimed her share of a community estate valued in excess of $3 million, despite agreeing to a *mahr* of 500 Egyptian pounds (approximately $86). The husband introduced the Islamic marriage contract into evidence and sought to prove through parol evidence that by accepting *mahr*, Mrs. Shaban also consented to their marriage being dissolved according to Islamic law's separate property presumption (403). Practically speaking, that would mean that "there would be no community interest in Ahmad's medical practice or retirement accounts" (404).

The LFEA court refused to recognize *mahr* and rendered the Egyptian Islamic wedding contract void primarily because it failed to satisfy the *Statute of Frauds*. The Court concluded that an agreement whose only substantive term in any language is that the marriage has been made in accordance with "Islamic law" is hopelessly uncertain as to its terms and conditions. It held:

> Given the need for reasonable certainty of terms and conditions, it is evident that the phrases "in Accordance with his Almighty God's Holy Book and the Rules of his Prophet" and "two parties [having] taken cognizance of the legal implications," no matter how much they might indirectly indicate a desire to

be governed by the rules of the Islamic religion, simply bear too attenuated a relationship to any actual terms or conditions of a prenuptial agreement to satisfy the statute of frauds. (406)

The Court further commented that an additional impediment to the validity of the Shaban marriage contract would be that, in California, "dowry provisions have not fared well by themselves" (407); the Court referred specifically to the decisions in *Dajani* and *Noghrey*. The Court refused to allow the expert to testify, and concluded that the purported premarital agreement was in fact a marriage "certificate" (404). The Court thus entered a judgment applying California community property law to the acquisitions during the marriage and dividing what it then held as the community estate.

The Unenforceability of Mahr *Due to Lack of Consent and Consideration: The United States*   In *Akileh v Elchahal,* a case whose facts are described in the LLPA section above, the Florida Court relied on basic contract law doctrine to conclude that *mahr* was unenforceable. In fact, the "trial court held that the *sadaq* was unenforceable for lack of consideration and because there was no meeting of the minds" (248). Justice Foster specified, in the final judgment of dissolution of marriage, that the "Wife's claim to the *sadaq* is denied. The *sadaq* does not meet the statutory requirements of Florida law for the enforcement of a contract because there was no meeting of the minds and Wife supplied no consideration" (*Akileh* Family Law Division: 3).

The Unenforceability of Mahr *on Grounds of Abstractness: Germany*   In *IPRax 1988*, the German Federal High Court examined *mahr* as a legal contractual debt under the German *Civil Code* and concluded that it did not meet the contract law requirements. A debt under German law consists of "a naked or abstract promise to perform and a description of what is to be performed, independent of motives, economic circumstances or any legal considerations. A measure of abstractness lies in the absence in the contract of the motive for the performance" (Jones-Pauly unpublished: 25). In this case, the husband had specifically included in the marriage contract the motives for agreeing to *mahr*: he entered into the contract in consideration of Islamic legal rules. Consequently, the test of abstractness failed, although the wife had tried to convince the Court that "the contract did not limit itself to Islamic law only. The contract gave her the alternative of applying the German divorce law, whereupon she could also claim the 10,000 DM" (Jones-Pauly unpublished: 25). On the basis of this exception to contract law *mahr* was not enforced.

Concluding Remarks on the LFEA

In adjudicating *mahr*, the most direct expression of the LFEA is the *secular* conception of this religious institution: deprived of its Islamic flavour, *mahr* becomes a (Western) contract enforceable (or not) irrespective of race, gender or religion. In capturing *mahr* under the umbrella of Western contract law, as opposed to Islamic family law, the judge pictures the liberal system as devoid of a representative role for the Muslim-ness of the parties. Contract law, the judge assumes, is not a matter of identity politics. As was apparent in this section, the LFEA judge chooses, in interpreting *mahr*, between rules and standards arranged around the rule/exception or rule/counter-rule configurations specific to contract law doctrine: *mahr* is enforced either as a "marriage agreement" (rule—Canada), as an "antenuptial agreement" (rule—US), as a "legal debt" (rule—Germany), or as a "contractual condition of marriage" (rule—France); or *mahr* is rendered unenforceable because of "vagueness" (exception—US), due to lack of consent and consideration (exception—US), and "abstractness" (exception—Germany).

Liberal-Substantive Equality: The Feminist Understanding of *Mahr*

The LSEA is concerned with power differentials—how subjects are constituted through structural and hierarchical systems of inequality, and how the law specifically (re)produces systemic conditions of oppression and can remedy or dissolve them. In its normative mode, the LSEA opposes both the LLPA and the LFEA: according to the LSEA, if the LLPA wrongly places the autonomy of the group over the autonomy of the individual, and in so doing suppresses the rights of women by promoting conservative visions of the community over progressive ones, the LFEA fails to take power into account in projecting a universal, delocalized and objective legal reality. (One ironic view of this was expressed by Justice Douglas of the United States Supreme Court, who remarked in *International Association of Machinists v Street*: "[O]ne who of necessity rides busses and streetcars does not have the freedom that John Muir and Walt Whitman extolled" (775)). Susan Moller Okin (1999: 10) has attempted to show that multiculturalism and feminism cannot coexist:

> I think we—especially those of us who consider ourselves politically progressive and opposed to all forms of oppression—have been too quick to assume that feminism and multiculturalism are both good things which are easily reconciled. I shall argue instead that there is considerable likelihood of tension between them—more precisely, between feminism and a multiculturalist commitment to group rights for minority cultures.

Okin (1998: 675) also notes the negative effects on women who live in minority cultures: they are "socializ[ed] into inferior roles, resulting in [a] lack of self-esteem [and] a sense of entitlement." In her view, then, in a society truly committed to sex equality, multiculturalism must give way, and feminism must triumph.

In constitutional law matters, the LSEA starts from the perspective of the oppressed, and critiques existing doctrines, practices and structures through the lens of subordination theory (Dworkin 1984). The real world is marked by attempted or real domination—of one race over another, of men over women. Therefore, the state *must* deliver outcomes that are substantively equal, even if the group striving for equality is not necessarily internally united in its approach—feminist theory, for example, is diverse, with liberal, radical, Marxist and socialist strands (Halley 2006). In *Bakke*, the United States Supreme Court recognized this explicitly with regard to race, advocating the adoption of race-specific legislation: "In order to get beyond racism, we must first take account of race. There is no other way. And in order to treat some persons equally, we must treat them differently. We cannot—we dare not—let the Equal Protection Clause perpetuate racial supremacy." In terms of the recognition of gender inequalities, this can emerge as either constitutional equality protection, or legislation that, in its application, results in inequitable outcomes. For the former, textual support for substantive equality in Canada is found in subsection 15(1) of the *Canadian Charter of Rights and Freedoms*, which guarantees "equal benefit of the law": "Every individual is equal before and under the law and has the right to the equal protection and equal benefit of the law without discrimination and, in particular, without discrimination based on race, national or ethnic origin, colour, religion, sex, age or mental or physical disability."

Examples of legislative inequities to which the LSEA responds, abound. In the United States, feminist litigators have struggled to have courts accept evidence about battered women's syndrome as relevant to the self-defence issue when a battered woman is being prosecuted for the murder of her batterer (Schneider 1986a, 1986b), illustrating the LSEA in action. In the debate over maternity leave policies, known as the "special treatment/equal treatment debate," the LSEA aims to demonstrate that the typical worker behind the law is a man (Finley 1986). In divorce law, the LSEA claims that formal equal treatment, or gender-neutral property division and custody laws, has had drastically adverse consequences on the economic well-being of women. Women and men are not equally situated in terms of marketable skills, economic resources, access to affordable childcare, and high paying jobs: the law should recognize this discrepancy (Fineman 1983).

The purpose of the LSEA is thus to name, expose and ultimately eradicate the socially and economically inferior position of oppressed groups in society. In such a context, affirmative action programs are not only considered constitutionally permissible, they are mandatory.

In contract law matters, the LSEA focuses on the actual power of the individual parties—men and women, husbands and wives, etc.—to make decisions about the agreements they make. LSEA judges see their role as one of deciding how the parties *would* have contracted had they not been constrained by the overall unequal structure of social and economic power. Consequently, the LSEA embraces a general fairness policy in enforcing contracts: because men and women in intimate relationships are not considered to be operating at arm's length in bargaining contracts, especially with regard to those related to the family, the state intervenes to monitor the outcomes. In the long run, this systemic imposition will reduce some of the power traditionally held by the strongest party (often the man, the LSEA would claim) by eliminating the legal backing necessary to uphold unfair agreements (Kennedy 1982). The LSEA does not concern itself with the possibility that such external monitoring could be seen as paternalism, mainly because paternalism can be understood not as a negative power-grab, but in a positive light:

> It is not hard to imagine a society in which everybody agreed that there were particular classes of people who were likely to make choices not in their best interests, and that the legal system should protect them from themselves. Indeed, with respect to children and the insane, this is the condition of our society (though the consensus is beginning to break down). The objects of this protection might be in complete agreement that it was necessary. Or imagine a society in which everyone agreed that in particular situations or states of mind, everyone was likely to make mistakes and needed to be protected from themselves. The category of paternalism might come up mainly with strong positive connotations of loving care for others. (Kennedy 1982: 588)

The Enforcement of Mahr *According to Gender Equity Standards*

The fairness dimension of the LSEA transfers *mahr* to the centre of the "public" and highly interventionist standpoint of the state: *mahr* is not a contract existing comfortably under the individual, "private" umbrella of antenuptial agreements (LFEA), nor is it located merely behind the collective, group expression of Muslim subjectivity (LLPA). In the German and Québec cases discussed below, courts have embraced the legitimacy of *mahr*, but have intervened to regulate its enforcement. Such intervention carries with it the mark of substantive equality. While Germany has modified the initial amount of *mahr* to align with equitable considerations, Québec has rejected the Islamic family law logic of *khul mahr* to welcome the enforcement of *mahr* in a context where the Muslim wife is the one asking for divorce.

The Enforcement and Readjustment of Mahr *as Alimony: Germany* In *OLG Koeln*, a 1983 appeal decision from Cologne,[6] the notarized marriage contract between an Iranian wife and a German husband specified as *mahr* a Qur'an worth 1000 rials, jewellery worth 88,000 rials, and 4 million rials (equivalent to approximately 42,000 DM or 21,000 Euros). Christina Jones-Pauly (2008: 305) notes: "The four million rials were specifically referred to as a 'debt' on the husband, payable at any time the wife requested." The wife asked for and obtained a divorce before the German Family Law Chamber, and separately claimed the enforcement of *mahr* plus interest as a legal debt before the Civil Law Chamber.

---

6   The trial decision is described in the section entitled "the unenforceability of Mahr as unjust enrichment of the wife."

At trial, the husband had convinced the Court that the enforcement of *mahr* constituted an unjust enrichment for the wife, one which would violate German public order. On appeal from the Civil Law Chamber, the appellate court viewed *mahr* as an Islamic institution which serves as post-marital maintenance—but only insofar as its enforcement meets the German standards of equity. It held that enforcing its full amount in this case—the full 4 million rials—would be repugnant to German principles of justice. Consequently, the amount would have to be counted against any maintenance which the husband might be ordered to pay. To discern this amount—that is, exactly how much of the *mahr* would be awarded to the wife—the appeal court sent the matter back to the Family Law Chamber. *Mahr* was thus translated as alimony and its amount adjusted based on fairness considerations.

The Enforcement of Mahr *even though the Wife Initiated Divorce: Québec*   In *M.H.D. v E.A.*, a case discussed under the LLPA section on the unenforceability of *mahr* in the case of *khul* divorce, the Québec trial court concluded that Syrian Islamic law could not apply in Canada: its application would create a negative effect on Muslim wives availing themselves of the *Divorce Act*. In fact, had the court correctly applied Syrian Islamic law, it would have refused to enforce *mahr* according to the logic of the *khul* divorce. The Court considered this outcome contrary to the *Canadian Charter of Rights and Freedoms* because enforcing *khul mahr* would require the Western state to punish a wife because *she* is the one initiating the divorce proceedings, an outcome that would not similarly apply to the husband. In insisting on the impact of religious law on the woman involved, the LSEA judge explicitly rejected the authority of Islamic beliefs:

> With all due respect to the beliefs of the religious authority as well as to those of the husband, the court believes that such traditions, customs and doctrine put before us are not applicable to the wife, and that the court must consider the wedding present discussed above only with respect to the *Québec Civil Code*. (para. 27, translated from the French by the author)

Accordingly, gender equity principles dictate that the LSEA court enforce *mahr* despite the *khul* divorce:

> However, this court believes that the legislation cannot be in conflict with sections of the *Canadian Charter* whereby fundamental rights and freedoms are guaranteed. The *Canadian Charter* is the supreme law of Canada. All must abide by it, including the legislator. The *Divorce Act* gives the opportunity to both spouses to initiate divorce proceedings, and punishing a spouse on the basis that she exercises her rights according to the *Act* is a violation of her freedom. In cases of conflict between spouses, each has the right to the equal protection and equal benefit of the law (s. 7 and 15(1)). Also, to deny the wife her right to equality by asking her to give back her wedding presents or gifts received

or agreed upon in the marriage contract on the basis that she exercised rights recognized by the law, constitutes a form of discrimination. (para. 26, translated from the French by the author)

Embracing egalitarian considerations in the interpretation of contract law, the state accepts to intervene in family/religious matters in order to police the outcomes. If *khul mahr* is seen as violating principles of substantive equality and relegating Muslim women to a gendered legal position, the court rejects such an institution altogether. In its place, it substitutes its own feminist doctrinal approach and delivers its LSEA treatment: the enforcement of *mahr* despite the *khul* divorce, firmly rooted in the constitutional bedrock of the *Canadian Charter of Rights and Freedoms*.

These German and Québec cases embraced gender-equity principles in enforcing *mahr*. In so doing, they significantly changed *mahr*'s function in regard to Islamic family law. In the next subsection, I describe how the identical allusions to substantive equality produce the opposite outcome in Canada (including Québec), Germany, the United States and France: *mahr* is unenforceable based on "equity," "unjust enrichment," "substantial justice" and "public policy" considerations.

The Unenforceability of Mahr *According to Fairness Principles*

In the cases described here, the unenforceability of *mahr* is attached to the application of fairness principles as between the spouses: sometimes equity toward the Muslim *man* dictates the non-enforcement of *mahr*; sometimes equity toward the Muslim *woman* dictates such an outcome. I will review cases from the United States, Canada, Germany and France that have all attempted to bring about an egalitarian outcome in the form of the non-enforcement of *mahr*.

The Unenforceability of Mahr *on the Basis of Equity: Québec*   In *M. F. v MA. A.*, a 2002 Québec trial court decision, the LSEA offers a distributional pattern against which *mahr* is judged and ultimately rejected on the basis of equity toward the Muslim husband. In 1997, Mrs. Ajabi married in Montreal at the age of 23, and gave birth to a son the following year. The "Musulman contract of marriage" (to use Mrs. Ajabi's term) read: "There is a Mahr of Holy QURAN Book, one piece Sugar Candy, one Kilo of Gold payable by the groom to the bride." The marriage lasted a little less than three years, throughout which Mrs. Ajabi stayed at home to raise her son. In applying the family law rules of the Québec *Civil Code*, Justice Hurtubise divided the family patrimony equally, which resulted in an award to the wife of $27,304.85, and determined the alimony due her to be $150 per week. The Court, however, refused to enforce *mahr*, an amount that would have been worth $15,960 (para. 32). Justice Hurtubise concluded: "The message is clear: given what the husband has already given to the wife, he should not be required to give more. He has fulfilled his obligation" (para. 32, translated from the French by the author).

In *M.F.*, the Court admittedly focused on distributive effects. Instead of viewing *mahr* as a form of identity based on community standards, or as a secular contract reflecting the intentions of the parties, the Court viewed the adjudication of *mahr* through a lens filtered by outcomes. The Court thus implicitly asked: Would it be *fair* for this *particular* man to pay $15,960 as *mahr* in addition to $27,304.85 on account of the division of assets *and* $150 per week as alimony? Such an outcome, which would require the enforcement of *mahr*, is considered to unjustly profit the wife.

The Unenforceability of Mahr *as Unjust Enrichment: Germany*   The legal reasoning and outcomes of the cases described in this section are similar to those of the Québec court in *M.F.* However, while the judge in *M.F.* implicitly ascribed to the doctrine of unjust enrichment, the two cases reviewed here explicitly refer to this doctrine. Both cases examined the bargaining power that existed between the marital parties, and both concluded that enforcing *mahr*, in the *particular* circumstances, would unjustly enrich the Muslim woman.

The facts of *OLG Koeln*, a 1983 decision from Cologne, have already been described in the section on the enforcement and readjustment of *mahr* as alimony. Briefly, the notarized marital contract between an Iranian wife and a German husband specified as *mahr* a Qur'an worth 1,000 rials, jewellery worth 88,000 rials, and 4 million rials (approximately 42,000 DM or 21,000 Euros). The wife asked for and obtained a divorce before the German Family Law Chamber, and separately claimed the enforcement of *mahr* plus interests as a legal debt before the Civil Law Chamber. Arguing for the non-enforcement of *mahr*, the husband attempted to demonstrate that enforcing *mahr* would be repugnant to German public order due to the unjust enrichment of the wife. The Civil Law Chamber agreed. The parameters, categories and legal analysis of the doctrine of unjust enrichment were similarly applied in *OLG Cell*, a 1998 German decision. In that case, the Family Law Chamber had already awarded the Muslim wife maintenance of 37,000 DM as part of the divorce proceedings. The judge, operating under precepts of the LSEA, concluded that the wife could not, in all equity, claim an additional 30,000 DM as *mahr*.

The Unenforceability of Mahr *on the Basis of Substantial Justice: Canada*   In *Vladi v Vladi*, a 1987 decision from the Canadian province of Nova Scotia, the Court refused to enforce mahr on the basis of "substantial justice." In 1973, Mr. and Mrs. Vladi, Iranian nationals residing in West Germany, married religiously and civilly in Germany. In 1978, the parties began visiting Nova Scotia and subsequently became Canadian citizens. *Vladi* represents an application under Nova Scotia's *Matrimonial Property Act*, made by Mrs. Vladi subsequent to a divorce granted to her husband by a West German court in September 1985. At the time of separation, the parties had assets in Nova Scotia and elsewhere in the world. Although Mrs. Vladi and the couple's child had taken up residence in

Nova Scotia, the parties were found to have their last common residence in West Germany.

Pursuant to subsection 22(1) of the province's *Matrimonial Property Act*, the division of matrimonial assets in Nova Scotia is governed by the law of the place where the parties had their last common habitual residence, in this case West Germany. Since West German law would have applied Iranian law—that is, the law of citizenship—application of the doctrine of *renvoi* would result in the case being decided according to Iranian Islamic family law. Justice Burchell thus concluded that *mahr* was attached to Iranian Islamic family law, and that such legal regime was altogether contrary to "substantial justice" because women could not benefit from the principle of equal sharing: "To put it simply, I will not give effect to Iranian matrimonial law because it is archaic and repugnant to ideas of substantial justice in this province" (para. 30). Justice Burchell further described the foreign law regime in the following manner: "In Iran, a wife in the position of Mrs. Vladi would be entitled to minimal support and a nominal award in relation to a so-called 'mahr' or 'morning-gift'. Otherwise she would have no direct claim against assets standing in the name of her husband" (para. 11).

Having found Iranian law inapplicable, Justice Burchell reverted to German domestic law instead of to the Nova Scotia internal rule. According to West German law, Mrs. Vladi was entitled to an equal division of matrimonial assets, which resulted in an equalization payment to her:

> The difference between the value of assets now held by Mrs. Vladi at the date of division and those held by her former husband is thus $493,037 and it follows according to the law of West Germany that Mrs. Vladi is entitled to an equalization payment of one half of that amount, viz., the sum of $246,518.50, which I round to $246,500. (para. 70)

The Court did not enforce *mahr*. In fact, it does not even state what the amount of *mahr* is or what its value would have been to Mrs. Vladi, having concluded that *mahr* shall be understood as part of a wider system of Islamic family law which is considered to contradict understandings of substantial justice in the Canadian province of Nova Scotia.

The Unenforceability of Mahr *on Grounds of Public Policy: France and the United States*   In 1976, a French court of appeal refused to enforce *mahr*, citing its incompatibility with conceptions of French public order (*Douai*). In applying international private law principles, the Court concluded that marriage contracts requiring the existence of *mahr* for forming a valid marriage contradict French public order because they reduce marriage to a financial transaction and obligation.

Public policy was similarly used in *In re Marriage of Dajani*, a 1988 Court of Appeal decision from California, which understood *mahr* to be facilitating divorce.[7] As such, the Islamic marriage contract containing the *mahr* provisions was void as against public policy. In *In re Marriage of Dajani*, the trial court had not enforced *mahr* because the wife, Awatef, had initiated the divorce proceedings. Awatef argued on appeal that the decision in the lower court led to an unjust result and was against public policy (1389). The Court agreed that a public policy argument was appropriate, but not the one urged by Awatef. Justice Crosby's opening remarks, in which two other judges concurred, tip the Court's hand in a bluntly worded question: "Will a California court enforce a foreign dowry agreement which benefits a party who initiates dissolution of the marriage? No" (1388). The *Dajani* decision held that the Jordanian marriage contract must be considered as one designed to facilitate divorce, because "with the exception of the token payment of one Jordanian dinar ... the wife was not entitled to receive any of the agreed upon sum unless the marriage was dissolved or husband died. The contract clearly provided for wife to profit by divorce, and it cannot be enforced by a California court" (1390).

The California court leaves us with the impression that *mahr* is no longer an individual, private matter incorporating Islamic family law rules. Rather, it is regulated by a public law doctrine; its unenforceability is the direct result of a violation of a *collective* notion of public morals. Regarding the concept of what falls under public law, the adoption of the *Uniform Premarital Agreement Act* assists in defining its scope. Matters barred by public policy include (among others) agreements to pay for domestic services or companionship; agreements altering mutual obligations during marriage (premarital agreements purporting to alter the obligations between spouses of mutual respect, fidelity and support during marriage; agreements to raise children in a particular religion; agreements penalizing a party for a "fault" committed during marriage (upholding the public policy underlying California's no-fault dissolution laws); and agreements that purport to waive parties' legal disclosure obligations in the event of marriage breakdown. More broadly speaking, agreements against public policy can be understood according to the parameters judicially defined in the 1974 New Jersey decision in *Garlinger v Garlinger*:

> An agreement is against public policy if it is injurious to the interest of the public, contravenes some established interest of society, violates some public statute, is against good morals, tends to interfere with the public welfare or safety, or, as it is sometimes put, if it is at war with the interests of society and is in conflict with public morals. (40)

---

7   See the previous LLPA section for a detailed description of the facts of the decision.

The *Dajani* decision welcomed LSEA in its internal understanding of contract law, and explicitly closed the door on a brewing battle of expert witnesses who would opine on the meaning and enforceability of *mahr* according to Islamic family law: "Wife devotes a considerable portion of her brief to a challenge of the qualifications of husband's expert. It is not necessary for us to enter that fray, however" (1389).

In 2002, the California Court of Appeal in *In re Marriage of Bellio* distinguished between the *Dajani* and *Noghrey* decisions, ruling that the former was wrongly decided. The Court stated that *Noghrey* correctly held that the promise of a *substantial* benefit to a party on filing for dissolution of the marriage is void as against public policy. In *Bellio*, the premarital agreement provided for a $100,000 payment to the wife in the event of the dissolution of the marriage. At the time of the marriage the husband was 71 and a multimillionaire; the prospective wife was earning $12/hour, and receiving $933 in monthly alimony from a former husband to whom she had been married for 24 years. In view of the fact that remarriage would terminate spousal support, the wife, as a condition of marriage, negotiated for an amount roughly equivalent to the foregone alimony, to support her in the event of the death of the husband or dissolution of the marriage. In these circumstances, the Court held the payment was not an incentive to promote and encourage divorce, but a reasonable measure of compensation to make up for the wife's lost support. The purpose of the $100,000 payment provision was to assure the wife that, if her husband died or the marriage was dissolved, she would be no worse off than she would have been had she remained single. Such a provision cannot reasonably be construed as threatening to induce the destruction of the marriage. Rather, the provision made it economically feasible for the wife to enter into the marriage. In effect, it encouraged the marriage in the first place.

Thus, according to the Court in *Bellio*, the public policy test is not whether a sum of money is offered at the time of marriage to provide for the eventuality of divorce, but rather whether the amount "threaten[s] to induce the destruction of a marriage that might otherwise endure" (635). To return to its relevance to the *Noghrey* decision and why the Court favours the analysis contained in that case, the property involved in *Noghrey* (the husband's house and the greater of $500,000 or one half of his assets) was so substantial that the premarital agreement was considered void. In *Dajani*, on the other hand, the $1,700 in play was insufficient to seriously jeopardize a viable marriage (*Bellio*: 635).

Concluding Remarks on the LSEA

The LSEA operates against a background of gender-sensitive and general fairness considerations: in adjudicating *mahr*, it tellingly referred to the equality of bargaining power between the Muslim husband and wife as identified by their social position and positioning. In this context, *mahr* is a religious custom that has an effect on substantive equality. Because family law aims also to protect the category of formerly married women, the LSEA engages in identity sexual politics in reviewing whether or not *mahr* should be enforced. However, although a general stance can be thus articulated, individual outcomes are no more predictable according to the LSEA than they were when approached from any other ideological standpoint: the LSEA, too, produces inconsistent outcomes in the adjudication of *mahr*, whether in reference to considerations of gender-equity standards or fairness principles (whether from the perspective of the Muslim woman *or* the Muslim man).

Conclusion

Three conclusions stand out from the investigation of *mahr*'s journey to Western courts. First, the "multiculturalist" understanding of *mahr* (LLPA), the "secular" understanding of *mahr* (LFEA), and the "feminist/fair" understanding of *mahr* (LSEA) have *all* produced, in inconsistent and unpredictable manners, the enforcement and non-enforcement of *mahr*. Second, the four Western jurisdictions under study—Canada, the United States, France and Germany—although differing in their relationship toward immigrants and minority citizenship as well as in the scope of applicable legal rules, have *all* generated cases on the adjudication of *mahr* in every liberal camp (LLPA, LFEA, LSEA). Finally, comparative law has failed to provide a setting of inquiry that could suggest or predict in which direction *mahr* is likely to be displaced and interpreted in the four Western states. As a result, "Canadian *mahr*," "American *mahr*," "German *mahr*" and "French *mahr*" do not enjoy a cohesive status. There may be an explanation for why this is: we unearth only paradoxical answers when we study *mahr*'s journey to Western courts because of the deeply ideological nature of adjudication.

Chapter 4
Contradictions in the Reception of *Mahr* as Ideology and Subjectivity

Introduction

In its many fragmented forms—as a form of identity under the liberal–legal pluralist approach (LLPA), as a secular contract under the liberal–formal equality approach (LFEA) and as a symbol of fairness under the liberal–substantive equality approach (LSEA)—the adjudication of *mahr* in Western states offers a panoply of conflicting images and speaks the competing considerations that pre-exist its judicial encounter. This chapter is intended as a critique of the LLPA, LFEA and LSEA in regard to *mahr* in Canada, the United States, France and Germany. At the heart of this critique is the project of uncovering the numerous contradictions which underlie the reception of *mahr* as ideology and subjectivity. In exploring the contradictory nature of the adjudicative process, my aim is to complicate and attempt to transcend the ruling binaries that have organized the disciplinary fields in which *mahr* is projected and produced. My objective is not to propose alternative and innovative legal ways to "resolve" the contradictions discovered in the analysis of the cases in Chapter 3, nor is it to develop a project of coherent and consistent adjudication in the case of *mahr* intended for judicial actors. Rather, my interest here is to demonstrate that these dualistic contradictions emerge persistently, and that they both highlight and obscure the distributional stakes in adjudicating *mahr*.

Four contradictions have accompanied much of *mahr*'s journey to Western courts. First is the doctrine–outcome contradiction: as the legal doctrine adopted by the court projects the mandate to recognize or not to recognize, the outcome resulting from that recognition does not logically follow the doctrine. In fact, it is often reversed. Second is the ends–means perversity contradiction, that is, the probability, in the global context of rules moving across borders, that the legal means available to judges to achieve a given end cannot and will not produce the hoped for result. Moreover, the parties involved in the dispute over the enforcement of *mahr* act out this contradiction, individually and relationally, in related but somewhat different terms. Third is the state–church/disentanglement–intensification contradiction: the secular court, by doctrinally rejecting the religious in the public sphere, likely contributes to its intensification and legitimation in the so-called private sphere. Finally, in the state–church/Western–Islamic contradiction, the Western state, by obsessively "looking when the gaze is not returned" (Cossman 1997: 525), conveniently registers the differences *between* the "East" and the "West," but fails to see the differences *within* the two legal orders in a comparative law context.

The Doctrine–Outcome Contradiction

The doctrine–outcome[1] contradiction may well be the effect of the deeply contradictory nature of law in general, and adjudication in particular. In making this observation, I am led by the critical thinking of Duncan Kennedy:

> My answer is that they [judges], and their informed audience, "deny", in the psychological sense of the word, the influence of ideology. They do so for good reasons, of which the most important is that they would otherwise have to confront the contradictory character of the role constraints under which judges operate. Acknowledging that judges can't coherently be asked to "just say no" to ideology would threaten, in turn, the plausibility of Liberal legalism in general and, in particular, the favorite "legally correct" outcomes of liberals and conservatives alike. (Kennedy 1997: 180)

In fact, the LLPA, the LFEA and the LSEA share some common ground, which I wish to lay bare here: (1) all of the approaches portray judges as "independent" actors, denying the existence of strategic behaviour used to achieve certain outcomes; (2) they all deny the effect of ideology in order to present legal doctrine as a coherent, logical and consistent body of knowledge; (3) they all pretend that the legal doctrine chosen to adjudicate *mahr* generates predictable outcomes. However, the reality is that liberal ideologies hide behind judicial law-making while *inconsistently* generating the enforcement or non-enforcement of *mahr*.

In this section, I test the doctrine–outcome contradiction by using cases analyzed in Chapter 3. I address the indeterminacy between the legal doctrine used by the judge, on the one hand, and the outcome of particular LLPA decisions as represented by the holding of the case, on the other. I have chosen the LLPA camp to exemplify this contradiction because it frequently adopts the doctrine of Islamic law to interpret *mahr*, and yet other doctrines and policies held by judges will block the causal relationship between doctrine and outcome. In order to study the doctrine–outcome contradiction, I bring in the indeterminacy thesis popularized by critical legal studies (CLS) to capture the "spin" that the holding receives in relation to the doctrine.

---

1   In this section, I use the term "outcome" to refer to the case ruling in a given decision. The expression "outcome" is not used to convey the same meaning it does in Chapter 3 in the description of the liberal–substantive equality approach.

The Liberal–Legal Pluralism Approach and the Critical Legal Studies Indeterminacy Thesis

The CLS indeterminacy thesis posits that the interpretation of legal doctrine by judges may, in a given case, support opposing outcomes; this is so because legal materials presented to judges show the existence of numerous gaps, conflicts and ambiguities. Therefore, when confronting a legal question in a particular case, the adjudicator may perform her legal work by interpreting legal doctrine in such a way as to produce, strategically, the holding of the case. In the words of Duncan Kennedy (2005: 374):

> [l]egal work, as I am using the term, whether aimed at cores or frames or at penumbras or conflicts or gaps, is undertaken "strategically." The worker aims to transform an initial apprehension of what the system of norms requires, given the facts, so that a new apprehension of the system, as it applies to the case, will correspond to the extra-juristic preferences of the interpretive worker.

Kennedy (2005: 382) continues his analysis, taking it to the contextually logical conclusion and applying it to judges:

> The "biases" of judges are relevant because they orient legal work by judges (and other jurists) to transform initial apprehensions of what the materials require in the particular direction suggested by the judge[']s material or ideal interests (loosely, the judge's or jurist's ideology). Whether the jurist will succeed in the work of making the materials conform to his ideological or material extra-juristic strategic motive is never knowable in advance (though as with any uncertain future event, we can make odds). Jurists constantly accept interpretations according to which the positive law is contrary to their view as to what it ought to be.

In this section, I will identify this strategic field by exploring the ways in which the CLS indeterminacy thesis presents itself in the LLPA cases: while the Islamic legal doctrine applicable to judges should have driven us in a certain direction, other doctrines came into play to direct an opposite ruling.

The first example is *IPRax 1983*, the German case analyzed in Chapter 3 that I have classified as representing "the enforcement of *mahr* as an Islamic custom." In this case, the legal reasoning used by the Court to enforce *mahr* borrowed deeply from an identitarian politics of recognition toward Muslim identity. As suggested in Chapter 2, the German choice of law rule is pluralist in its aim to recognize and legalize cultural/religious differences: German courts will rely, in family law matters, on the law of the state of origin. Mathias Rohe (2003: 47) suggests that this concept allows for predictability in the way individuals order their personal lives:

> In the area of civil law, which essentially regulates legal relations between private persons, the welfare of those persons is of prime importance. If someone has organized his/her life in accordance with a certain legal system, this should be protected even when the person in question changes his/her place of abode. Accordingly the law of the state of origin which is familiar to the person in question should continue to be applied when the person crosses the borders.

In *IPRax 1983*, both parties were Iranian citizens and had been married in Iran. The Court therefore applied the law of citizenship to resolve the issue, according to international private law rules which directly incorporate Islamic family law. In the absence of any written or oral contract, the judge accepted the religious expert evidence arguing for the existence of an Islamic *mahr al-mithl*. (As a reminder, this is a concept designated as a form of "proper *mahr*" determined by comparing "the *mahr* paid to other female members of the wife's family, for instance sisters, paternal aunts and female cousins" (Pearl and Menski 1998: 180).) The mandate to recognize underlying much of the legal doctrine even led the German Court to consult, study and evaluate the Iranian family code. The wife argued that, given her privileged socio-economic status, the application of the Islamic legal doctrine should produce a holding that would entitle her to 75,000 Euros plus 4 percent interest as *mahr al-mithl* "the Islamic way."

However, in order to work properly in its new environment, *mahr al-mithl* was rewritten by the judge against the backdrop of the national (Germany) and, more specifically, the local (Hamburg). Consequently, the outcome—the determination of *mahr al-mithl* according to the similarly situated German woman living in Hamburg—became 10,000 Euros as *mahr al-mithl* "the German way," divided into 10 monthly payments of 1,000 Euros each. Here, the contradictory relationship between doctrine and outcome can be expressed thus: given the indeterminacy of legal doctrine(s), other (German) doctrines intervene between the (Islamic) doctrine and the ruling of the case to produce a holding that is very different from what we could have expected from the (Islamic) Iranian doctrine alone. In this instance, the economic interests that lie behind the legal decision are clearly apparent. For the Muslim woman involved, the distributive consequences of such shift of rules by the Court brings her claim of 75,000 Euros plus 4 percent interest as *mahr al-mithl* "the Islamic way" down to an award of 10,000 Euros as *mahr al-mithl* "the German way." Could those specific material stakes have motivated the spin of legal doctrine and hence the outcome that flew from it?

My second example, the 1998 *Kaddoura* decision from Ontario, Canada, exemplifies judges' choice of interpretation through policy analysis rather than through deduction in legal reasoning. In *Kaddoura*, the Ontario Court concluded that all the elements related to the definition and enforcement of a "domestic agreement" pursuant to subsection 52(1) of Ontario's *Family Law Act* were met: both Sam and Manira had acknowledged the agreement as to *mahr*; the parties entered into the agreement freely and willingly; and no evidence demonstrated that the provision requiring the payment of $30,000 as deferred *mahr* was vague or that the agreement was signed under circumstances suggestive of inequality, improvidence, or duress. The Court thus held:

> In his testimony, Sam said he understood and agreed that the *Mahr* would be $35,000 and that he would pay $5,000 and understood he would "write" $30,000. By that, he understood that the $30,000 would be written as the amount ascribed to the deferred portion of *Mahr* in the religious ceremony but he said he never understood he would ever be compelled to pay it. Sam testified that he knew his sister had been divorced and had been unable to collect the deferred or written portion of the *Mahr* that was due her according to Islamic custom. Sam did not seem to contemplate that the *Mahr* represented an obligation that he could be obliged, by civil process, to meet. Much time was spent at trial over whether Sam would understand spoken or written references to *Mahr* in Arabic. *I am satisfied that he understood clearly how much the* Mahr *was and that it was written into the marriage certificate which he signed.* (para. 16, 20, emphasis added)

Given this judicial pronouncement, we could have predicted, with a certain degree of certainty, that *mahr* would be enforced as a simple "domestic agreement" similar to those that are routinely dealt with in family law. Yet, somehow, the chain of causality between the legal doctrine and the holding broke down through the introduction of another legal doctrine: the (American!) principle of the separation of church and state. Deploying the argument in unfamiliar and unexpected ways, Justice Rutherford wrote:

> While the first amendment to the Constitution of the United States of America provides a clearer or at least more visible footing on which to separate matters of Church from matters of State than is apparent in Canada, I am inclined to borrow a term used by the United States Supreme Court in *Serbian Eastern Orthodox Diocese for U.S. of America & Canada v. Milivojevich*, 426 U.S. 696 (U.S. Ill. 1976) and ask whether the resolution of the issue of obligation relating to *Mahr* will necessarily lead the court into the "religious thicket". True, the courts in Canada have, not infrequently, taken on and determined disputes involving church properties or civil rights, but, in cases in which such disputes can be resolved according to generally applicable legal principles. Where, however, as seems to be the case here, the issue must be determined with reference to religious doctrine and principle, the civil court is, in my view, at least lacking in expertise and, in the United States context and perhaps Canadian as well, constitutionally beyond its proper territory. (para. 26)

By first identifying and then applying this set of specific policy arguments, Justice Rutherford contrasted *mahr* with Christian marital commitments to "love, honour and cherish, or to remain faithful" and refused to enforce it on the basis that it constituted a "religious" obligation, not a civil one:

The *Mahr* and the extent to which it obligates a husband to make payment to his wife is essentially and fundamentally an Islamic religious matter. Because *Mahr* is a religious matter, the resolution of any dispute relating to it or the consequences of failing to honour the obligation are also religious in their content and context. While not, perhaps, an ideal comparison, I cannot help but think that the obligation of the *Mahr* is as unsuitable for adjudication in the civil courts as is an obligation in a Christian religious marriage such as to love, honour and cherish, or to remain faithful, or to maintain the marriage in sickness or other adversity so long as both parties live, or to raise children according to specified religious doctrine. Many such promises go well beyond the basic legal commitment to marriage required by our civil law, and are essentially matters of chosen religion and morality. They are derived from and are dependent upon doctrine and faith. They bind the conscience as a matter of religious principle but not necessarily as a matter of enforceable civil law. (para. 25)

The legal doctrine first invoked could not have borne such an outcome: case law under subsection 52(1) of Ontario's *Family Law Act* does not provide for this religious exception, and the Court does not cite any precedent aside from the vague reference to the American separation of church and state doctrine. It seems only fair to ask: How did the situation get framed in this way? Duncan Kennedy (2005: 373–74) writes:

[F]or our purposes, what counts is not how policy analysis is done, but how the situation is framed as one in which it is possible, or required. In other words, before the policy analysis begins, whatever its content, the interpreter explicitly or implicitly frames the situation as one in which there is a conflict or a gap that exempts him from the elementary duty to apply a clear norm when the facts clearly fit within its definitions.

In *Kaddoura*, not only did the indeterminacy of doctrine(s) generate an unexpected holding—that is, *mahr* as jurisdictionally unenforceable—but the policy analysis also exempted the Court from the "elementary duty to apply a clear norm."

It would no doubt be interesting to explore the doctrine–outcome contradiction from the perspective of the LFEA camp. This could take the form of measuring whether the contract law doctrine used to interpret *mahr* ("law in books") corresponds to a secular understanding of the outcome by the parties themselves ("law in action"). In fact, as the legal doctrine de-recognizes and individualizes *mahr*, the outcome may well be treated as recognition of the group by the Muslim woman herself. In other words, although the (secular) court insists on the fact that the Muslim woman is merely a contractual party, the enforcement of *mahr* may subjectively be understood by her as a victory for identity politics. This conceptualizing, however, is purely speculative at this point as empirical research would be required to test this hypothesis.

The Ends–Means Perversity Contradiction

The first contradiction, which has revealed the effect of judges' ideology on the "broken" relationship between doctrine and outcome, is intimately related to the second one, the ends–means perversity contradiction, which can be explored through the analysis of how ideology manifests itself concretely in the framing of a legal problem. Under the umbrella of this second contradiction, I address more specifically the limits and frustrations of *not* achieving the outcome that strategic behaviour was expected to produce in the process of ideological interpretation, due to the perverse relationship between ends and means in the adjudication of *mahr* in Western courts.

For most of the cases I have analyzed under the LLPA and LFEA, the frustration of the ends by means can be explained as follows: for any end that a court aims to achieve, ideologically and discursively, the available (Western) means to reach that end are powerless to achieve it. As a result, *mahr* cannot travel through either recognition or through non-recognition. For instance, if the end is to enforce *mahr* as a form of classical Islamic family law—*as if* it were situated in Egypt, let us imagine—the means of the Western court cannot be used to achieve it. In fact, the legal tools available to judges cannot reproduce Egyptian *mahr*—that is, the enforcement of *mahr* incorporating the background Islamic legal regime of *talaq mahr, khul mahr, faskh mahr,* and inherited *mahr*. In this section, I present three parts of the contradiction. The first presents the perverse relationship between ends and means as it operates against the backdrop of the LLPA and ultimately fails to reproduce *mahr* as a legal transplant. The second explores the possibility that *mahr* could project a "religious" contractual intention, highlighting the mysterious dimensions of "religion" and "Islamic intentions" as they permeate the relationship between means (contract law as acknowledging contractual intentions) and ends (*mahr* as merely secular). The third part emphasizes the puzzling role of parties involved in the adjudication of *mahr* as they behave strategically, from opposite ends of the spectrum, in relation to means and ends. For this, I consider the contradiction enacted by the parties themselves, using as a backdrop the Holmesian character of the "bad man" (whom I also portray as a "bad woman").

The Liberal–Legal Pluralism Approach: Mahr *as a Culturally Transformed Legal Transplant?*

The LLPA cases presented in Chapter 3 all attempted to transplant *mahr* as a legal construct into new ground—that is, to recreate it through many different routes of cultural recognition: as a manifestation of identity in Canada; as an Islamic custom in France and Germany; as related to a *khul* divorce in Québec and the United States. Yet, along the way of its transportation, Western courts transformed *mahr*.

Nathoo and *M.(N.M.)*[2] exemplify well the ends–means perversity contradiction. In both cases, courts advanced an image of religion as an organized, comprehensive and organic entity: Muslim subjects *chose* to be Muslims, and one consequence of performing Muslim identity is the enforcement of *mahr* by the court. Ironically, the *mahr* that was institutionally transferred unfolded as an exceptional penalty imposed on the husband, a result which cannot be explained or legitimated from the point of view of the original Islamic milieu of departure.

In *Nathoo*, the Court required the Muslim husband to pay $37,747.17 to his former wife upon reapportionment of family assets, *and* enforced *mahr* as an additional and separate payment of $20,000 due to the wife. This holding is extremely confusing. In fact, as previously demonstrated, had only Canadian family law applied, a marriage agreement as defined by subsection 61(2) of British Columbia's *Family Relations Act* would have supplanted the marital equitable regime; had only Islamic family law applied, Mrs. Nathoo would have obtained only *mahr* and maintenance during the *iddah* period. Such an unusual outcome in *Nathoo*—the enforcement of *mahr* in addition to the division of property under the statutory regime—is explained by the ends–means perversity contradiction: the (Western) means available to legally transplant *mahr* cannot (and in fact did not) achieve that end.

Similarly, in *M.(N.M.)*, the British Columbia court added the "amount of $51,250 on account of the Maher" (para. 31) to an amount of $101,911 due by the husband upon the division of family assets *and* to an additional $2,000 in monthly spousal support. Confronted with the particularities of the Canadian legal culture, *mahr* faces resistance as it moves from an Islamic regime of "you get *mahr* and only *mahr* in cases of *talaq* and *faskh* divorce," to a family law system applying doctrines of equitable division in British Columbia. Where did *mahr* go in this instance? Can this form of penalty be called *mahr* at all, if such a conception cannot be found under Islamic family law doctrine? Was Mr. Nathoo aware of this interaction between *mahr* and the Canadian family law provisions? If not, can we still affirm that he "agreed" to *mahr*? How will fragmented *mahr* return to the religious culture in which it originated? Will Mr. *M.(N.M.)* of tomorrow include *mahr* in a marriage contract?

To function properly in the LLPA paradigm, Muslim parties have to accept multiculturalism's insistence on viewing them in absolute and homogeneous terms: the complex, contradictory and shifting *mahr*, which exists as a bargaining endowment "in the shadow of the law" (complete with a cost-benefit analysis), does not easily travel. *Mahr*, once a "provision for a rainy day" (Fyzee 1974: 133) conceived by classical Islamic jurists as a "powerful limitation" (Schacht 1982: 167) on the possibly capricious exercise of *talaq* divorce by the husband as well as a form of "compensation" (Esposito and DeLong-Bas 2001: 35) to the wife once the marriage has been dissolved, becomes under the LLPA a feature of

---

2   These cases are described in Chapter 3, in the section entitled *The Enforcement of* Mahr *as a Manifestation of Identity: Canada.*

multiculturalism that supposedly reflects Muslim identity, yet in fact distorts it. Can the LFEA cases, which attempt to formally reject notions of religious identity and recognition, achieve such a desired end through the means of contract law doctrine?

The Liberal–Formal Equality Approach: Mahr *as Projecting a "Religious" Contractual Intention?*

The ends–means perversity contradiction also affects the LFEA cases. In following a mandate *not* to culturally recognize *mahr*, the judicial narratives embracing formal equality have attempted to secularize *mahr*, and to correctly and merely give effect to "the intention of the parties." The contract law doctrinal analysis invokes questions such as: Were the parties capable of contracting *mahr*? Was there a "meeting of the minds" between the two parties regarding prompt and deferred *mahr*? Was there consideration, even in cases where no amount was specified (*mahr al-mithl*)? This analysis, as applied to the specific context of *mahr*, has carried a religious intention into the law. In effect, although pretending not to, courts have opened the door to the existence of this contractual/religious intention of the parties.

Aziz, Odatalla, and *Akileh* all denied this perverse relationship between means and ends. In fact, the three American decisions all insisted on the fact that the religious character of *mahr* was irrelevant: "Why should a contract for the promise to pay money be less of a contract just because it was entered into at the time of an Islamic marriage ceremony?" asked the judge in *Odatalla* (309). "Its secular terms are enforceable as a contractual obligation, notwithstanding that it was entered into as part of a religious ceremony," responded the *Aziz* court (1013). After all, suggested the judicial reasoning in *Akileh*, the *mahr* "agreement was an antenuptial contract" (248). In the LFEA, secular *mahr* becomes an antenuptial agreement immediately enforceable as long as the conditions of contract law doctrine are met. The irony lies in the fact that the *secular* promise-to-pay-money-in-the-form-of-an-antenuptial-agreement can be understood, contractually, contextually, only by referring to the *religious* intentions of the Muslim parties. By *a priori* rejecting the pertinence of the Islamic shadow behind which husband and wife negotiate, bargain and determine *mahr* and its amount, courts have paradoxically refused an appreciation of contract law that would account for the parties' particular, peculiar private ordering regime. What is blocked from view by the ends–means perversity contradiction in these cases?

In this apparent refusal to explore the religious role of contracts in the social order, the LFEA gaze in *Aziz, Odatalla,* and *Akileh* projected *mahr*-as-contract, but could not observe *mahr*-as-status: the complexity of "the will of the parties" under Islamic law—that is, the fact that *mahr* was possibly understood by Mr. Aziz or Ms. Odatalla as being enforceable under a *talaq* or *faskh* divorce, but not under a *khul* divorce—has been uprooted from the discourse of secular *mahr*. As established in Chapter 1, *mahr* is portrayed under Islamic family law as a "mark of respect for the wife" (Pearl and Menski 1998: 179), a sign of "honour to the bride" (Wani 1995: 193), a "free gift by the husband" (Doi 1984: 159), "a manifestation of his love for the wife" (Wani 1995: 193) and a symbol of the "prestige of the marriage contract" (Nasir 2002: 43). But the primary effect of a deferred *mahr* during marriage is to delineate a bargaining structure that exists in the shadow of the law, one that hides and preserves a capital in the event of *some* specific and culturally, traditionally recognized forms of divorce or of death. Instead, LFEA projects and imposes a liberal consent to a contractual obligation that did not necessarily originate in the intention of the (Muslim) parties themselves: in *Aziz*, *Odatalla*, and *Akileh*, *mahr* is dissociated from the Islamic social and legal meaning from which it emerged and becomes enforceable in *all* cases (e.g., in *talaq*, *khul* and *faskh* divorce), so long as the neutral principles of law are met and respected. These cases illustrate the perverse relationship between ends and means: the contradiction seems unresolvable. In the next section, I investigate whether the Muslim parties themselves, in the course of their involvement in the interpretation and adjudication of *mahr*, perform, in strategic and opposing terms, the ends–means perversity contradiction.

The Performance of the Contradiction by the Parties Themselves: Holmes' "Bad Man" and "Bad Woman"

In Oliver Wendell Holmes' "The Path of the Law" (first published in 1897), the legal system is depicted as "an instrument ... of business" whose "prophecies" the lawyer attempts to rigorously predict and master. If adjudication is about judges' "duty of weighing considerations of social advantage," parties must know not only the adequate rules and precedents, but also "the relative worth and importance of competing considerations" that are likely to affect judges. Emphasizing the existence of battles between individuals and/or groups, Holmes introduces the famous "bad man" to explore his theory of the law. This mercenary fellow cares only about the material (and not the ethical) consequences of his act:

> If you want to know the law and nothing else, you must look at it as a bad man, who cares only for the material consequences which such knowledge enables him to predict, not as a good one, who finds his reasons for conduct, whether inside the law or outside of it, in the vaguer sanctions of conscience. ... The confusion with which I am dealing besets confessedly legal conceptions. Take the fundamental question, What constitutes the law? You will find some text writers telling you that it is something different from what is decided by the courts of Massachusetts or England, that is a system of reason, that it is a deduction from principles of ethics or admitted axioms or what not, which may or may not coincide with the decisions. But if we take the view of our friend the bad man we shall find that he does not care two straws for the axioms or deductions, but that he does want to know what the Massachusetts or English courts are likely to do in fact. I am much of his mind. The prophecies of what

the courts will do in fact, and nothing more pretentious, are what I mean by the
law. (Holmes 1993: 17)

Holmes' predictive theory of law and his advocacy of the bad-man perspective
constitute powerful strategies undermining the misleading picture of law. I thus
add another internal dimension to the ends–means perversity contradiction: the
agency and active role of the Muslim parties themselves in relation to each other,
as well as in relation to the Western court. Because of their individual motives,
the husband and wife are continually, sometimes simultaneously, speaking both
the mandate to recognize and the mandate not to recognize. They advocate or
oppose the judicial enforcement of *mahr* depending on how their interests would
be affected by its recognition. Two questions suggest themselves: Is the Muslim
husband arguing for the non-enforcement of *mahr* mainly on religious grounds the
equivalent of Holmes' "bad man"? And, conversely, does the Muslim wife arguing
for the enforcement of *mahr* mainly on secular grounds personify a Holmesian
"bad woman"?

Is the Muslim (Religious/Secular) Husband the "Bad Man"?   In most of the
matrimonial disputes adjudicated in the cases discussed in Chapter 3, Muslim
parties made contradictory claims about Islam and the role of religion in a secular,
Western state more generally. The Muslim husband typically argued that the
obligations imposed by *mahr* arise solely from religious/Islamic law and can
therefore be interpreted only by reference to religious dogma. Consequently,
mahr is a matter touching upon purely religious doctrine that can be enforced
only by religious authorities—its enforcement by a civil court would violate the
principle of the separation of church and state, *laïcité* or some other persuasive
legal doctrine. It is, quite ironically, *in the name of religion* that the Muslim
husband argued for the non-enforcement of *mahr*—an outcome that would
coercively disengage his financial responsibility. Such was the argumentation of
the husband in *M.(N.M.)* (British Columbia—the husband testified that, for him,
mahr was merely symbolic), *Kaddoura* (Ontario—the husband argued that *mahr*,
a religious obligation, was not justiciable in the civil courts), *Aziz* (New York—the
husband urged the court to view *mahr* as a religious document and not enforceable
as a contract) and *Odatalla* (New Jersey—the husband made the constitutional
argument that the First Amendment precluded the court from reviewing the *mahr*
agreement under the separation of church and state doctrine). At times, however,
the prediction of economic sanctions will dictate to the Muslim husband to borrow
from the secular rhetoric. How, if at all, did the cases on the adjudication of *mahr*
speak to issues that interested Holmes?

Holmes' "bad man" theory offers interesting analytical insights into *Odatalla*,
the 2002 New Jersey decision. With what could have been cynicism, Mr. Odatalla
asked the court not to enforce *mahr*—alleging that, according to his religious faith,
mahr could only be decided by an Islamic authority—but, on the same account,
requested "alimony and equitable distribution of certain jewelry, furniture,

wedding gifts and marital debt" (94), demands that he could not have made under Islamic family law. Mr. Odatalla's litigation strategy is that of Holmes' "bad man" in that he uses law as a tool to gain the best possible economic outcomes and material consequences while undermining the importance of religious law (Holmes' morality).

In caring only about what the law might *do* to him, not what it abstractly *is* for him, Mr. Odatalla presented his argument to the court in such a way that he would be compelled to pay the least and consequently gain the most. Imagine his strategy assessment in this situation: Mr. Odatalla considered the possible, predictable sanctions that the law might impose on him. The recognition/non-recognition of Islam as a religion, of him as a believer and of *mahr* as an Islamic institution, was crucial in his calculation. Will the mandate to recognize pay off, he asked himself? Surely not—*mahr* might be declared unenforceable on the basis of the separation of church and state, but he might *also* be prevented from enjoying the equitable dissolution of family assets. Will the mandate not to recognize pay off, he may have further inquired? Surely not—he might be ordered to pay the sum of $10,000 as *mahr* on the basis of contractual antenuptial agreement doctrine *in addition to* the division of family property. Considering these complex and highly material predictions, Mr. Odatalla assumed an efficient hybrid position, one in which he would wear the religious and secular hats concurrently: the mandate to recognize/ not to recognize translated into the non-enforcement of *mahr*, for religious reasons; and "alimony and equitable distribution of certain jewelry, furniture, wedding gifts and marital debt," on secular grounds. This represents, he may have thought, the maximization of outcomes.

In *Amlani*, the "bad man" strategy served as a focus of inquiry in a context of rules recreated by the parties themselves prior to the adjudication of *mahr*. In 2000, Mr. Amlani asked the British Columbia Supreme Court for a declaration acknowledging that the marriage contract made during the religious wedding ceremony did not constitute a "marriage agreement" under section 61 of British Columbia's *Family Relations Act*. In consequence, *mahr* should not be enforced. The marriage contract, however, specified that Mr. Amlani would "pay the agreed sum of money by way of Maher to my said wife. It shall be *in addition and without prejudice* to and not in substitution of all of my obligations provided for by the laws of the land" (para. 30, emphasis added). Thus removed and repositioned in British Columbia, *mahr* is named by the husband himself as a different and surprising institution compared to what it is under Islamic family law, its native place of departure. In anticipation of (Western) adjudication, *mahr* is no longer attached to a regime of *talaq/khul/faskh* divorce. The transfer has already occurred across jurisdictions: *mahr* embraces the complexity and perversity of flirting with the laws of the land. It adds *itself* to a well-established family law regime, one of no-fault divorce and equitable division of family assets. It accepts to define itself as an exceptional penalty for the husband: in this particular case, *mahr* becomes a debt of $51,000 *added* to the equitable division of family property. Along the road to Western states, *mahr* lost its coherence in relation to the law of origin, Islamic law.

Ironically, against this background of previous legal transplanting, Mr. Amlani presented himself to the court as a religious man, claiming the existence of a purely religious *mahr*. The relationship between Islamic law—"you will get *mahr* and only *mahr* if *I* divorce you"—and Canadian law—"*you* can divorce me *and* get *mahr and* benefit from the division of property"—clearly delineates to the "bad man" the least profitable path of the law. Mr. Amlani indeed chose the path that paid off most lucratively for him: Islamic law divorced from the laws of the land. Such a regime, in the specific circumstances of the case, would have meant that Mr. Amlani was required to pay nothing. This is so because his wife embarked on what Islamic law classifies as a *khul* divorce; she should therefore have waived the $51,000 and not made a claim for alimony or division of property. Mr. Amlani thus argued that "the Mehr amount is a traditional custom of Muslim law that was intended to provide financial compensation for a wife and children in the event of a marriage break-up. Muslim religious law did not allow a wife to pursue support for herself and any children, nor any rights to property" (para. 28).

The Court rejected this sudden redesign, which it regarded as profoundly lacking in good faith:

> The contention that [*mahr* is] ... only payable in the absence of civil remedies being available to Ms. Hirani directly contradicted his obligations as set out in the Marriage Contract. In particular, in the Marriage Contract Mr. Amlani agreed, confirmed, and declared that his "undertaking to pay the agreed sum of money by way of Maher to my said wife shall be in addition and without prejudice to and not in substitution of all of my obligations provided for by the laws of the land". (para. 30)

Not only did Mr. Amlani virtually change his reading of the original contract for his personal economic benefit, but he went still further by asking the Court to judge his case on the rule that none of the laws of the land applied. Could the Court reproduce the practical consciousness of Islamic *mahr*? Could it crystallize the cultural codes of conduct that surround Islamic *mahr*? Could it do so *despite* the marriage contract, as if it were somehow expressing false consciousness? In the eyes of the Court, such an interpretation could not be sustained: "Ms. Hirani has civil remedies available to her. If the payment of the Maher/Mehr Amount only applied in the absence of civil remedies, as suggested by Mr. Amlani in his Examination for Discovery, there would have been no reason for these parties to have entered into the Marriage Contract" (para. 31).

Until now, I have only used instances where the Muslim husband has wrapped himself in the strategic cloak of Holmes' bad man. Can we imagine the Muslim wife behaving in the same fashion, alternatively drawing upon and occasionally transcending the secular/religious performance? Can the Muslim wife, in asking for the enforcement of *mahr* in Western courts, constitute a Holmesian "bad woman"?

Is the Muslim (Secular/Religious) Wife the "Bad Woman"?   In most of the matrimonial disputes discussed in Chapter 3, the Muslim wife claimed that nothing in law or public policy prevents judicial recognition and enforcement of the secular terms of *mahr*. After all, *mahr* is a contractual matter. It should be enforced and distributed to her. This was the argumentation put before the court in *M.(N.M.)* (British Columbia—the wife's father's undisputed evidence was that the *mahr* document was presented and explained by an Islamic religious authority and that the parties read the printed form and agreed to it prior to the marriage ceremony), *Kaddoura* (Ontario—the wife argued that the $30,000 *mahr* constituted a "marriage contract" and that her husband should be required to honour his agreement), *Aziz* (New York—the wife contended that *mahr* was enforceable as a contract therefore the court had jurisdiction) and *Odatalla* (New Jersey—the wife sought enforcement of *mahr* on the basis of contract law). At times, however, in response to the Islamic argument that she should waive *mahr* because she was the one asking for divorce (*khul* divorce), the Muslim wife donned the religious hat and presented a profoundly surprising description and analysis of Islamic law. The examples of *Akileh, Dajani, M.H.D., Douai*, and *Vladi* illustrate this point.

The key to understanding the performance of the "bad woman" is to measure the *predicted* economic gains and losses of advocating the enforcement or the non-enforcement of *mahr* in a given situation, in relation to both Islamic family law *and* Western law. In response to the waiver rule of *khul mahr*, the "bad woman" has two options: either pretend that the waiver rule is *not* part of Islamic family law (the religious route), or suggest that the waiver rule is so discriminatory that it should be regarded as inherently contrary to public order in relation to international private law rules (the secular route). Cases fall into both of these camps.

In *Akileh* and *Dajani*, the Muslim wife offered her version of a striking and fascinating dimension of the legal transplantation of *mahr*, one which entirely disregards Islamic theory. In *Akileh*, the wife testified that a Muslim woman's right to receive the postponed portion of *mahr* was "absolute and not affected by the cause of a divorce" (*Akileh* Appeal: 248). The wife further suggested that "the exception was that a wife would forfeit the dowry if she cheated on her husband" (248). In her testimony, the wife said that she was unaware of any other instances in which deferred *mahr* would be forfeited. Moreover, Raji Akileh, the wife's father, also testified that deferred *mahr* is "an absolute right of a wife to request from the husband whenever she wished and especially in the event of divorce" (248). Similarly, in *Dajani*, the Muslim wife claimed that she was entitled to *mahr* upon her husband's death or the dissolution of the marriage, notwithstanding the reason for, or form of, divorce. Her expert on the subject was "an attorney admitted to practice in California and Egypt who testified that the dowry provided for a cash payment to the wife in the event of the husband's death or dissolution of the marriage. In the latter case, the sum was due no matter which party initiated the dissolution proceedings" (1389).

In *M.H.D.*, a Québec trial court decision, the Muslim wife embarked on a secular argumentation and convinced the court that Syrian Islamic law could not apply in Canada because its application would create a negative effect on Muslim wives availing themselves of the *Divorce Act*:

> However, this court believes that the legislation cannot be in conflict with sections of the *Canadian Charter* whereby fundamental rights and freedoms are guaranteed. The *Canadian Charter* is the supreme law of Canada. All must abide by it, including the legislator. The *Divorce Act* gives the opportunity to both spouses to initiate divorce proceedings, and punishing a spouse on the basis that she exercises her rights according to the *Act* is a violation of her freedom. In cases of conflict between spouses, each has the right to the equal protection and equal benefit of the law (s. 7 and 15(1)). Also, to deny the wife her right to equality by asking her to give back her wedding presents or gifts received or agreed upon in the marriage contract on the basis that she exercised rights recognized by the law, constitutes a form of discrimination. (para. 26, translated from the French by the author)

As this passage suggests, the Muslim wife argued that *khul mahr* as a legal institution violates principles of substantive equality in that it requires the Western state to punish a wife because she is the one initiating the divorce proceedings, an outcome that would not similarly apply to the husband. In the name of gender equality, which the conflict of laws held at the heart of the principle of *l'ordre public* (public order), such discriminatory Islamic traditions should be formally and rigidly rejected by the host legal system, despite rules of international private law incorporating Syrian Islamic law:

> With all due respect to the beliefs of the religious authority as well as to those of the husband, the court believes that such traditions, customs and doctrine put before us are not applicable to the wife, and that the court must consider the wedding present discussed above only with respect to the *Québec Civil Code*. (para. 27, translated from the French by the author)

Mahr should therefore be viewed as a contractual donation, despite the *khul* divorce.

The same public order logic was successfully used by the Muslim wife in a 1976 French Court of Appeal decision (*Douai*) and a Canadian trial court decision (*Vladi*) in 1987. In *Douai*, the Court applied international private law principles, concluding that marriage contracts requiring the existence of *mahr* for forming a valid marriage simply contradict the French public order because they reduce marriage to a financial purchase. In *Vladi*, the Court refused to enforce *Mahr* on the basis of "substantial justice." The Court held:

> To put it simply, I will not give effect to Iranian matrimonial law because it is archaic and repugnant to ideas of substantial justice in this province. ... In Iran, a wife in the position of Mrs. Vladi would be entitled to minimal support and a nominal award in relation to a so-called "mahr" or "morning-gift". Otherwise she would have no direct claim against assets standing in the name of her husband. (para. 30)

Rather, the Court championed the principle of equal sharing of the marriage assets.

In *M.H.D.*, the route to the material maximization of outcomes implied the following claim on the part of the Muslim wife: the rejection of *khul mahr* (which amounts to zero), on the one hand, and the adoption of the equitable division of family patrimony *plus* the enforcement of *mahr* as a contractual donation, on the other. In *Douai* and *Vladi*, the wives' strategies precisely produced this highly sympathetic economic result: conflict of laws rejected *khul mahr* (which amounts to zero), on the one hand, and adopted the equitable division of family patrimony, which in the case of *Vladi* meant a generous equalization payment:

> As may be apparent from the foregoing, my conclusion is that Mrs. Vladi is entitled to a division of matrimonial assets (as defined in the Matrimonial Property Act of Nova Scotia) in accordance with the law of West Germany. ... The difference between the value of assets now held by Mrs. Vladi at the date of division and those held by her former husband is thus $493,037 and it follows according to the law of West Germany that Mrs. Vladi is entitled to an equalization payment of one half of that amount, viz., the sum of $246,518.50, which I round to $246,500. (paras 46, 70)

In this case, the Court does not even state what the amount of *mahr* is, having concluded that *mahr* shall be understood as part of a wider system of Islamic family law which is considered against substantial justice in the Canadian province of Nova Scotia.

Such an unusual view of Islamic family law in Western courts (the non-enforcement of *khul mahr* attached only to circumstances of adultery; the enforcement of *mahr* as an absolute right, thus denying the existence of the waiver rule; the rejection of *khul mahr* as inherently contrary to gender equality) certainly underlines the perverse relationship between means and ends. In what appears as the perfect equivalent of an attempt to materially obtain the most out of the interplay between Islamic law and Western law (the desired end), the Muslim wife subversively recreated the scope of this comparative law encounter to *her* economic advantage (the means).

The distributive character of adjudication as applied to this specific example of *mahr* allows us to ask ourselves certain questions: Would the Muslim wife have performed the "bad woman" script had no money been connected to the postponed portion of *mahr*? Does the shift in where the enforcement should take place tell us something about how strictly the woman adheres to the tenets of her religion? Does it matter to us that she might be strategically shaping her religiosity to achieve a maximal outcome? Do we care whether she is *really* a believer, and that we know that we cannot possibly know? Do we consider the possibility, as she insists on the "big M" (her as a Muslim; us as Multiculturalists), that she might only *pretend* to be devoted to Allah in order to get a devastating public revenge (make her husband pay, for instance, because he left her for her best friend; humiliate him by obtaining a secular *mahr* to which they had never agreed, etc.)?

Our intellectual impulse and political desire to project certainties may lead us to answer these questions in certain ways. While our answers to those questions would be interesting for present purposes—perhaps by either cementing or eroding the strength of the contradiction I have explored here—they are, in the end, unknowable: another mystery in the series of unpredictable fragments of doctrine, law and culture that surround the issue of *mahr*.

Concluding Remarks

The ends–means perversity contradiction has produced several concurrent phenomena. First, in relation to the LLPA, it has revealed the "impossibility of legal transplants," an expression I borrow from Pierre Legrand (1997), although I do not entirely agree with his vision. While I am sympathetic to the "law and society" perspective adopted by Pierre Legrand, my approach rejects the idea of an external, coherent and real "culture," "society" or "religion" which exists in corresponding features to law. Second, it has exposed the unavoidability of a religious/contractual intention in relation to the LFEA and, third, the strategic postures of the "bad" (religious/secular) Muslim husband as well as the "bad" (secular/religious) Muslim wife in relation to the LLPA, the LFEA and the LSEA. These, in turn, are all connected to the third contradiction I wish to explore. In the next section, I take the perverse relationship between means and ends to another location, one marked by the complex and often contradictory coexistence between the "public" and "private" spheres.

The State–Church/Disentanglement–Intensification Contradiction: Marx's "On the Jewish Question"

In his radical piece "On the Jewish Question," Karl Marx investigated the ways in which the French and the American revolutions are defined and understood as a critical move from feudalism: "Political emancipation is at the same time the dissolution of the old society, upon which the sovereign power, the alienated political life of the people, rests. Political revolution is a revolution of civil society. What was the nature of the old society? It can be characterized in one word: *feudalism*" (Marx 1978: 42). In effect, the political and civil societies are now split apart; the political society is supposedly neutral in its enforcement of rights;

and the Jew is Jewish in civil society only. Marx (1978: 32) explores this concept in terms of the "twofold life":

> The perfect political state is, by its nature, man's species-life, as opposed to his material life. All the preconditions of this egoistic life continue to exist in civil society outside the sphere of the state, but as qualities of civil society. Where the political state has attained its true development, man—not only in thought, in consciousness, but in reality, in life—leads a twofold life, a heavenly and an earthly life: life in the political community, in which he considers himself a communal being, and life in civil society, in which he acts as a private individual, regards other men as a means, degrades himself into a means, and becomes the plaything of alien powers.

This is liberation and, as such, is liberalism. Yet for Marx (1978: 30), political emancipation is *not* human emancipation:

> The political emancipation of the Jew or the Christian—of the *religious* man in general—is the *emancipation* of the state from Judaism, Christianity, and *religion* in general. The *state* emancipates itself from religion in its own particular way, in the mode which corresponds to its nature, by emancipating itself from *state religion*; that is to say, by giving recognition to no religion and affirming itself purely and simply as a state. To be *politically* emancipated from religion is not to be finally and completely emancipated from religion, because political emancipation is not the final and absolute form of *human* emancipation.

What is it that we cannot see? Marx argued that political emancipation is in fact an illusion: it intensifies and legitimizes what it sets outside itself—private property, which it does not abolish, rather "the political suppression of private property ... presupposes its existence" (Marx 1978: 31); and "man's real religiosity" (Marx 1978: 33). Both of these continue despite the struggle to attain political emancipation. Marx (1978: 29) suggested:

> The question is: what is the relation between *complete* political emancipation and religion? If we find in the country which has attained full political emancipation, that religion not only continues to *exist* but is *fresh* and *vigorous*, this is the proof that the existence of religion is not at all opposed to the perfection of the state. But since the existence of religion is the existence of a defect, the source of this defect must be sought in the *nature* of the state itself. Religion no longer appears as the basis, but as the *manifestation* of secular narrowness. This is why we explain the religious constraints upon the free citizens by the secular constraints upon them. We do not claim that they must transcend their religious narrowness in order to get rid of their secular limitations. We claim that they will transcend their religious narrowness once they have overcome their secular limitations.

Performing this secular/religious reversal, I propose that we can employ a state–church/disentanglement–intensification contradiction to ask whether "the *displacement* of religion from the state to civil society" (Marx 1978: 32), in the specific context of the adjudication of *mahr* in Western states, has had the consequence of generating more religiosity. In other words, did Islam get intensified in the private sphere by courts' refusal to enforce it in the public judicial system? I will use the LLPA decision of *Kaddoura* to suggest that the answer may sometimes be "yes."

The Kaddoura Decision: Excluding Mahr *from the Public Sphere*

In *Kaddoura*, the Court constructed a fence around *mahr*, relegating it to the private, to the religious, to the civil society, to the family; it was deemed *not* to belong to the public, to the secular, to the political society, to the market. The Court justified the unenforceability of *mahr* in reference to the sharply demarcated separation between state and church: "Where, however, as seems to be the case here, the issue must be determined with reference to religious doctrine and principle, the civil court is, in my view, at least lacking in expertise and, in the United States context and perhaps Canadian as well, constitutionally beyond its proper territory" (para. 26). The Ontario Court of Justice admittedly conferred a secularist dimension to the Canadian state. Yet the secular needs the religious, in order to be secular. In the state–church/disentanglement–intensification contradiction, not only does the existence of the state presuppose the existence of the church, but the former constitutes the latter. More specifically, the secular-public-judicial-branch-of-Ontario requires and depends on the production and subjugation of the religious-private-domestic-branch-of-the-Muslim-community. As a result, *Kaddoura* concurrently makes and suppresses *mahr*: it makes it religious and suppresses it from the courthouse. The Court makes this distinction clear: "I don't think, even if I had received clear and complete Islamic doctrine from these experts, that I could, as if applying foreign law, apply such religious doctrine to a civil resolution of this dispute. … In my view, the claim that Sam owes Manira $30,000 is not a matter that is justiciable in the civil courts" (paras 27, 29).

Confronted with this *fin de non-recevoir*, with this coercive declaration of impossible encounter, *mahr* leaves the Ontario Court of Justice as nothing: non-enforced. The translator could not read its (uncommon) language—as if applying foreign law, admits the Court. The verdict: *mahr* is not enforced because it is unenforceable, not from the standpoint of contract law, constitutional law, family law, or even Islamic law doctrines, but rather from the standpoint of procedure— the performance of the judicial exercise of translation could not even *begin*. But does *mahr* leave the courthouse frustrated? Where did it travel? Did it go back home, to the local Imam, to the Muslim extended family or to the Islamic-based arbitration system? Could *Kaddoura*'s vision of real and unproblematic dichotomies—religious versus civil disputes, Islamic doctrine versus contractual obligation, foreign law versus domestic law, Us versus Them—have the effect of sentimentalizing *mahr* as something *more* religious and sacred than it otherwise would be for the Muslim parties involved? Could the non-enforcement of *mahr* in *Kaddoura* have the perverse counter-effect of producing *more mahr* as a discursive practice?

In attempting to partially answer these queries, I advance the possibility that *mahr* gathers strength in the so-called private sphere through the emergence of arbitration as a sub-jurisdictional system in Canada. In June 2005, the Ontario government appointed the Honourable Marion Boyd, former Attorney General of the Province of Ontario, to determine whether parties should be allowed to submit to *shari'a* arbitration in family law matters. The study recognized and explored the reactions to the stirring of a debate in Canada on the use of religious/Islamic rules in family law matters. Later that same year, after reviewing the issues and consulting with various stakeholders, Marion Boyd prepared and released a report entitled *Dispute Resolution in Family Law: Protecting Choice, Promoting Inclusion.*[3] This report provides a basis for my own exploration of where *mahr* lands in Ontario's family law landscape.

The Shari'a *Court Debate in Ontario:* Protecting Choice, Promoting Inclusion

In Ontario, the *Arbitration Act* regulates arbitration between individual parties. Because the *Act* does not exclude family-related disputes from the scope of arbitration, the door has been open to *shari'a*-based tribunals set up as arbitration boards for family matters since it was passed in 1991. This legal framework stands in stark contrast to that of the Province of Québec. Section 2639 of the *Québec Civil Code* reads: "Disputes over the status and capacity of persons, family matters or other matters of public order may not be submitted to arbitration. An arbitration agreement may not be opposed on the ground that the rules applicable to settlement of the dispute are in the nature of rules of public order." Moreover, a motion was passed unanimously in the Québec legislature on May 26, 2005, stating that no *shari'a* court in family matters will be allowed in the province, and that the laws of Québec will apply to all its residents, regardless of religion, ethnicity or culture (Séguin 2005).

On September 11, 2005, Dalton McGuinty, Premier of the Province of Ontario, announced: "[T]here will be no Sharia law in Ontario. ... There will be no religious arbitration in Ontario. ... There will be one law for all Ontarians" (Freeze and Howlett 2005: A1). However, as Ontario's *Arbitration Act* stood at the time, an arbitrator could apply any set of norms: *shari'a* law, rabbinical law or any other set of values or "rules of law" that the parties "agreed" to. In fact, subsection 32(1) of the *Arbitration Act* allowed parties to agree to have their family law disputes resolved using any "rules of law" with no consideration to the applicable standards of the *Family Law Act*, the *Divorce Act*, or the *Children's Law Reform*

---

3   The full text of the report is available online at http://www.attorneygeneral.jus.gov. on.ca/english/about/pubs/boyd/ (accessed October 19, 2009).

Act. This effectively neutralized the operation of a whole panoply of federal and provincial laws designed to protect the rights of parties involved in family-related disputes.[4] Furthermore, this broad freedom resulted from the absence of procedural guidelines: there was no requirement to keep a record of arbitral awards, no requirement for the arbitrator to be trained or educated in Canadian law or *shari'a* law, and no requirement to verify the validity of consent by both parties before signing the arbitration agreement. The potential pitfalls of this system, especially when compared to the public forum of a court, are not unique to Ontario:

> The vocation of private justice is, well, to remain as private as possible. This means that potentially unjust awards are never submitted to the broader, quasi-democratic scrutiny of the public institutions. In that, arbitral awards stand in stark contrast with public judgments issued by State courts. While private arbitrators need only to justify their awards, if at all, to the parties who appear before them, state judges, not only must ground their reasoning on publicly debated norms, they must also appeal to a form of public reason. Indeed, the legitimacy of a judicial judgment is in large part related to the court's ability to persuade. (Gaudrault-Desbiens 2005: 20)

Moreover, while a right of appeal exists under the *Arbitration Act* (s. 45), since "the purpose of arbitration is typically to avoid the traditional court system, it is likely that parties will contract out of their appeal rights in arbitration agreements, resulting in very limited judicial oversight through the mechanism of judicial review" (Bakht 2004: 6). In any case, if an arbitral decision is put forward for judicial review (as provided for in s. 46), courts will likely afford a high degree of deference to the arbitrator's decision on the basis that the arbitrator can claim a specialized expertise, such as religious knowledge and experience in interpreting religious texts. While the degree of deference a court will show to an arbitration decision is usually based on "a complex test that incorporates a variety of different factors ... courts will usually respect and enforce the terms of an award unless the decision of the arbitrator is unreasonable or patently unreasonable" (Bakht 2004: 6).

The roots of Marion Boyd's report, however, went further back than the date when she was recruited to study the issue of *shari'a* law in arbitration. On October 21, 2003, the Islamic Institute of Civil Justice,[5] a Muslim organization established by Syed Mumtaz Ali, a retired Ontario lawyer, had proposed an Islamic tribunal that would apply Islamic law in adjudicating family law matters through voluntary arbitration. This was envisioned to begin in Ontario, and eventually move into

---

4   Since then, the *Family Statute Law Amendment Act, 2005* proposed amendments to the *Arbitration Act*, the *Family Law Act* and the *Children's Law Reform Act*. These Acts were amended and substantially modified.

5   Information about this organization can be accessed online at http://muslim-canada. org/DARLQADAform2andhalf.html (accessed October 19, 2009).

other Canadian provinces. This proposal gave rise to strong reactions in the mainstream press and the Muslim community.[6] The Attorney General of Ontario's response to these concerns came in the form of the appointment of Marion Boyd. Her task was to review the *Arbitration Act* and decide "what differential impact, if any, arbitration may have on women, elderly persons, persons with disabilities, or other vulnerable groups" (Boyd 2004: 5).

At the national level, numerous non-governmental organizations offered their political visions to Marion Boyd by way of oral and written submissions. The Canadian Council of Muslim Women, the National Association of Women and the Law and the National Organization of Immigrant and Visible Minority Women issued a statement outlining a number of substantive concerns about the proposed arbitration tribunal. Their report recommended that family matters be excluded from the scope of the *Arbitration Act* (Bakht 2004: 1). According to their submissions, separate arbitration tribunals for settling family matters under *shari'a*/Muslim family law would ghettoize and further marginalize Muslim women. Homa Arjomand founded the International Campaign Against the Shariah Court in Canada, and called for a moratorium on family arbitration, whether in existing rabbinical courts or Islamic tribunals. Similarly, the Muslim Canadian Congress expressed its opposition to the *shari'a* court on the basis that such division was in fact racist:

> In practical and realistic terms, what began as a demand to introduce "Sharia Law" has now dishonestly mutated into the same thorn by any other name, and is still offensively unacceptable for the following reasons. ... This insidious and discriminatory ghettoization and marginalization, into "out of sight" only plays into: (i) The hands of the extremist political and ideological agenda of a certain sector of Muslim-Canadian proponents of "Muslim Law" that is antithetical to the Canadian Constitution and values; and (ii) Equally into the hands of the reactionary, intolerant and otherwise racist segments of Canadian non-Muslim society who want nothing better than to exclude Muslims from the mainstream; all of this, behind the dishonest guise of religious tolerance and accommodation.[7]

Despite such strongly worded opposition, other representatives of the Muslim population backed the project. Several individual Imams and Islamic leaders voiced their support, and other Muslim organizations argued in favour of the

---

6   Collections of opinions and newspaper articles on this topic began to crop up on the Internet. Two sites that collected such information include International Campaign Against Shari'a Court in Canada (http://www.nosharia.com (accessed May 11, 2010)) and The Canadian Society of Muslims (http://muslim-canada.org (accessed May 11, 2010)).

7   Quoted from the unpublished submission of R. Galati and the Muslim Canadian Congress to Marion Boyd during the Review of Arbitration Process on August 26, 2004, a copy of which is on file with the author.

implementation of a *shari'a* court in Canada. These organizations, led mostly by men, included the Canadian Society of Muslims and the Masjid El Noor Muslim arbitration board, which had this to say:

> It is ludicrous to suggest that the majority of Muslim women oppose the Shariah, otherwise they would not be Muslim. … The fact is, Shariah Tribunals have been in operation already for many years and nothing terrible has occurred. It is clear that the hyperbole and polemic that has been promoted has totally skewed the reality of what is happening, "on the ground." The Islamic nature of this Tribunal attracts people to pursue their disputes through it versus the courts. The added privacy and confidentiality is paramount (particularly for women) if this is to have credibility.[8]

Locating Protecting Choice, Promoting Inclusion*: The Aftermath of Kaddoura*

Protecting Choice, Promoting Inclusion is based on the conclusion that there is no legal evidence of systemic discrimination against women: "The review did not find any evidence to suggest that women are being systematically discriminated against as a result of family law issues" (Boyd 2004: 133). The arbitration agreement is signed by the parties to authorize the arbitrator to act, whereas the arbitral award is the decision or reasons of the arbitrator. The irony lies in the fact that arbitration is by definition a private system that is entered into by agreement, without any duty on the part of the arbitrator to render the arbitral award public. Hence, it is hardly surprising that Marion Boyd did not find any "legal evidence," the evidence being of a private nature. Despite this, and as a consequence of the findings, the report suggests that the use of Islamic family law in arbitration matters be maintained. I will first outline the conclusions of the report and explore how *Kaddoura* explicitly participated in the elaboration of such conclusions.

Protecting Choice, Promoting Inclusion rests upon two interdependent and complementary theses: the primacy of multiculturalism as a constitutional guiding principle, and the significance of "freedom of contract" in religious and family law matters. Recall that section 27 of Canada's *Charter of Rights and Freedoms* entrenches the legitimacy and primacy of multiculturalism as an interpretive principle: "This Charter shall be interpreted in a manner consistent with the preservation and enhancement of the multicultural heritage of Canadians." Thus, first and foremost, *Protecting Choice, Promoting Inclusion* relies extensively on currently circulating narratives about the true meaning of "multiculturalism" as a Canadian political project whose central unit is not the individual or the state but the minority group. Such a project, referred to as "differentiated citizenship" by Iris Young (Kymlicka 1995: 26), aims to grant traditionally marginalized cultural

---

8   Quoted from the unpublished submission of M. Shaikh to Marion Boyd during the Review of Arbitration Process on August 24, 2004, entitled *Shariah Tribunals and Masjid El Noor: A Canadian Model*. A copy is on file with the author.

communities jurisdictional autonomy over legal domains such as education and family law. As demonstrated in the identity-based arguments expressed below, the premises and normative commitments of *Protecting Choice, Promoting Inclusion* explicitly push for the recognition of distinct racial or religious groups in Canada, and insist on the articulation of a multicultural project that protects expression and values in the name of community standards:

> The use of religious principles in arbitrations of family law matters illustrates the fundamental role of family law in delineating who is inside and who is outside the community according to the community's own norms. Being able to police these boundaries is a basic aspect of cultural self-determination for all communities. ... Allowing and supporting communities' and individuals' links to cultures (including their religions) of origin is a central aspect of multiculturalism. (Boyd 2004: 89–90)

Yet in deciding to advocate, embrace and adopt racial multiculturalism, and in naming religious subjects, desires and realities, *Protecting Choice, Promoting Inclusion* produces benefits with implicit costs. As a response to the claim that well-meaning accommodation policies by the state may allow systematic discrimination against women in a minority group, *Protecting Choice, Promoting Inclusion* simply transcends the liberal dichotomy between gender equality and religious freedom/multiculturalism by (re)organizing and (re)locating the first *as part of* the latter. Under this view of racial multiculturalism, the absence of equality becomes a defining feature of the minority group's identity:

> Leaders within the Muslim community have repeatedly made statements that justify unequal treatment of women under Muslim law. As a result, many Ontarians have understandable difficulty in believing that the rights of women in arbitrations undertaken by Imams or other male members of the Muslim communities, will be respected. ... Nonetheless, incorporating cultural minority groups into mainstream political processes remains crucial for multicultural, liberal democratic societies. (Boyd 2004: 93)

Second, by embracing identity politics, *Protecting Choice, Promoting Inclusion* portrays the multicultural state as having little justification for intervening in a minority group's affairs, on the theory that such intervention would unduly restrict transactional relationships in arbitration. This approach is based on a liberal conception of freedom of contract that regards unequal bargaining power as economically justified in the name of "freedom to choose":

> People are entitled to make choices that others may perceive not to be correct, as long as they are legally capable of making such choices and the choice is not prohibited by law. In those areas where the state has chosen to allow people to order their lives according to private values, the state has no place enforcing any

particular set of values, religious or not. ... Accepting this form of agreement rests on the notion that the parties entering into such an agreement are capable of making such decisions for themselves. State scrutiny of each privately ordered arrangement implies that no one is capable of making decisions on their own behalf. This is a degree of paternalism which I would find intrusive and inappropriate. (Boyd 2004: 75–76)

This stance evidences, if not disingenuity, at least dangerous over-simplification: so-called non-intervention of the state is already a form of intervention (Hale 1943: 603). Furthermore, the private sphere that allows people to make bad choices is, ironically, the very creation of the state. Absent the *Arbitration Act*, people would be required to take their family law disputes to Ontario's Superior Courts of Justice and engage in a public and transparent process. Why is *Protecting Choice, Promoting Inclusion* so sceptical, at a normative level, of the existence of the judicial public legal system that is able to fairly adjudicate disputes for Muslim parties? Performing the state–church/disentanglement–intensification contradiction, the report explicitly responds to the secular take of *Kaddoura*, citing the decision itself and the unenforceability of *mahr* that resulted from it:

Although the court system offers interpretation services to accommodate the needs of Ontario's diverse community, it is widely accepted that many concerns with respect to its cultural sensitivities remain. Many of those working with immigrant and refugee people, particularly those who may be perceived as hostile to Canada by virtue only of their race or national origin, identified incidents of discrimination and racism that impede access to justice. In the court system, parties have no control over which judge will preside over their case. In some instances, presiding judges have indicated discomfort in dealing with cultural and religiously based issues, such as *Mahr*. Some contributors have pointed out that there is "an 'apparent cultural anxiety' in Ontario associated with entering the 'religious thicket', a place that the courts cannot safely and should not go." (Boyd 2004: 106)

Protecting Choice, Promoting Inclusion presents itself as a response to *Kaddoura* in that the discursively available binary arguments (secular/religious; public/ private; judicial/arbitral) left no choice aside these two poles of the contradiction. In fact, the report seems to suggest that if racism/orientalism has admittedly permeated the secular-public-judicial sphere and relegated Muslims to the religious-private-arbitral domain, the Canadian state should react by accepting the use of Islamic law in family law matters through arbitration. *Mahr*'s travel through the state–church/disentanglement–intensification contradiction unfolds in this mysterious way: *Kaddoura* (state) refused to enforce *mahr* because it is religious (church), supposedly disentangling itself from religion (disentaglement), yet *mahr* becomes intensified in the private sphere by *Protecting Choice, Promoting*

Inclusion's acceptance of the use of Islamic family law in arbitration matters (intensification).

Concluding Remarks

The state–church/disentanglement–intensification contradiction entertains instances where the liberal state envisions the judiciary and religion as two distinct, autonomous and mutually exclusive domains. The religious is thus seen as a private realm, as the *outside* of politics, the market, the public street and so on. The next contradiction I will explore—the state–church/Western–Islamic contradiction—represents an extension of the binary and foundational proposition of the third contradiction.

The State–Church/Western–Islamic Contradiction: Edward Saïd's *Orientalism* and Barbara Johnson's *The Critical Difference*

In *Orientalism*, a key text on colonial and post-colonial discourse, Edward Saïd suggested that the West codifies and discursively produces knowledge about the East through the paradigm of colonial/imperial structures; he thus inaugurates "colonial discourse theory" as an area of academic inquiry. In exploring discursive boundaries for colonial discourse analysis, Saïd (1978: 41) wrote:

> In a sense Orientalism was a library or archive of information commonly held and, in some of its aspects, unanimously held. What bound the archive together was a family of ideas and a unifying set of values proven in various ways to be effective. These ideas explained the behavior of Orientals; they supplied Orientals with a mentality, a genealogy, an atmosphere; most important, they allowed Europeans to deal with and even to see Orientals as a phenomenon possessing regular characteristics. But like any set of durable ideas, Orientalist notions influenced the people who were called Orientals as well as those called Occidental, Europeans, or Western; in short, Orientalism is better grasped as a set of constraints upon and limitations of thought than it is simply as a positive doctrine. (Said 1978: 41)

Borrowing from Saïd's methodology, I consider the existence of a state–church/ Western–Islamic contradiction, exploring the construction of both "Western" and "Islamic" law as revealed in cases adjudicating *mahr*. My question is arguably simple: Has the rhetorical emphasis on the East as the "outside" of the West created a monolithic vision of both systems of law?

I will also use the approach Barbara Johnson articulated in the series of essays she entitled *The Critical Difference* to elicit the differences and similarities that exist *within* the West and the East as entities. Johnson brilliantly proposed, in an essay on the contemporary rhetoric of reading, that the existence and production of binary relations suppose, on each part of the dualist difference, something like its opposite which it hides. She wrote:

> Far from eliminating binary oppositions from the critical vocabulary, one can only show that binary difference does not function as one thinks it does and that certain subversions that seem to befall it in the critical narrative are logically prior to it and necessary in its very structure. ... Reading, here, proceeds by identifying and dismantling differences by means of other differences that cannot be fully identified or dismantled. The starting point is often a binary difference that is subsequently shown to be an illusion created by the workings of differences much harder to pin down. The differences *between* entities (prose and poetry, man and woman, literature and theory, guilt and innocence) are shown to be based on a repression of differences *within* entities, ways in which an entity differs from itself. (Johnson 1981: ix–xi)

I thus draw on Saïd's and Johnson's innovative perspectives on comparative law to deconstruct the discursive effects of the West/East binary and further assess the repression of differences *within* the entities of Western and Islamic law.

The Production of the West/East as a Binary Relation

In the scholarship dedicated to legal transplants, including approaches that view comparative law as a subversive discipline (Sacco 1991; Mattei 1994a, 1994b; Monateri 1998a, 1998b; Muir-Watt 2000), the binary East/West permeates the images and understanding of the ways in which Islamic legal rules travel, permeate and are received by the West in a comparative law dialogue (Shalakany 2001a, 2001b; Abu-Odeh 1992, 1997). Differences are thus assigned *between* the legal regimes of the East and the West, two entities considered as sharply divided. This can be seen both in Saïd's perceptions and in more modern times. For example, in *Orientalism*, as noted above, Saïd elaborated on how Western representations of the East not only served to define the East but the West itself, which was defined through its opposition to the "backward" and "barbaric" East. In the contemporary context, as the East has become more and more synonymous with "terrorism," the West has increasingly defined itself as the antithesis of terrorism, that is, through the self-image of democracy (Porras 1995: 297).

In the specific context of the LLPA, cases have produced *mahr* as a space of identity that can only be accessed and acknowledged through recognition. *Mahr is*; it exists *prior* to Western contact. If done correctly and carefully, the LLPA exercise of comparative law believes that it can transplant *mahr* from the Islamic to the Western forum. Yet Western representations of *mahr* as purely Islamic prevent the reader from seeing the complexity of both Western and Islamic law. I thus explore the rhetorical insistence on the homogeneity of Islamic law or Canadian, American, German or French law, and ask whether, rather than constituting a binary opposition whereby the West is *not* the East (and, inversely, the East is *not* the West), the elements attributed to each side of the binary can be transposed. What I call the state–church/Western–Islamic contradiction specifically deals with the secular/religious dichotomy and addresses the blind spots created, in the process of adjudicating *mahr*, by the overemphasis on *mahr* as religious, Islamic, and divinely made. Brenda Cossman (1997: 526) provides a way of differently inhabiting the ethnocentric gaze of comparison where "the geopolitical location of the author becomes the unstated norm against which the exotic 'other' is viewed." Taking her words to heart, in using the strategy of "turning the gaze back upon itself," my hope is to approach the "hybridity" (Bhabha 1994) of both the East and the West.

The Production of Western Law in the LLPA Cases

In most of the LLPA cases analyzed in Chapter 3, the production of Western law posits itself as the outside of *mahr*. In *Nathoo v Nathoo* and *M.(N.M.) v M.(N. S.)*, cases from the British Columbia Supreme Court from 1996 and 2004, respectively, *mahr* is represented as the religious and cultural expression of the Muslim minority group, one that Canadian society (and courts) must respect in the name of multiculturalism. In *Nathoo*, the Court insisted on the fact that *mahr* is a religious act performed in "the traditions of the Ismaili community," that both parties attended "Mosque regularly and adhere to the tenets of their faith" and that they "courted for approximately two years prior to their marriage" (para. 8). Justice Dorgan further suggested that section 48 of the British Columbia *Family Relations Act*, like all Canadian laws, should "evolve in a manner which acknowledges cultural diversity" and be "respectful of traditions which define various groups who live in a multi-cultural community" (para. 25).

In *M.(N.M.)*, the Court presented *mahr* as "required by the tenets of the Ismaili faith" (para. 7) and enforced it on the basis that "both parties wished to marry in the Ismaili faith and they understood and accepted that a condition of doing so was to agree to the Maher" (para. 28). Similarly in *Cour de Cassation 1978-000137*, *OLG Bremen*, *Kammergericht* and *M.H.D. v E.A.*, cases from France, Germany and Québec, courts embarked on the exercise of translating the foreign nature of *mahr*, based on the application of international private law rules. *Mahr* has thus become "Iranian *mahr*" or "Syrian *mahr*."

All of these cases projected Western law as having no history of dowry or dower practices. But is that really the case? Referring to the American context, Thomas Lund (2006: 659) wrote: "To this day, dower remains a fundamental principle within Anglo-American law, although the name has fallen into the lexicon of archaic terms, replaced by such general concepts as the widow's elective share against her husband's will, or her claim against his intestate estate." In "Home As Work: The First Women's Rights Claims Concerning Wives' Household Labor," Reva Siegel explored the nineteenth-century statutes recognizing women's rights to their earnings outside the home, and their relationship to the wider feminist movement claiming a joint property system. Siegel's analysis situated the legal developments surrounding dower in the United States, in the context of the existence of a gendered model of male providers and female dependents within the nuclear family:

> In the opening decades of the nineteenth century, the common law of marital status was starkly hierarchical, imposing pervasive constraints on the lives of free women subject to its terms. The common law charged a husband with responsibility to represent and support his wife, giving him in return the use of her real property and absolute rights in her personality and "services"—all products of her labor. Unless her family was wealthy enough to provide property in an equitable trust, a wife negotiated marriage as a dependent: without property or the legal prerogative to earn it, and impaired in her capacity to contract, to convey or devise property, and to file suit. If she survived her husband, she acquired a life estate in one-third of any real property he held during the marriage ("dower"); so long as the marriage produced offspring, a husband who survived his wife was entitled to tenancy for life of any lands she held ("curtesy"). (Siegel 1994: 1082)

According to the American legal doctrine, dower was an interest that the law creates for the benefit of the widow in the real estate that the husband held in his sole name (*In re Estate of Del Guercio, Estate of Johnson v Commissioner*), whereas curtesy was the corresponding right of the husband by which he was entitled, upon the death of his wife, to a life estate in lands of which she was seized during her coverture (*Estate of Johnson v Commissioner*). Dower thus consisted of the wife's right to use, after the death of her husband, one third of all the real property to which her husband was beneficially entitled by inheritance at any time during their marriage. Although several statutes dealt with the subject explicitly (if only as mere restatements of the common law definition), dower was a common law right (*Boan v Watson*) which was not guaranteed by the privileges of citizenship (*Akers v Morton*).

The right that a wife has after her husband has become seized of real property and is still living is called "inchoate dower" (*In re Estate of Wulf*). However, while the husband was still alive, the dower attached to all real property of which the husband was seized: he could therefore, in practice, not sell without his wife's approval (*Wilson v Wilson*). After the husband's death, the "assignment of dower" referred to the common law procedure of physically marking off one third of the husband's lands and setting this portion aside for the widow's use during her lifetime. In American law, dower was also used to design the widows' statutory rights in the real property of their husbands (*McGuire v Cook, In re Noble's Estate, McAllister v Dexter & P.R. Co.*), and to surviving spouses' statutory rights in personal property as well as real property (McCauliff 1992, *Loughran v Loughran, Schneider v Schneider, Perlberg v Perlberg*).

Because a widow's common law dower provided no security against destitution, woman's rights advocates asked for formal equal testamentary and inheritance rights in the joint estate at death. This formal equality specifically meant claiming for the wife a right of survivorship in the husband's property akin to his estate by curtesy in hers. However, the women's movement did not demand "equality of treatment" (that is, that wives' household labour be emancipated in the form of a separate property right that might be exchanged for a wage). Ariela R. Dubler has suggested that the feminist struggle for dower reform was, however, intimately related to a wider critique of the male-provider/female-dependent model of the family, as well as to women's second-class citizenship rights:

> As their somewhat sporadic discussions of inheritance law reveal, nineteenth-century woman's rights activists offered two principal arguments against dower, both related to their larger critiques of marital status law, and both grounded in the recognition that inheritance law constructed the family and family roles. First, woman's rights activists offered a formal sex-equality argument based on the doctrinal differences between dower and curtesy, and, second, they argued that the common law of inheritance functioned as an orchestrated assault on the private family and, especially, on the family home. Read alongside one another, these arguments reveal a deep tension within woman's rights activists' reformist vision of the relationship between the law and the family, as well as a significant ambiguity in the meaning of equality within marriage. Their critiques of dower suggest that these reformers at once envisioned a dramatic transformation of the family—in which principles of sex equality would be imported into the marriage relationship—and simultaneously clung to a traditional vision of the private family and of women's entitlements within a family shielded from the law's intrusion. (Dubler 2003: 1674)

By the 1840s, many American states had enacted married women's property acts and had thus replaced the common law of marital status. The "earnings statutes," based on the separate property principles, conferred to wives property rights in earnings from their "separate" or "personal" labour, and thus enabled them to take on many legal transactions in their own right. The legal and customary allocation of title in a separate property system, however, "left a wife who spent her life working for the family unable to 'call a dollar her own'—holding nothing but a paltry life-interest in dower at her husband's death" (Siegel 1994: 1119). By 1935, "few states retained a woman's traditional dower right in its pure form" (Dubler 2003: 1669) and a facially sex-neutral elective share, which provided to a widow or widower a certain share of her or his deceased spouse's real and personal property, was often adopted to replace the legal institution of dower.

What can be gained from considering this historical knowledge about American dower in the interpretation of Islamic *mahr*? What specific lessons can be learned from the history of dower's demise in the United States? Dubler (2003: 1652) argues that "[d]ower, like coverture, sought to ensure a woman's economic reliance on a particular man. In so doing, it bolstered the assumption that the state had no responsibility for her financial needs." Could it be that the relationship between the family and the state in the case of American dower, premised on marriage's ability to privatize women's material needs, is similar to the relationship between the Muslim family and the state in the case of *mahr*? If so, how does the provider function of both legal institutions resonate with feminist activism? Can this history of Western dower provide a new framework within which to analyze the contemporary legal and political dimensions of the adjudication of *mahr* in Western states, by ultimately stepping out of the liberal parameters of either religious difference, on the one hand, or gender equality/fairness, on the other?

Out of all the cases that have adjudicated *mahr*, only *In re Marriage of Dajani*, the 1988 California Court of Appeal decision belonging to the LFEA, embarked on this concrete exercise of comparing *mahr* to dower/dowry practices in American law. The Court thus stated:

> Black's Law Dictionary explains, "'Dower,' in modern use, is distinguished from 'dowry.' The former is a provision for a widow on her husband's death; the latter is a bride's portion on her marriage. *Wendler v. Lambeth [1901] 163 Mo. 428, 63 S.W. 684.*" (Black's Law Dict. (4th ed. 1951) p. 581, col. 1.) … The estate of dower is not recognized in California, pursuant to *Cal. Prob. Code § 6412*, but parties to a premarital agreement may contract with respect to the disposition of property upon death, pursuant to *Cal. Civ. Code § 5312(a)(3)*. (1388)

As this passage suggests, the deconstruction of the Western/Islamic binary renders explicit what otherwise would remain hidden: that there exists a similarity of legal rules between Islamic law and Western law. Although the Court refused to enforce *mahr* based on public policy in *Dajani*, it nevertheless refrained from painting *mahr* in the tantalizing but mysterious shades of the Exotic Other, a recurring depiction in the LLPA cases. Allowing for the existence of hybridity, this methodological difference reverses the relation between the West and the East and facilitates the emergence of another story, one which creates a space where Muslim men and women might be able to negotiate their claims outside the recognition/non-recognition binary. It is therefore possible to draw the conclusion that it might be useful to view the opposition between the West and the East *not* as a binary relation between traditionalists/modernists, Islam/secularism, gender inequality/gender equality, terrorism/democracy, etc., but rather quite simply as "two conceptions of language, or between two types of reading" (Johnson 1981: 84).

The existence of the state–church/Western–Islamic contradiction makes it difficult for courts "to turn the gaze back upon itself" and embark on the exercise of tracing back the analogy between *mahr* and other Western legal institutions that share some of its characteristics or functions. In fact, in order effectively to preserve the binary opposition suggested by the West/East discourse, the (non-localized) Western judge must deny the differences *within* the West.

The Production of Islamic Law in the LLPA Cases

What follows logically from the exploration of Western law is a complementary exploration of how the dominant legal discourse around Islamic law in the adjudication of *mahr* has created, perpetuated or regulated prevailing conceptions of personal identity and group affiliation along the West/East binary. In the LLPA cases analyzed in Chapter 3, courts conceptualized Muslim identity to be derivative of an already circumscribed subjectivity, equated in many ways to truth claims about "subordinated" Muslim groups living in "dominant" Western states. Yet, the words of Judith Butler (1990: 5) resonate here:

> The question of the "subject" is crucial for politics, and for feminist politics in particular, because juridical subjects are invariably produced through certain exclusionary practices that do not "show" once the juridical structure of politics has been established. … In effect, the law produces and then conceals the notion of "a subject before the law" in order to invoke that discursive formation as a naturalized foundational premise that subsequently legitimates that law's own regulatory hegemony.

Thus, not only is law itself predicated upon the very process of "making subjects" that it purports merely to regulate, but, further, the production of Islamic law from the location of the Western judge constructs *mahr* as a purely religious and non-civil law institution. This conclusion is questionable from a legal perspective. For instance, in *Kaddoura*, the Ontario court focused precisely on the inherent religious nature of *mahr* in refusing to enforce it:

> The *Mahr* and the extent to which it obligates a husband to make payment to his wife is essentially and fundamentally an Islamic religious matter. Because *Mahr* is a religious matter, the resolution of any dispute relating to it or the consequences of failing to honour the obligation are also religious in their content and context. … Many such promises go well beyond the basic legal commitment to marriage required by our civil law, and are essentially matters of chosen religion and morality. They are derived from and are dependent upon doctrine and faith. They bind the conscience as a matter of religious principle but not necessarily as a matter of enforceable civil law. (para. 25)

What sense can be made of this disturbing opposition between *mahr* and civil law? Is *mahr* legally divorced from civil law? Is it indeed, as *Kaddoura* has suggested, "a matter of religious principle but not necessarily a matter of enforceable civil law"? Ironically, and as noted in Chapter 1, the *mahr* that *pre-exists* the road to Western states is strongly contractual in form. Islamic law stipulates that anyone with the requisite knowledge of Islamic law is competent to perform religious ceremonies, including marriage. One is not required to have an official position in a religious institution such as a mosque (*masjid*) in order to be qualified to perform such ceremonies—Islamic marriage is a civil contract which, unlike Christian marriages, is not sacramental in nature (Afifi 1996). Therefore, parties may insert a variety of clauses—commonly, such stipulations include agreements related to *mahr*, polygamy, and the wife's financial independence, right to work and right to education—as long as they do not contradict the purpose of marriage itself. However, by insisting on the differences between the secular/religious, the civil/Islamic, the Us/Them, the national/foreign *within* Western states, none of the cases on the adjudication of *mahr* has noticed the civil character and the significant importance of contract law *within* Islamic family law.

Moreover, from a purely geopolitical and historical perspective, the equation between Islam/religion and the West/secularism cannot be sustained. In fact, there are Western democracies which have constitutionally adopted a clear separation of church from state—the United States, France, Mexico, Portugal and Turkey all specifically affirm the principle of the separation of church and state in their constitutions. Others, whether Western or not, have explicitly recognized the importance of religion in their constitutions. For example, England, Denmark, Finland and Iran all recognize an official state religion. More ambiguously, the preamble of Canada's *Charter of Rights and Freedoms*, as previously noted, states that "Canada is founded upon principles that recognize the supremacy of God and the rule of law." The complex relationship between religion and the West/East divide can be highlighted in further examining, from both a legal and historical perspective, the case of Egypt. Amr Shalakany (2001b: 157) states:

> With respect to the question of law in particular, … abstract terms take on the relatively more concrete concerns of "legal reform." Since the mid-nineteenth century, most Arab legal systems have gone through a series of reforms that effectively uprooted the pre-colonial "tradition" of Islamic law, and replaced it with a set of "modern" legal transplants borrowed from Western legal systems. Often the Western legal transplant was installed side-by-side with some Islamic doctrine, institution, or other. For example, while Western civil, commercial, and criminal codes were introduced into the Egyptian legal system, the codes did contain various doctrines derived from Islamic law. Furthermore, personal status law remained Islamic in origin, but its reform was based on a modernist cut-and-paste methodology between often conflicting schools of Islamic jurisprudence. Additionally, while new secular law schools and a judiciary were established, an Islamic judiciary and law school remained intact for quite some time. The end result is the current legal system: a hybrid mishmash of secular and Islamic jurisprudence, doctrines, law schools, and case law.

Moreover, even when Islamic law does present itself as divinely made, many contradictory and conflicting interpretations muddy its content from within. Schools of interpretation vary widely. The traditionalist approach deals with the Qur'an verse by verse, follows the Qur'anic text and expounds it in a piecemeal fashion, employing those instruments of exegesis that it believes to be effective (such as reliance on literal meanings, traditions or other verses that have some word or meaning in common with the verse under study) to shed light on the part being commented upon (Zahra 1955; Schacht 1982). The liberal tradition in Islam is traced back to nineteenth-century leaders and writers, such as Jamal al-Din al-Afghani, Sayyid Ahmad Khan and Muhammad Abduh, who emphasized the ideas of freedom from *taqlid* (tradition) and expansion of the right to practice *ijtihad*, which is the process of making a legal decision by interpreting the legal sources, the Qur'an and the Sunnah independently. Ideas of this kind were spread mainly through education, journalism and international networking. Al-Ashmawi (1994: 108) wrote:

> Such political conceptions of religion [that all of Egypt's civil code should be re-promulgated after an expression of the intention that the *shari'a* control] are extremely dangerous for Islam and for its *shari'a*. They imply the worst threats to Egypt; they would break in two its legal and judiciary systems, as well as the country itself, and declaring [*sic*] an end to contemporary Egyptian Islamic Law, all without this being required by anything in religion or in *shari'a*.

The utilitarian type of exegesis emphasizes the philological and literary aspects of the Qur'anic text, thus concentrating on meaning and content. An example of this type of interpretation is provided by Ausaf Ali (2003), who comments broadly on Islam's take on gender equality:

> Islam, I think, provides perspectives on both equality as well as inequality of men and women. In this respect, there is, indeed, a tension between certain verses, such as 2:223, 2:228 and 4:34 of the Koran, on the one hand, and certain other verses, such as 9:71 and 33:35 of the Koran, on the other. The former set of verses lays the basis of social and economic inequality of men and women and the latter of their moral and spiritual equality. My considered opinion is that it is the message and intent of the equalitarian verses of the Koran that ought to be taken as the more beneficent, compassionate, and judicious paradigmatic basis and determiner of Muslim life and living in the 21th century of the Common Era upon us. Judged by the standards of civilization and civility, in our time, for instance, verse 33:35 provides a better guide for genderization, sexuality, and marriage in contemporary Islam and Muslim society than verse 4:34, that is, if human equality is the goal of the message of Islam, and, I am convinced, it is.

As a final example in this non-exhaustive review of schools of interpretation, I include feminist readings, which advocate not just revisionist interpretations, but wholly new methods of reading traditional texts. Fatima Mernissi demonstrates that for each misogynist *hadith*, one should check the identity of the Companion of the Prophet who uttered it, and in what circumstances and with what objective in mind, as well as the chain of people who passed it along. She queries:

What conclusion must one draw from this? That even the authentic *hadith* must be vigilantly examined with a magnifying glass? That is our right, Malik ibn Anas tells us. ... All the monotheistic religions are shot through by the conflict between the divine and the feminine, but none more so than Islam, which has opted for the occultation of the feminine, at least symbolically, by trying to veil it, to hide it, to mask it. (Mernissi 1998: 123)

Given the convolutions that exist within and among the various schools of interpretation, it is hardly surprising that an understanding of this complex/hybrid character of Islamic law surely has not travelled to Western courts. Rather, what the case law has demonstrated is that *mahr* is equated with Islam, the religious, the non-Western and, ultimately, with the place allocated for non-civil law.

Concluding Remarks

In a comparative law context of adjudicating *mahr*, the state–church/Western–Islamic contradiction functions as follows: because the real opposition at the heart of the comparative exercise has reorganized the "State" as "Western" and the "Church" as "Islamic" (and, in so doing, has pitted them against one another), differences *within* the East (a mixed system of civil/religious law) and differences *within* the West (the existence of dower as a similar yet non-Islamic practice) are not located and are, in fact, deemed non-existent. Reactions to this lack of acknowledgement or perceived neglect can be manifest differently. In some cases, it has taken the form of feminist critique. In others, we may simply find ourselves musing on what hypothetical variations of national law, personal history or religious adherence could lead to a different result in any given situation—marital or otherwise—and whether it reached the courts or not. In the circumstances, however, merely recognizing the dichotomy takes on new meaning and overarching purpose: "turning the gaze back upon itself" means identifying the differences that have been silenced and thus opening unexplored spaces across the divide.

Can Contradictions Be Laid to Rest?

The analysis of the reception of *mahr* as ideology and subjectivity has not only highlighted the existence of four contradictions in courts' present jurisprudence: it has also provided a way in which to think about adjudication. The doctrine–outcome contradiction and the ends–means perversity contradiction both undermine some of the assumptions of the LLPA and the LFEA, namely the causal relationship between legal doctrine and outcome, and the capacity of Western means to either reproduce a legal transplant or a non-religious contractual *mahr*. Hence, the representation of *mahr* and the power it organizes has formed the basis for understanding how *mahr* cannot travel, through either recognition or non-recognition. The state–church/disentanglement–intensification contradiction and the state–church/Western–Islamic contradiction demonstrate how, in adjudicating *mahr*, the LLPA has further intensified religion by attempting to push it to the private sphere and has simultaneously missed the paradoxical split of Islamic law and Western law. Perhaps because liberalism is so eager *not* to get involved in religious matters, the adjudicative process consequently fails to appreciate the richness and heterogeneity of both legal systems.

Chapter 5
Samir and Leila Revisited:
The Adjudication and Reception of
Mahr and its Subjective Significance for
Muslim Women

In earlier chapters, I analyzed *mahr* as "adjudication" and "reception" by the Western court, without inquiring into its subjective significance for the Muslim woman involved. This chapter brings back into focus what has been hidden by the adjudicative discourse of *mahr* as "recognition" (LLPA), as "equality" (LFEA), and as "fairness" (LSEA)—the complex and shifting function of *mahr* as if it were being used by the parties in the "shadow of the law." In a fictional style that borrows from Chapter 1, I revisit the story of Samir and Leila with additional scripts to delineate the power dynamics at play. I thus follow the way *mahr* operates in the distribution of power and desire *between* the Muslim husband and the Muslim wife, as well as in the constitution of their respective identities through law. I argue that *mahr* is disciplinary in that it incorporates norms and rules regarding the family, both in relation to the Islamic law regime presented in Chapter 1, as well as in relation to the Western legal systems outlined in Chapter 2. Those function as the "rules of the game" (Kennedy 1997) in the conflict between the Muslim husband and the Muslim wife—before, during and after the concrete adjudication of *mahr*. In developing this framework, my aim is to study the specific ways in which background legal rules and background social norms (employment, age, immigration, and social security, among others) might affect and have affected the shape of *mahr* disputes, and multiply their distributional stakes. To carry out this analysis, I borrow from Christine Jolls' and Robert Hale's methodologies to create diverging scripts of *mahr* as empowerment and as disempowerment, the enforcement or non-enforcement of which can act variously as a bonus or a penalty for either party.

Christine Jolls' Accommodation Mandates: The Economic Asymmetry of *Mahr*'s Adjudication

In a paper about United States discrimination law and its remedial structure, Christine Jolls proposed a theoretical framework for understanding the distributive effects of laws mandating employers to provide benefits to disadvantaged groups of workers (Jolls 2000). Specifically, Jolls analyzed the (disparate) impact of accommodation mandates and anti-discrimination laws on the wages and employment levels of their intended beneficiaries by breaking down the category of "workers" as a whole. The article provided a counterpoint for the existing literature, which assumed either that desirable effects for accommodated workers are unlikely since the costs are shifted to the accommodated group in the form of reduced wages or reduced employment (the law and economics camp), or that accommodation requirements are morally good regardless of the potential adverse effects of these laws on the wages and employment levels of the accommodated group since what is at stake is human dignity (the liberal camp). Her approach strikes me as eminently suitable to my subject, thus I propose to adopt it as a convenient and apt starting point for examining the distributional analysis of the recognition or non-recognition of *mahr* in Western courts. Using Jolls' model, my analysis intervenes in the liberal–legal pluralist approach (LLPA), the liberal–formal equality approach (LFEA), and the liberal–substantive equality approach (LSEA) to demonstrate that, in family law cases involving the enforcement of *mahr*, the legal reasoning of the courts has failed to perform a systematic distributional analysis.

The first step in the application of Jolls' model is to use an economic analysis of the outcomes determined by the three liberal camps to show disparities in the distributional consequences for the Muslim women concerned. In fact, as demonstrated in the analysis of Chapter 3, the same Muslim woman will get very different outcomes—that is, she will be better or worse off economically—depending on the ideological position adopted by the judge. Whereas the economic outcome for the individual Muslim woman is rarely a factor in the legal reasoning of the liberal–legal pluralist approach and the liberal–formal equality approach, the liberal–substantive equality offers a standard-based fairness approach which does account for the impact of legal doctrine on *that particular* Muslim woman. The reason is simple: the LSEA, by virtue of its consideration of outcomes, focuses on consequences, on the impact of enforcement, on the effect of courts' intervention into a private arrangement, on the concrete rather than abstract significance of using legal doctrine to enforce, reject or modify deferred *mahr*, depending on the particular circumstances of the case. However, equity as fairness, by definition, is an exercise that must be undertaken on a case-by-case basis and which masks the discretionary power of the judge: equity is equity for *that* judge (Kennedy 1976).

A second step in the analysis would be to break down the Muslim woman category into several subcategories, such as the secular Muslim woman, the religious Muslim woman, the rich professional Muslim woman, the poor head-of-household Muslim woman, and others. The legal enforcement of *mahr* as a legal rule can be deemed to have asymmetric economic effects among different groups of women. For instance, the enforcement of 30,000 Euros as deferred *mahr* by the German Family Law Chamber, in so far as it is understood by the court as a substitute for post-divorce division of the surplus of marital profits and maintenance, would probably benefit the rich Muslim woman (who would keep her personal assets on top of deferred *mahr*) and could potentially hurt the Muslim husband if he would have to sell all his assets in order to pay *mahr* to his ex-wife. On the other hand, the poor head-of-household Muslim woman married to a rich Muslim man would be highly disadvantaged by the very same enforcement of *mahr*: in this example, she would get 30,000 Euros upon divorce, and nothing else.

My objective is not to propose an alternative way of adjudicating *mahr* that could be translated into a concrete judicial policy model. However, I confess to a certain affinity to the LSEA since it sometimes most closely resembles the distributional model I have in mind. The LSEA's focus on outcomes makes it particularly appealing. However, by *only* paying attention to economic/gender fairness towards *this particular* Muslim woman, the LSEA cases have failed to incorporate the religious significance of *mahr* in the bargaining strategies that exist between the parties. The LSEA analysis and predictions might thus be unconnected from what happens on the ground in Muslim religious communities. In this chapter, I wish to test this hypothesis by reintroducing Samir and Leila, who are now bargaining in the shadow of Western courts.

Leila and the Many Different Routes to *Mahr* as Bonus and Penalty: The Enforcement of *Mahr*

While the first step of the analysis was to identify the different economic outcomes for differently situated Muslim women in the enforcement of *mahr* cases, the second step is to analyze *mahr* in the wider context in which it operates, that is, as part of background legal rules and background social norms that pervasively structure the bargaining power of husband and wife. As Robert Hale convincingly suggested, focusing solely on labour contract to the exclusion of property rules that differentially and asymmetrically empower individuals in the economic struggle maintains the illusion that the outcomes of negotiations/transactions are "chosen" or "free." This perspective ignores the power of "coercion" (Hale 1923). Hale's approach can be transposed seamlessly into the family law context by examining the possible background legal rules that condition the distributional consequences of any given *mahr* dispute. For this kind of analysis, two additional types of rules become relevant: (1) the background legal rules governing the conduct of husband and wife that directly increase or decrease their respective power during the divorce procedures (I am thinking, for example, of immigration laws, social security factors, employment laws and the like); and (2) the background social norms that define the Muslim woman's situation in the communities in which she finds herself during and after the divorce procedures (this could be the presence/ absence of extended family members, the presence/absence of domestic violence or other such factors). Accounting for these background rules determines the actual bargaining power of the Muslim woman and makes apparent the distributive conflict that exists between her and her husband, as well as the *projected* significance of the enforcement or non-enforcement of *mahr*.

I thus perform a distributive shift to argue that in the social life of Islamic marriages, *mahr* is not unitary and autonomous, but rather a functional institution that produces a series of inconsistent characteristics which we can study. Through this distributive reading of *mahr*, my hope is to offer a narrative concerned primarily with the social effects created by the judiciary as it claims to merely *translate mahr* according to ideological preferences when in fact it *produces mahr* as bonus or penalty. In an attempt to underline the complexity of *mahr* as it moves ideologically to the LLPA, the LFEA or the LSEA—and the contradicted meanings each position conceals—I have deconstructed the "Muslim-woman-reacting-to-*mahr*" into many conflicting players, situated along a continuing spectrum between the two poles of empowerment and disempowerment. In each category of empowerment or disempowerment, I present Leila in relation to her specific background rules and norms and situate how *mahr* could be employed and deployed by her in strategic terms given that location. These perspectives are fictional, although I draw partly upon existing characters from autobiographies, public cases, feminist manifestos, religious advocacy groups and best-selling books. In so doing, I mean to show that my six Leilas are in some ways connected to real people out there in the world. All of these scripts also reflect, directly or indirectly, the legal reasoning or outcome of real cases emanating from Western courts.

Mahr *as Penalty for the Wife and Bonus for the Husband*

Leila: The-Feminist-President-of-the-Canadian-Council-of-Muslim-Women[1]   Leila is a Canadian citizen who founded the Canadian Council for Muslim Women in 1982. The organization views Islam as a religion of peace, compassion, social justice and equality, while acknowledging that many of the interpretations and practices of Muslim law do not always reflect these principles. Leila and her husband, Samir, met in Toronto where they were both working for the same company. After a brief courtship, they decided to get married in Tunis, where both of their families lived. Samir paid Leila $65 in prompt *mahr* on their wedding day, in accordance with Tunisian law. Although Leila and Samir were happy together for the first few years of their marriage, their relationship slowly deteriorated and Leila decided to seek a divorce.

---

   1   This script is *not* based on the life of the President of the Canadian Council of Muslim Women, although I have used some of the insights I have collected, throughout the years, from my work with several female members of the Council. This script borrows from the following decisions, which have all adopted the internal logic of the Islamic law regime in applying the waiver of *mahr*: *M.H.D. v E.A.*; *I.(S.) v. E.(E.)*; *Akileh*; and *In re Marriage of Dajani*. Hence, *mahr* is unenforceable because the wife is the one asking for divorce.

Leila sees herself as a strong feminist—she is fascinated by the many progressive and intelligent women who exercised a positive influence on the life and teachings of the Prophet Mohammed. She especially draws inspiration from the Prophet's first wife, Khadija, who "had her own business, traded, dealt with society at large, employed the Prophet Mohammed when he was a young boy, and subsequently, herself sent a proposal (of marriage) to the Prophet" (Bhutto 1998: 110). For Leila, this is a direct and convincing example that women should have the ability to propose and end a marriage unilaterally and ask for deferred *mahr* whenever they so wish, without any relation to *talaq*, *khul* or *faskh* divorce. If the Prophet Mohammed himself accepted this initial bargaining structure, why shouldn't future generations of women follow the model he established? Leila is committed to the revival of Khadija!

Although the trend in her native Tunisia was for the payment of only a nominal amount of *mahr*, Leila viewed *mahr* as a personal guarantee against financial ruin in the case of divorce. So, Leila insisted on a $10,000 deferred *mahr* in her marriage contract. Her belief in the legacy of Khadija also motivated her to include numerous feminist stipulations in her marriage contract:

- the right to request *mahr* whenever she wishes and for whatever reason;
- the right to divorce for both spouses, either through mutual consent or upon the husband's desire or the wife's request;
- the right to maintenance for herself and the children;
- the right to treat each other well and avoid inflicting harm on each other (absence of obedience); and
- the right to be paid for breastfeeding.

When Leila and Samir divorced—at Leila's initiation—Leila turned her back on the religious conservative voices in her Muslim community, including well-known and well-respected Imams in Toronto. She entered the courthouse almost demystified, asking for the enforcement of *mahr* from a religious feminist perspective. She was hoping to introduce a new terminology: the non-existence of *khul mahr* on religious grounds. In an act of liberation and subversion, Leila presented the existence of Khadija as "the very image of somebody who is independent, assertive, and does not conform to the passive description of women in Muslim societies that we have grown accustomed to hearing about" (Bhutto 1998: 110). She further gave the example of Khadija's marriage proposal to the Prophet Mohammed as a matriarchal approach to Islam. But the court did not accept her novel take on Islamic law because of her lack of "expertise" and "legitimacy." The non-Tunisian Imam who testified at court soon came to deliver the truth: Leila should waive *mahr* because she initiated the divorce, and the feminist stipulations of the marriage contract were ludicrous! The court respected the sacred testimony and refused to order Samir to pay Leila the deferred *mahr* on the basis that she was the one who chose to pursue the divorce, even though Leila would have likely been entitled to *mahr* had she divorced in Tunisia. There were risks to Leila's strategy of invoking the life of Khadija to support her case. Leila miscalculated and paid a high price. She left the courthouse in shock, hurt and enraged. And with no money. Undaunted, however, her struggle for *mahr* as empowerment for other Muslim women shall continue!

Leila: The-German-Egyptian-"Foreign Bride" [2]   Leila has been married to Samir for 15 years. Although of Egyptian origin and citizenship, she lives in Kreuzberg, the Turkish Muslim suburb of Berlin. She rarely goes out, and makes contact with her German neighbours more hesitantly than her sons and her husband. At home, men often gather to talk of politics, the war in Afghanistan, the disastrous state of Iraq, the integration of Turkey into the European Union. Women cook, support, clean—mute shadows, outsiders. In recent years, Leila has been exposed to the new wave of feminist critiques coming from German women of Muslim background, such as Necla Kelek's *The Foreign Bride*. Kelek addresses the everyday violence of arranged marriages, as well as the oppressive and sexist behaviour of Muslim men in Germany. Leila was powerfully seduced by her critique and the promising and assertive voice Kelek developed. Leila saw herself in the guise of the "foreign bride"—this young Muslim woman imported to Germany as a bride, who led a fully insular and subservient life as a wife and a mother. The book represented an ultimatum for Leila: she would either embrace women's rights (and other Western, German conceptions of freedom) or remain forever "a foreign bride" whose equality is constantly being jeopardized. Leila opted for the former. She left Samir, her sons, her home—with perfect irresponsibility. [3]

---

2   This script is partly based on *OLG Bremen* and partly on Necla Kelek's book *Die fremde Braut: Ein Bericht aus dem Inneren des türkischen Lebens in Deutschland* [The Foreign Bride: A Report from the Inside of Turkish Life in Germany], which received the prestigious Scholl Award in Germany and topped the German bestseller list. In her book, Kelek strongly criticizes both the so-called fundamentalist Muslim society for perpetuating a culture of female slavery, and the liberal German society, which in her opinion has adopted a hands-off approach based on tolerance.

3   I borrow this expression from Ralph Ellison's *The Invisible Man*, in which he argued that irresponsibility is, for subordinated groups, a consequence of their invisibility:

> I am one of the most irresponsible beings that ever lived. Irresponsibility is part of my invisibility; any way you face it, it is a denial. But to whom can I be responsible, and why should I be, when you refuse to see me? And wait until I reveal how truly irresponsible I am. Responsibility rests upon recognition, and recognition is a form of agreement. Take the man whom I almost killed: Who was responsible for that near murder—I? I don't think so, and I refuse it. I won't buy it. You can't give it to me. He bumped me, he insulted me. Shouldn't he, for his own personal safety, have recognized my hysteria, my "danger potential"? He, let us say, was lost in a dream world. But didn't he control that dream world—which, alas, is only too real!—and didn't he rule me out of it? And if he

While contemplating divorce, Leila was obsessed by the memory of her sister, Fatima, who had been left financially destitute in Egypt after obtaining a *khul* divorce. Fatima's husband had been emotionally abusive to her, but, not having the financial resources to prove the abuse in a *faskh* divorce, Fatima had opted for the quicker, less expensive *khul* divorce. The court ruled that Fatima lost the right to seek any maintenance or deferred *mahr* from her husband and she had to repay the prompt *mahr* she had received. Even now, five years later, Fatima was still heavily indebted to her ex-husband. She worked 12 hours a day as a cleaner, just to make payments on the debt and to maintain a small apartment for herself and her daughter in Cairo.

Despite Fatima's painful experience, Leila was not worried about suffering the same fate as her sister because she was seeking a divorce in Germany where divorce law, she had been told, was much more favourable toward women. Faced with the impossibility of surviving with very limited economic resources, Leila approached the courthouse, confident that state alimony and division-of-property laws in Germany would guarantee her generous benefits. How wrong were her predictions! Leila soon realized that, as a non-German citizen, Egyptian Islamic law would apply to her case. Since she had no claim under Egyptian law at the time to post-divorce alimony or to her share of the profits accruing to the marital property, the court held that *mahr* constituted a substitute for post-divorce maintenance and division of the surplus of marital profits. Furthermore, because Leila was the one seeking the divorce, the court held that she had given up her right to deferred *mahr* and was obligated to pay back the prompt *mahr* she had been given at her wedding.

Leila felt trapped in a complex and seemingly incomprehensible reality. It had come as a rude shock to her that, as a non-citizen, she was considered a "guest" in Germany, although she had made it her home for so many years. The very Islamic laws from which she hoped to escape into newfound freedom were being applied to her in the course of an already-painful marital dispute. Was Leila fooled into thinking that she, too, could embrace German conceptions of freedom, as Kelek's book had so delightfully suggested to her? Is Leila forever condemned, by virtue of the application of private international law rules in Germany, of representing this tragic foreign bride whom she so fervently sought to elude?

Mahr *as Penalty for Husband and Bonus for Wife*

Leila: The Canadian-Pakistani-Journalist-Writing-as-a-Lesbian-Refusenik[4]   Leila asserts herself as a "Lesbian Refusenik" living in British Columbia, Canada: "The

---

had yelled for a policeman, wouldn't I have been taken for the offending one? Yes, yes, yes! (Ellison 1952: 17)

4   This script is partly based on Irshad Manji's autobiographical book, *The Trouble with Islam: A Muslim's Call for Reform in her Faith*, an internationally acclaimed bestseller that has been published in 26 countries. However, many of the facts that I have included

good news is I knew I lived in a part of the world that permitted me to explore. Thanks to the freedom afforded me in the West—to think, search, speak, exchange, discuss, challenge, be challenged, and rethink—I was poised to judge my religion in a light that I couldn't have possibly conceived in the parochial Muslim microcosm of the madressa" (Manji 2004: 19). Leila married Samir at the age of 18, and he repudiated her three years later, as soon as she made her sexual preferences known to him: "I'm openly lesbian. I choose to be 'out' because, having matured in a miserable household under a father who despised joy, I'm not about to sabotage the consensual love that offers me joy as an adult. I met my first girlfriend in my twenties and, weeks afterwards, told my mother about the relationship" (Manji, 2004: 21). Leila has infinite gratitude toward Canadian society, where one can be a lesbian (and even marry!), write radical and provocative essays against Islam and choose an alternative life path even if it goes against the wishes of one's parents.

Leila becomes furious with proponents of multiculturalism who romanticize Islam and excuse brutality as a "cultural feature":

> I have to be honest with you. Islam is on very thin ice with me. I'm hanging on by my fingernails, in anxiety over what's coming next from the self-appointed ambassadors of Allah. … When I speak publicly about our failings, the very Muslims who detect stereotyping at every turn label me as a sell-out. A sellout to what? To moral clarity? To common decency? To civilization? Yes, I'm blunt. You're just going to have to get used to it. (Manji 2004: 1)

Leila is angry, embarrassed by the fact that she was once "in the closet," married to Samir, sleeping next to Samir, faking it with Samir, because of her misconception that one cannot simultaneously be a Muslim and a lesbian: "You may wonder who I am to talk to you this way. I am a Muslim Refusenik. That doesn't mean that I refuse to be a Muslim; it simply means I refuse to join an army of automatons in the name of Allah" (Manji 2004: 3). Leila is very angry. She decides to ask the secular court for the enforcement of *mahr*, in the amount of $50,000, as a calculated revenge. Given that "the parties chose to marry within the Muslim tradition" (*Nathoo*, para. 24), knowing "full well that provision for Maher was a condition of so doing" (*Nathoo*, para. 24), the Court chose to enforce *mahr*. Leila is happy. But something new and quite surprising will make Leila even happier: not only is *mahr* culturally recognized and financially due to her, but it is added to an amount of $37,747.17 owed by Samir to Leila as a result of the division of family assets. Leila will thus receive $87,747.17 on that very special day—an exceptional and costly penalty for Samir.

---

in this story are purely fictional, including a first marriage to a man, and should not be interpreted as reflecting the life of Irshad Manji. I chose this perspective because I believe it does capture some of the anger of some Muslims who consider themselves as "Muslim Refusenik."

Leila and the Many Different Routes to *Mahr* as Bonus and Penalty: The Non-Enforcement of *Mahr*

Mahr *as Penalty for Wife and Bonus for Husband*

Leila: The-American-"Terrorist"-Convicted-under-the-Patriot-Act[5]   On September 25, 2001, Leila was arrested and detained on the basis of allegations that she constituted a threat to the security of the United States, by reason of her involvement in terrorist activities linked to Al-Qaeda. She was convicted soon after under the *Patriot Act*. Having recently married Samir, whom she had met a few months before being arrested, Leila is currently in detention. In response to these unfounded suspicions linking her to terrorist groups, Leila finds peace in reading the Qur'an and in writing letters to Samir, her soulmate. Leila is a romantic. For her, *mahr* symbolizes the beauty and purity of Samir's love, like "a bone in the upper part of the breast, or gristles of the ribs; or something presentable as a gift like a pearl" (Wani 1995: 193). Last week, she received a letter informing her that Samir wishes to divorce her religiously, with no further explanation. Samir came on Sunday for his weekly visit and irrevocably pronounced the three *talaq*. Leila was repudiated. Heartbroken, she asked a California lawyer to represent her in a claim for the enforcement of deferred *mahr*, a symbolic amount of $1,700. She was informed that the court could not enforce *mahr*. It held that the marriage contract is considered as one designed to facilitate divorce: with the exception of prompt *mahr*, "the wife was not entitled to receive any of the agreed upon sum unless the marriage was dissolved or husband died. The contract clearly provided for wife to profit by divorce, and it cannot be enforced by a California court" (*Dajani*: 1390).

Leila is perplexed. How can *mahr* provide for *her* to profit from divorce? And how can it *clearly* do so? It is Samir who religiously divorced her! The least she can ask for is the enforcement of deferred *mahr*, a condition of issuing *talaq* in the first place. By distorting *mahr*'s function, the court penalized Leila.

Leila: The-German-Secular-Young-Professional-Rising-Star[6]   Leila   is   a young German professional. A physician, her peers consider her a rising star in Germany's medical circles. She was born in Iran into a family that was very well off, and too closely related to the Shah to remain in Tehran safely following Ayatollah Khomeini's arrival. Although Leila arrived in Cologne soon after the Islamic revolution, she never obtained German citizenship. Leila considers herself a secular woman, although she was married to Samir in a religious ceremony. Samir has been working sporadically as a taxi driver. Their notarized marital contract specified 21,000 Euros as deferred *mahr*. Leila asked for and

---

5   This script is partly based on *In re Marriage of Dajani*, a California Court of Appeal case analyzed in Chapter 3.

6   This script is partly based on *OLG Koeln*, a German case analyzed in Chapter 3.

obtained a divorce before the German Family Law Chamber and separately claimed the enforcement of *mahr*, plus interest, as a legal debt before the Civil Law Chamber. She reached the courthouse with a clear notion of her privileged position: she 'legally' argued for the enforcement of *mahr*, although she never really conceived of *mahr* as a form of identity, as a religious affiliation to the Prophet Mohammed or as a sign of gender (in)equality. Moreover, *mahr* was not meant to protect her economically in the case of a *talaq* divorce, because not only was she the main breadwinner, but, further, the existence of a religious *talaq* divorce in Germany would not have been recognized by the state. Aware of the different angles of the bargaining power structure that existed between her and Samir, she attempted to use *mahr* purposefully and subversively.

She wanted to test her power. Indirectly and ambiguously, *mahr* produced differing and exciting incentives for her. Were her interests erotic? Aesthetic? Both? Leila admittedly desired the court's gaze: to watch her, uncover her, make her publicly *bad*. The court pierced her veil: it held that the enforcement of *mahr* would create an unjust enrichment so as to violate German public order. It thus refused to enforce *mahr*.

Mahr *as Penalty for Husband and Bonus for Wife*

Leila: The-French-Member-of-Ni-Putes-Ni-Soumises[7]   To envision the non-enforcement of *mahr* as a penalty for the husband and a bonus for the wife, imagine Leila attempting to break her marriage in order to escape a hostile domestic environment. At the age of 19, Leila could never have guessed where life would take her when she married Samir, a family friend, in Malaysia. At the time of the wedding, Leila was proud that she had garnered both a fairly high amount of *Mas Kahwin* (*mahr*) as a young, unmarried woman, as well as an additional substantial amount of promised *Pemberian* (a customary form of dowry). The very idea of divorce seemed unthinkable at the time.

Leila and Samir moved to France seven years later so that Samir could pursue an advanced engineering degree. Bored with her life as a housewife, Leila decided to take night courses to become a secretary. She excelled in her studies and blossomed in her new job working for a women's organization. Samir became more and more jealous and possessive after Leila started working. His physical abuse escalated and he started to make degrading remarks on how she had become a "Western slut." Samir would also make persistent comments, especially in the presence of her immediate and extended family, about the fact that she has been "brainwashed" by the corrupt secular French society.

He was particularly incensed that Leila had been introduced by a colleague to the organization *Ni Putes Ni Soumises* (Neither Whores Nor Slaves)[8], a French

---

7   This script is partly based on *Douai*, a French appeal decision analyzed in Chapter 3.

8   The French organization *Ni Putes Ni Soumises* has become a nationwide force, in France, of Muslim women refusing to give in to violence and submission. "Neither Whores

feminist movement founded in 2002 which soon secured recognition by the French press and parliament. With ambivalence at first (the slogan used by the movement is meant both to shock and mobilize), but with growing enthusiasm and passion, she gradually became an active member of the organization and an engaged activist. She organized several conferences and publicly shared her experience of suffering with other Muslim women, especially those from her native Malaysia. In the home and out in the streets, she was no longer afraid. Leila knew too well that Samir would never pronounce the three *talaq*, and she did not even attempt to negotiate a *khul* divorce. One day, she simply walked away and never came back.

She decided to reach out to the French court system, however, to claim the unenforceability of *mahr*! She argued that, precisely because she is "neither a whore nor a slave," she should never have been subjected to the unequal and degrading treatment that the promise of *Mas Kahwin* and *Pemberian* represent. Undoubtedly, such foreign institutions should be declared contrary to *l'ordre public français*! Leila won her case with pride. Considering the *Mas Kahwin* and *Pemberian* payments together, the Court relied on conflict of laws principles to reject the application of *mahr* as against "public order," on the one hand, and apply Western equity standards, on the other. The Court's reasoning translated into the generous sum of €200,000 for Leila instead of the $0 due to her under Islamic family law.

Nor Slaves" is an expression which is meant to reflect the tragedy of Sohane Benziane, a 19-year-old girl who was set on fire and killed by a boy she knew in a run-down apartment estate in the outskirts of Paris in October 2002. The movement expresses its anger at the "tolerance" of French society towards violence and stigmatization suffered by Muslim women in the name of Islamic tradition in the neglected French suburbs. The political platform of the organization can be found at: http://www.niputesnisoumises.com/ (accessed May 12, 2010). A translation of the key points (as translated from the French) could be expressed as follows: "No more moralizing: our condition has worsened. The media and politics have done nothing, or very little, for us. No more wretchedness. We are fed up with people speaking for us, with being treated with contempt. No more justifications of our oppression in the name of the right to be different and of respect toward those who force us to bow our heads. No more silence in public debates about violence, poverty and discrimination."

Chapter 6
Deep Roots and Tall Branches: Conclusions on the Reception of *Mahr* by Western Courts

Recently, with the explosion of global migration, discussions surrounding the recognition of minority cultures in Western Europe and North America have blossomed. All across the western world, courts, policy makers, and theorists are struggling with how to respond to the existence of "unofficial" forms of law. In England, discussions multiplied following the speech by the Archbishop of Canterbury, who proposed that the British legal system adapt to changing social/cultural realities (Shah 2009). In France, concerns over religious symbols in public schools, specifically the Islamic headscarf, fuelled a public debate over the very nature of the French secular state. In Germany, public furore erupted following a ruling by a family court judge who refused to expedite a divorce on the basis of abuse and who cited passages of the Qur'an in defense of her decision. In Canada, the use of *shari'a* arbitration in Ontario sparked public outcries and gave rise to an ongoing discussion on the limits of multiculturalism (Bader 2009). It is clear that the challenge of how to deal with the accommodation of minority cultures, like most legal and social issues today, is becoming global in nature.

On a theoretical level, the debate often remains concentrated on notions of equality, especially in regards to gender. Feminists such as Susan Moller Okin (1999), Martha Minow (1997), and Martha Nussbaum (2000) have argued that uniformly accepting minority cultures could wrongly place the autonomy of a group over that of an individual, and in so doing suppress the rights of women and children by promoting conservative visions of the community over progressive ones. Postcolonial and critical race theorists have criticized such feminist polarized vision for perpetuating racist stereotypes about minority women and obscuring the role that colonization and exploitation by mainstream society have played in the influence of cultural/religious practices. Solutions to this problem have varied from regulated privatization of certain areas of family law to a form of state-supervised legal pluralism. Unfortunately, most of these proposals fail to consider how courts *actually* adjudicate religious claims inside their courtrooms and whether women participate in and resist conventional disciplinary mechanisms in subversive ways.

In this book I have argued for the introduction of a new language in discussing the extent to which Islamic legal norms can or should be recognized within Western legal systems. In borrowing from legal realist, postmodernist, and consequentialist tools, I have challenged the idea that Western states ought to recognize Islamic marriages by enforcing *mahr*. In fact, structuring the debate in this way assumes that Islamic marriage contracts can be enforced as a legal transplant, in static and homogeneous terms, across jurisdictions. I hope I have convinced you that adjudication concerning such contracts has resulted in quite diverse approaches and interpretations both *within* and *across* the home and host countries. The complexity of religious interactions with secular states, especially in the context of gender relations, requires an interdisciplinary and legal realist methodological posture. The book has developed such a framework of analysis by using one case study, *mahr en voyage* in Western courts, to follow the wider phenomenon of legal migration.

I have concentrated on women in their engagement of religious and state laws at the points of the dissolution of marriage, and how they deploy various strategies for personal benefit or satisfaction. One of my discoveries has been that these strategies succeed and fail—unpredictably and variously—in different places, at different times, and with different actors. My very specific focus, however, is not the only possible site of exploration. In many ways, this book serves to guide research projects on legal migration and religious interaction by setting a framework of analysis for the ways in which all kinds of laws migrate from one milieu to another. The methodological lens I have introduced helps to disenchant the formalist ideas that: a) legal rules, in their original place of departure, are determinate; b) legal rules can be transplanted by a host legal community and their so-called authenticity can be preserved; and c) doctrines relied upon by the judiciary can transparently control outcomes.

Mahr's religious and secular journey proceeded in four steps. Chapter 1 differentiated formalist interpretations of Islamic law from functionalist ones and demonstrated that *mahr* is internally plural. Hence, in Egypt, Tunisia, and Malaysia, the background legal systems provide an extremely wide-open spectrum of possible valid outcomes regarding the adjudication of *mahr*. A concept so diverse in its roots, not surprisingly, bears fruit in foreign jurisdictions in surprising ways. Chapter 2 offered a comparative review of contract law, family law, constitutional law, and private international law as they are applied in Canada, the United States, France, and Germany, which form the foundation for the subsequent discussion on the "legal state of play" in the (liberal) reception of *mahr*.

Chapter 3 studied every judicial decision on the adjudication of *mahr* from the four countries under study and classified them according to the doctrine relied upon by the court to ground its decision. I have named them the Liberal–Legal Pluralist, the Liberal–Formal Equality, and the Liberal–Substantive Equality Approaches. The three liberal strands differ in their ideological commitments and the subject of their political concern: the legal pluralist is concerned with the Muslim group; formal equality with the individual party; and substantive equality with the Muslim woman. Interestingly, each approach leads to indeterminate outcomes and quite logically produces both the recognition *and* the non-recognition of *mahr*. Furthermore, despite their different attitudes towards immigrants and minority citizenship and their respective legal rules, the four countries have *all* generated cases on the adjudication of *mahr* in *every* "liberal" camp. This is so, I have suggested, because judges choose among a wide pool of conflicting considerations to perform and justify their judicial role. This ideological bent, in turn, is concurrently restricted by several highly complex contradictions which I have designated in Chapter 4 as the Doctrine–Outcome Contradiction, the Ends–Means Perversity Contradiction, the State–Church/Disentanglement–Intensification Contradiction, and the State–Church/Western–Islamic Contradiction.

Finally, Chapter 5 reintroduced a fictitious couple, Leila and Samir, already presented in Chapter 1, and brought to the foreground the bargaining structures which colour the parties' respective regulatory regimes. I have invited you, as reader, to imagine with me several Leilas who are placed in various social and family settings. In unexpected ways, the Leilas performed their agency in the shadow of their poverty or wealth, their national affiliations, their sexual freedom or submission, their marital conditions, their relation to God, their political network. The Muslim women behind the *mahr* are multiple and their interactions with the western courts will only intensify this multiplicity. For one Leila, the enforcement of *mahr* is a bonus; for the other, it is a penalty. For a third, the unenforceability of *mahr* is a penalty; for another, it is a bonus. Moreover, on a subjective level, Leila's dilemma and negotiating strategies range from subversive uses of *mahr* as a moral victory to treasuring *mahr* as personal revenge or an act of liberation.

Now, where are we going from here? When I presented chapters of the book at national or international conferences, I would almost systematically get the following question: What do you think Western courts ought to do with *mahr?* I always resisted formulating an answer that would provide a predictable and perfect judicial posture for all anticipated scenarios. That was precisely my point and the relevance of my inquiry: courts ought to pay attention to distributional consequences rather than doctrinal consistency. One thing is clear: women face the courtroom with different bargaining endowments and it is the complexity of this location that we must study before suggesting a normative answer to the legal pluralist inquiry. And to be sure, the various dynamics of institutional, background, and discursive power cannot be reduced to hierarchy. The discourses around law, religion, and politics must be attentive to what produces agency and how different scripts are performed in real and imagined ways. Let us penetrate a little further these unknown religious margins, the conditions of their possibility and inherent limits. This profound disorientation is, perhaps ironically, our only stable point of reference.

Appendix A: *Mahr* and the Qur'an

This Appendix compiles the Qur'anic verses that explicitly address the issue of *mahr*: provisions enjoying payment of *mahr*; remission and variation of *mahr*; *mahr* and the dissolution of marriage; and restrictions on taking *mahr* back.

Provisions Enjoying Payment of *Mahr*

[4:4] You shall give the women their due dowries, equitably. [...]

[4:24] Also prohibited are the women who are already married, unless they flee their disbelieving husbands who are at war with you. These are God's commandments to you. All other categories are permitted for you in marriage, so long as you pay them their due dowries. You shall maintain your morality, by not committing adultery. Thus, whoever you like among them, you shall pay them the dowry decreed for them. You commit no error by mutually agreeing to any adjustments to the dowry. God is Omniscient, Most Wise.

[4:25] Those among you who cannot afford to marry free believing women, may marry believing slave women. God knows best about your belief, and you are equal to one another, as far as belief is concerned. You shall obtain permission from their guardians before you marry them, and pay them their due dowry equitably. They shall maintain moral behavior, by not committing adultery, or having secret lovers. Once they are freed through marriage, if they commit adultery, their punishment shall be half of that for the free women. Marrying a slave shall be a last resort for those unable to wait. To be patient is better for you. God is Forgiver, Most Merciful.

[5:5] Today, all good food is made lawful for you. The food of the people of the scripture is lawful for you, and your food is lawful for them. Also, you may marry the chaste women among the believers, as well as the chaste women among the followers of previous scripture, provided you pay them their due dowries. You shall maintain chastity, not committing adultery, nor taking secret lovers. Anyone who rejects faith, all his work will be in vain, and in the Hereafter he will be with the losers.

[60:10] O you who believe! when believing women come to you flying, then examine them; Allah knows best their faith; then if you find them to be believing women, do not send them back to the unbelievers, neither are these [women] lawful for them, nor are those [men] lawful for them, and give them what they have spent; and no blame attaches to you in marrying them when you give them their dowries; and hold not to the ties of marriage of unbelieving women, and ask for what you have spent, and let them ask for what they have spent. That is Allah's judgment; He judges between you, and Allah is Knowing, Wise.

Remission and Variation of *Mahr*

[4:4] ... If they willingly forfeit anything, then you may accept it; it is rightfully yours.
[4:24] ... You commit no error by mutually agreeing to any adjustments to the dowry.

Mahr the Dissolution of Marriage

[2:236] You commit no error by divorcing the women before touching them, or before setting the dowry for them. In this case, you shall compensate them—the rich as he can afford and the poor as he can afford—an equitable compensation. This is a duty upon the righteous.
[2:237] If you divorce them before touching them, but after you had set the dowry for them, the compensation shall be half the dowry, unless they voluntarily forfeit their rights, or the party responsible for causing the divorce chooses to forfeit the dowry. To forfeit is closer to righteousness. You shall maintain the amicable relations among you. God is Seer of everything you do.

Restrictions on Taking *Mahr* Back

[4:20] If you wish to marry another wife, in place of your present wife, and you had given any of them a great deal, you shall not take back anything you had given her. Would you take it fraudulently, maliciously, and sinfully?
[4:21] How could you take it back, after you have been intimate with each other, and they had taken from you a solemn pledge?
[4:19] O you who believe, it is not lawful for you to inherit what the women leave behind, against their will. You shall not force them to give up anything you had given them, unless they commit a proven adultery. You shall treat them nicely. If you dislike them, you may dislike something wherein God has placed a lot of good.

Appendix B: *Mahr* and the *Hadiths*

This Appendix reproduces what the Prophet Mohammed has said and suggested about the existence of *mahr* in different scenarios. They are grouped thematically as follows: the obligatory nature of *mahr*; the amount of *mahr* when it has not been agreed upon; the subject matter of *mahr* (such as when *mahr* takes the form of teaching the Qur'an, offering the woman a pair of shoes); *mahr* and *khul* divorce; and *mahr* and *li'an*.

The Obligatory Nature of *Mahr*

In the *hadith* literature, on the other hand, there are numerous references to cases in which marriages were arranged without the payment of the bride-price. A'isha is reported to have condemned this practice, reproaching women who offered themselves to the Prophet without requesting a bride-price (Powers 1986: 81).

The Amount of *Mahr*

In a *hadith* it is related that the case of a woman, whose husband died before fixing a dowry and consummating marriage, was referred to Abd-Allah Ibn Mas'ud, who decided that she should be paid a dowry according to the dowry of the women of like status with herself (*Kasadaqi nisaiha*), and this decision was afterwards found to be in accordance with the decision of the Holy Prophet in a similar case (Doi 1984: 160).

The Subject Matter of *Mahr*

Mahr *in the form of teaching the Qur'an*

> [...] a woman came to the Prophet (S.A.W.) and said:
> "O Messenger of Allah, I wish to give myself to you."
> Then she stood for a long time waiting for an answer.
> Then a man stood up and said:
> "O Messenger of Allah, if you do not need her, get her married to me."
> The Prophet then asked him:
> "Do you possess something that you can give as *sadaq*?"

He replied that he has only a pair of trousers, which if given to her, he will be without one. He was asked to give even if he had an iron ring. Since he had none, the Prophet (S.A.W.) asked:

"Do you have anything from the Holy Qur'an?"

He said:

"Yes", and enumerated the *Surahs* that he remembered.

The Prophet then said:

"I declare you two married with what you possess from the Qur'an."

(Doi 1984: 163)

Mahr in the Form of Offering the Woman a Pair of Shoes

It is narrated by Amir bin Rabiah that a woman belonging to Banu Fazarah was married on a pair of shoes as her Mahr. The Messenger of Allah asked her:

"Are you happy with yourself with a pair of shoes?"

She said:

"Yes."

The Prophet then permitted her to marry.

(Doi 1984: 163, narrated by Ahmad, Ibn Majah and Thirmidhi)

Mahr and *Khul* Divorce

Narrated by Ibn Abbas (RA):

The wife of Thabit bin Qais came to the Prophet (SAW) and said:

"O Allah's Messenger (S.A.W.) I do not blame Thabit for defects in his character or his religion, but I being a Muslim, dislike to behave in un-Islamic manner if I remain with him i.e. I cannot endure to live with him or I am afraid that I may become unthankful for Allah's blessings."

On that Allah's Messenger (S.A.W.) said to her:

"Will you give back the garden which your husband has given you as *mahr*?"

She said:

"Yes".

The Prophet (S.A.W.) said to Thabit:

"O, Thabit accept your garden and divorce her once."

Ata (RA) narrates: Prophet (S.A.W.) said:

"Take not anything more than *mahr* for *khul* from women."

(Wani 1996: 45)

Mahr and *Li'an*

Narrated by Sa'id bin Jubair:

> I asked Ibn Umar,
> "What is the verdict if a man accuses his wife of illegal intercourse?"
> Ibn Umar said:
> "The Prophet (S.A.W.) separated (by dissolution of marriage) the couple of Bani Al-Ajlan and said to them Allah knows that one of you two is a liar; so will one of you repent?" But both of them refused, so he (S.A.W.) separated them by divorce.
> The man said:
> "What about the mahr that I have given to my wife?"
> It was said:
> "You have no right to restore any money for if you have spoken the truth you have also shared life with her and if you have told a lie, you are less rightful to have your money back."
> (Wani 1996: 45)

Appendix C: Statute Excerpts

Canada

Canadian Charter of Rights and Freedoms

15.(1) Every individual is equal before and under the law and has the right to the equal protection and equal benefit of the law without discrimination and, in particular, without discrimination based on race, national or ethnic origin, colour, religion, sex, age or mental or physical disability.

(2) Subsection (1) does not preclude any law, program or activity that has as its object the amelioration of conditions of disadvantaged individuals or groups including those that are disadvantaged because of race, national or ethnic origin, colour, religion, sex, age or mental or physical disability.

27. This Charter shall be interpreted in a manner consistent with the preservation and enhancement of the multicultural heritage of Canadians.

Family Law Act (Ontario)

2.(10) A domestic contract dealing with a matter that is also dealt with in this Act prevails unless this Act provides otherwise.

52.(1) Two persons who are married to each other or intend to marry may enter into an agreement in which they agree on their respective rights and obligations under the marriage or on separation, on the annulment or dissolution of the marriage or on death, including,

a) ownership in or division of property;
b) support obligations;
c) the right to direct the education and moral training of their children, but not the right to custody of or access to their children; and
d) any other matter in the settlement of their affairs.

(2) A provision in a marriage contract purporting to limit a spouse's rights under Part II (Matrimonial Home) is unenforceable.

56.(1) In the determination of a matter respecting the education, moral training or custody of or access to a child, the court may disregard any provision of a domestic contract pertaining to the matter where, in the opinion of the court, to do so is in the best interests of the child.

(4) A court may, on application, set aside a domestic contract or a provision in it,

a) if a party failed to disclose to the other significant assets, or significant debts or other liabilities, existing when the domestic contract was made;
b) if a party did not understand the nature or consequences of the domestic contract; or
c) otherwise in accordance with the law of contract.

Family Relations Act (British Columbia)

43.(1) Subject to this Part, each spouse is entitled to an interest in each family asset on or after March 31, 1979 when

a) a separation agreement;
b) a declaratory judgment under section 44;
c) an order for dissolution of marriage or judicial separation; or
d) an order declaring the marriage null and void
e) respecting the marriage is first made.

(2) The interest under subsection (1) is an undivided half interest in the family asset as a tenant in common.

(3) An interest under subsection (1) is subject to

a) an order under this Part; or
b) a marriage agreement or a separation agreement.

(4) This section applies to a marriage entered into before or after this section comes into force.

51. Where the provisions for division of property between spouses under section 43 or their marriage agreement, as the case may be, would be unfair having regard to the duration of the marriage; [...]

b) the duration of the period during which the spouses have lived separate and apart;
c) the date when property was acquired or disposed of;
d) the extent to which property was acquired by one spouse through inheritance or gift;

e) the needs of each spouse to become or remain economically independent and self sufficient; or

f) any other circumstances relating to the acquisition, preservation, maintenance, improvement or use of property or the capacity or liabilities of a spouse, the Supreme Court, on application, may order that the property covered by section 43 or the marriage agreement, as the case may be, be divided into shares fixed by the court. Additionally or alternatively the court may order that other property not covered by section 43 or the marriage agreement, as the case may be, of one spouse be vested in the other spouse.

61.(2) A marriage agreement is an agreement entered into by a man and a woman before or during their marriage to each other to take effect on the date of their marriage or on the execution of the agreement, whichever is later, for (a) management of family assets or other property during marriage, or (b) ownership in, or division of, family assets or other property during marriage, or on the making of an order for dissolution of marriage, judicial separation or a declaration of nullity of marriage.

Matrimonial Property Act (Nova Scotia)

Preamble
Whereas it is desirable to encourage and strengthen the role of the family in society; and whereas for that purpose it is necessary to recognize the contribution made to a marriage by each spouse; and whereas in support of such recognition it is necessary to provide in law for the orderly and equitable settlement of the affairs of the spouses upon the termination of a marriage relationship; and whereas it is necessary to provide for mutual obligations in family relationships including the responsibility of parents for their children; and whereas it is desirable to recognize that child care, household management and financial support are the joint responsibilities of the spouses and that there is a joint contribution by the spouses, financial and otherwise, that entitles each spouse equally to the matrimonial assets[.]

12.(1) Where

a) a petition for divorce is filed;
b) an application is filed for a declaration of nullity;
c) the spouses have been living separate and apart and there is no reasonable prospect of the resumption of cohabitation; or
d) one of the spouses has died,

either spouse is entitled to apply to the court to have the matrimonial assets divided in equal shares, notwithstanding the ownership of these assets, and the court may order such a division.

13. Upon an application pursuant to Section 12, the court may make a division of matrimonial assets that is not equal or may make a division of property that is not a matrimonial asset, where the court is satisfied that the division of matrimonial assets in equal shares would be unfair or unconscionable taking into account the following factors:

a) the unreasonable impoverishment by either spouse of the matrimonial assets;

b) the amount of the debts and liabilities of each spouse and the circumstances in which they were incurred;

c) a marriage contract or separation agreement between the spouses;

d) the length of time that the spouses have cohabited with each other during their marriage;

e) the date and manner of acquisition of the assets;

f) the effect of the assumption by one spouse of any housekeeping, child care or other domestic responsibilities for the family on the ability of the other spouse to acquire, manage, maintain, operate or improve a business asset;

g) the contribution by one spouse to the education or career potential of the other spouse;

h) the needs of a child who has not attained the age of majority;

i) the contribution made by each spouse to the marriage and to the welfare of the family, including any contribution made as a homemaker or parent;

j) whether the value of the assets substantially appreciated during the marriage;

k) the proceeds of an insurance policy, or an award of damages in tort, intended to represent compensation for physical injuries or the cost of future maintenance of the injured spouse;

l) the value to either spouse of any pension or other benefit which, by reason of the termination of the marriage relationship, that party will lose the chance of acquiring;

m) all taxation consequences of the division of matrimonial assets.

22.(1). The division of matrimonial assets and the ownership of moveable property as between spouses, wherever situated, are governed by the law of the place where both spouses had their last common habitual residence or, where there is no such residence, by the law of the Province.

(2). The ownership of immoveable property as between spouses is governed by the law of the place where that property is situated.

(3). Notwithstanding subsection (2), where the law of the Province governs the division of assets, the value of the immoveable property wherever situated may be taken into consideration for the purposes of a division of assets.

23. A man and a woman may enter into an agreement, to be known as a marriage contract, before their marriage or during their marriage while they are cohabiting, in which they agree on their respective rights and obligations

   a) under the marriage;
   b) upon separation;
   c) upon the annulment or dissolution of the marriage;
   d) upon the death of either spouse.

29. Upon an application by a party to a marriage contract or separation agreement, the court may, where it is satisfied that any term of the contract or agreement is unconscionable, unduly harsh on one party or fraudulent, make an order varying the terms of the contract or agreement as the court sees fit.

Québec Civil Code (Québec)

414. Marriage entails the establishment of a family patrimony consisting of certain property of the spouses regardless of which of them holds a right of ownership in that property.

415. The family patrimony is composed of the following property owned by one or the other of the spouses: the residences of the family or the rights which confer use of them, the movable property with which they are furnished or decorated and which serves for the use of the household, the motor vehicles used for family travel and the benefits accrued during the marriage under a retirement plan. The payment of contributions into a pension plan entails an accrual of benefits under the pension plan; so does the accumulation of service recognized for the purposes of a pension plan.

   This patrimony also includes the registered earnings, during the marriage, of each spouse pursuant to the Act respecting the Québec Pension Plan or to similar plans.

   The earnings contemplated in the second paragraph and accrued benefits under a retirement plan governed or established by an Act which grants a right to death benefits to the surviving spouse where the marriage is dissolved as a result of death are, however, excluded from the family patrimony.

   Property devolved to one of the spouses by succession or gift before or during the marriage is also excluded from the family patrimony.

   For the purposes of the rules on family patrimony, a retirement plan is any of the following:

- a plan governed by the Act respecting Supplemental Pension Plans or that would be governed thereby if it applied where the spouse works;
- a retirement plan governed by a similar Act of a legislative jurisdiction other than the Parliament of Québec;
- a plan established by an Act of the Parliament of Québec or of another legislative jurisdiction;
- a retirement-savings plan;
- any other retirement-savings instrument, including an annuity contract, into which sums from any of such plans have been transferred.

422. The court may, on an application, make an exception to the rule of partition into equal shares, and decide that there will be no partition of earnings registered pursuant to the Act respecting the Québec Pension Plan or to similar plans where it would result in an injustice considering, in particular, the brevity of the marriage, the waste of certain property by one of the spouses, or the bad faith of one of them.

423. The spouses may not, by way of their marriage contract or otherwise, renounce their rights in the family patrimony. One spouse may, however, from the death of the other spouse or from the judgment of divorce, separation from bed and board or nullity of marriage, renounce such rights, in whole or in part, by notarial act *en minute;* that spouse may also renounce them by a judicial declaration which is recorded, in the course of proceedings for divorce, separation from bed and board or nullity of marriage. Renunciation shall be entered in the register of personal and movable real rights. Failing entry within a period of one year from the time when the right to partition arose, the renouncing spouse is deemed to have accepted.

2807. Judicial notice shall be taken of the law in force in Québec.

2809. Judicial notice may be taken of the law of other provinces or territories of Canada and that of a foreign state, provided it has been pleaded. The court may also require that proof be made of such law; this may be done, among other means, by expert testimony or by the production of a certificate drawn up by a jurisconsult.

3083. The status and capacity of a natural person are governed by the law of his domicile.

The status and capacity of a legal person are governed by the law of the country under which it was formed subject, with respect to its activities, to the law of the place where they are carried on.

Protective supervision of persons of full age and tutorship to minors are governed by the law of the domicile of each person subject thereto. Whenever a minor or a protected person of full age domiciled outside Québec possesses property in Québec or has rights to be exercised and the law of his domicile does not provide for him to have a representative, a tutor or a curator may be appointed to represent him in all cases where a tutor or a curator may represent a minor or a protected person of full age under the laws of Québec.

A party to a juridical act who is incapable under the law of the country of his domicile may not invoke his incapacity if he was capable under the law of the country in which the other party was domiciled when the act was formed in that country, unless the other party was or should have been aware of the incapacity.

A legal person who is a party to a juridical act may not invoke restrictions upon the power of representation of the persons acting for it if the restrictions did not exist under the law of the country in which the other party was domiciled when the act was formed in that country, unless the other party was or should have been aware of the restrictions by virtue of his position with or relationship to the party invoking them.

Marriage is governed with respect to its essential validity by the law applicable to the status of each of the intended spouses. With respect to its formal validity, it is governed by the law of the place of its solemnization or by the law of the country of domicile or of nationality of one of the spouses.

The effects of marriage, particularly, those which are binding on all spouses regardless of their matrimonial regime, are subject to the law of the domicile of the spouses. Where the spouses are domiciled in different countries, the applicable law is the law of their common residence or, failing that, the law of their last common residence or, failing that, the law of the place of solemnization of the marriage.

Separation from bed and board is governed by the law of the domicile of the spouses. Where the spouses are domiciled in different countries, the applicable law is the law of their common residence or, failing that, the law of their last common residence or, failing that, the law of the court seised of the case. The effects of separation from bed and board are subject to the law governing the separation.

Filiation is established in accordance with the law of the domicile or nationality of the child or of one of his parents, at the time of the child's birth, whichever is more beneficial to the child. The effects of filiation are subject to the law of the domicile of the child.

The rules respecting consent to the adoption and the eligibility of the child for adoption are those provided by the law of his domicile. The effects of adoption are subject to the law of the domicile of the adopter.

Custody of the child is governed by the law of his domicile.

The obligation of support is governed by the law of the domicile of the creditor. However, where the creditor cannot obtain support from the debtor under that law, the applicable law is that of the domicile of the debtor.

No claim of support of a collateral relation or a person connected by marriage or a civil union is admissible if, under the law of his domicile, there is no obligation for the debtor to provide support to the plaintiff.

The obligation of support between spouses who are divorced or separated from bed and board, between spouses whose civil union is dissolved or spouses whose marriage or union has been declared null is governed by the law applicable to the divorce, separation from bed and board, dissolution of the civil union or annulment of the marriage or civil union.

3109. The form of a juridical act is governed by the law of the place where it was made.

A juridical act is nevertheless valid if it is made in the form prescribed by the law applicable to the content of the act, by the law of the place where the property which is the object of the act is situated when it is made or by the law of the domicile of one of the parties when the act is made.

A testamentary disposition may be made in the form prescribed by the law of the domicile or nationality of the testator either at the time of the disposition or at the time of his death.

3111. A juridical act, whether or not it contains any foreign element, is governed by the law expressly designated in the act or the designation of which may be inferred with certainty from the terms of the act.

A juridical act containing no foreign element remains, nevertheless, subject to the mandatory provisions of the law of the country which would apply if none were designated.

The law of a country may be expressly designated as applicable to the whole or a part only of a juridical act.

United States

California Family Code (California)

301. An unmarried male of the age of 18 years or older, and an unmarried female of the age of 18 years or older, and not otherwise disqualified, are capable of consenting to and consummating marriage.

302. An unmarried male or female under the age of 18 years is capable of consenting to and consummating marriage if each of the following documents is filed with the county clerk issuing the marriage license:

    a) The written consent of the parents of each underage person, or of one of the parents or the guardian of each underage person.
    b) A court order granting permission to the underage person to marry, obtained on the showing the court requires.

351. The marriage license shall show all of the following:

    a) The identity of the parties to the marriage.
    b) The parties' real and full names, and places of residence.

c) The parties' ages.

400. Marriage may be solemnized by any of the following who is of the age of 18 years or older:

a) A priest, minister, or rabbi of any religious denomination.
b) A judge or retired judge, commissioner of civil marriages or retired commissioner of civil marriages, commissioner or retired commissioner, or assistant commissioner of a court of record in this state.
c) A judge or magistrate who has resigned from office.
d) Any of the following judges or magistrates of the United States:

1) A justice or retired justice of the United States Supreme Court.
2) A judge or retired judge of a court of appeals, a district court, or a court created by an act of Congress the judges of which are entitled to hold office during good behavior.
3) A judge or retired judge of a bankruptcy court or a tax court.
4) A United States magistrate or retired magistrate.
5) A legislator or constitutional officer of this state or a member of Congress who represents a district within this state, while that person holds office.

422. The person solemnizing a marriage shall make, sign, and endorse upon or attach to the marriage license a statement, in the form prescribed by the State Department of Health Services, showing all of the following:

a) The fact, date (month, day, year), and place (city and county) of solemnization.
b) The names and places of residence of one or more witnesses to the ceremony.
c) The official position of the person solemnizing the marriage, or of the denomination of which that person is a priest, minister, rabbi, or member of the clergy.
d) The person solemnizing the marriage shall also type or print the person's name and address.

760. Except as provided by statute, all property real or personal, wherever situated, acquired by a married person during marriage while domiciled in this state is community property.

770.(a) Separate property of a married person includes all of the following:

1) All property owned by the person before marriage.

2) All property acquired by the person after marriage by gift, bequest, devise, or descent.
3) The rents, issues, and profits of the property described in this section.

(b) A married person may, without the consent of the person's spouse, convey the person's separate property.

1500. The property rights of husband and wife prescribed by statute may be altered by a premarital agreement or other marital property agreement.

1611. A premarital agreement shall be in writing and signed by both parties. It is enforceable without consideration. This section effectively operates as a statute of frauds, conditioning enforcement on a signed writing that embodies the material terms of the agreement.

1612. Parties to a premarital agreement may contract with respect to all of the following:

[…]

(3) The disposition of property upon separation, marital dissolution, death, or the occurrence or non-occurrence of any other event. The validity of pre-marital agreements executed before 1986 is subject to the statutes and case law in effect prior to January 1, 1986.

[…]

(6) The choice of law governing the construction of the agreement. (7) Any other matter, including their personal rights and obligations, not in violation of public policy or a statute imposing a criminal penalty.

2320. A judgment of dissolution of marriage may not be entered unless one of the parties to the marriage has been a resident of this state for six months and of the county in which the proceeding is filed for three months next preceding the filing of the petition.

Title 2A Administration of Civil and Criminal Justice (New Jersey)

2A:34–2. Causes for divorce from bond of matrimony.
2A:34–2. Divorce from the bond of matrimony may be adjudged for the following causes heretofore or hereafter arising:

a. Adultery;

b. Willful and continued desertion for the term of 12 or more months, which may be established by satisfactory proof that the parties have ceased to cohabit as man and wife;

c. Extreme cruelty, which is defined as including any physical or mental cruelty which endangers the safety or health of the plaintiff or makes it improper or unreasonable to expect the plaintiff to continue to cohabit with the defendant; provided that no complaint for divorce shall be filed until after 3 months from the date of the last act of cruelty complained of in the complaint, but this provision shall not be held to apply to any counterclaim;

d. Separation, provided that the husband and wife have lived separate and apart in different habitations for a period of at least 18 or more consecutive months and there is no reasonable prospect of reconciliation; provided, further that after the 18-month period there shall be a presumption that there is no reasonable prospect of reconciliation;

e. Voluntarily induced addiction or habituation to any narcotic drug as defined in the New Jersey Controlled Dangerous Substances Act, P.L.1970, c. 226 or habitual drunkenness for a period of 12 or more consecutive months subsequent to marriage and next preceding the filing of the complaint;

f. Institutionalization for mental illness for a period of 24 or more consecutive months subsequent to marriage and next preceding the filing of the complaint;

g. Imprisonment of the defendant for 18 or more consecutive months after marriage, provided that where the action is not commenced until after the defendant's release, the parties have not resumed cohabitation following such imprisonment;

h. Deviant sexual conduct voluntarily performed by the defendant without the consent of the plaintiff;

i. Irreconcilable differences which have caused the breakdown of the marriage for a period of six months and which make it appear that the marriage should be dissolved and that there is no reasonable prospect of reconciliation.

37:2–38 Enforcement of premarital or pre-civil union agreement; generally.

The burden of proof to set aside a premarital or pre-civil union agreement shall be upon the party alleging the agreement to be unenforceable. A premarital or pre-civil union agreement shall not be enforceable if the party seeking to set aside the agreement proves, by clear and convincing evidence, that:

a. The party executed the agreement involuntarily; or

b. The agreement was unconscionable at the time enforcement was sought; or

c. That party, before execution of the agreement:

1. Was not provided full and fair disclosure of the earnings, property and financial obligations of the other party;
2. Did not voluntarily and expressly waive, in writing, any right to disclosure of the property or financial obligations of the other party beyond the disclosure provided;
3. Did not have, or reasonably could have had, an adequate knowledge of the property or financial obligations of the other party; or
4. Did not consult with independent legal counsel and did not voluntarily and expressly waive, in writing, the opportunity to consult with independent legal counsel.

d. The issue of unconscionability of a premarital or pre-civil union agreement shall be determined by the court as a matter of law.

The 2009 Florida Statutes (Florida)

Title VI Civil Practice and Procedure

61.075 Equitable distribution of marital assets and liabilities.

(1) In a proceeding for dissolution of marriage, in addition to all other remedies available to a court to do equity between the parties, or in a proceeding for disposition of assets following a dissolution of marriage by a court which lacked jurisdiction over the absent spouse or lacked jurisdiction to dispose of the assets, the court shall set apart to each spouse that spouse's nonmarital assets and liabilities, and in distributing the marital assets and liabilities between the parties, the court must begin with the premise that the distribution should be equal, unless there is a justification for an unequal distribution based on all relevant factors, including:

a) The contribution to the marriage by each spouse, including contributions to the care and education of the children and services as homemaker.
b) The economic circumstances of the parties.
c) The duration of the marriage.
d) Any interruption of personal careers or educational opportunities of either party.
e) The contribution of one spouse to the personal career or educational opportunity of the other spouse.
f) The desirability of retaining any asset, including an interest in a business, corporation, or professional practice, intact and free from any claim or interference by the other party.
g) The contribution of each spouse to the acquisition, enhancement, and production of income or the improvement of, or the incurring of liabilities to, both the marital assets and the nonmarital assets of the parties.
h) The desirability of retaining the marital home as a residence for any dependent child of the marriage, or any other party, when it would be

equitable to do so, it is in the best interest of the child or that party, and it is financially feasible for the parties to maintain the residence until the child is emancipated or until exclusive possession is otherwise terminated by a court of competent jurisdiction. In making this determination, the court shall first determine if it would be in the best interest of the dependent child to remain in the marital home; and, if not, whether other equities would be served by giving any other party exclusive use and possession of the marital home.

i) The intentional dissipation, waste, depletion, or destruction of marital assets after the filing of the petition or within 2 years prior to the filing of the petition.

j) Any other factors necessary to do equity and justice between the parties.

(2) If the court awards a cash payment for the purpose of equitable distribution of marital assets, to be paid in full or in installments, the full amount ordered shall vest when the judgment is awarded and the award shall not terminate upon remarriage or death of either party, unless otherwise agreed to by the parties, but shall be treated as a debt owed from the obligor or the obligor's estate to the obligee or the obligee's estate, unless otherwise agreed to by the parties.

(3) In any contested dissolution action wherein a stipulation and agreement has not been entered and filed, any distribution of marital assets or marital liabilities shall be supported by factual findings in the judgment or order based on competent substantial evidence with reference to the factors enumerated in subsection (1). The distribution of all marital assets and marital liabilities, whether equal or unequal, shall include specific written findings of fact as to the following:

a) Clear identification of nonmarital assets and ownership interests;

b) Identification of marital assets, including the individual valuation of significant assets, and designation of which spouse shall be entitled to each asset;

c) Identification of the marital liabilities and designation of which spouse shall be responsible for each liability;

d) Any other findings necessary to advise the parties or the reviewing court of the trial court's rationale for the distribution of marital assets and allocation of liabilities.

(4) The judgment distributing assets shall have the effect of a duly executed instrument of conveyance, transfer, release, or acquisition which is recorded in the county where the property is located when the judgment, or a certified copy of the judgment, is recorded in the official records of the county in which the property is located.

(5) If the court finds good cause that there should be an interim partial distribution during the pendency of a dissolution action, the court may enter an interim order

that shall identify and value the marital and nonmarital assets and liabilities made the subject of the sworn motion, set apart those nonmarital assets and liabilities, and provide for a partial distribution of those marital assets and liabilities. An interim order may be entered at any time after the date the dissolution of marriage is filed and served and before the final distribution of marital and nonmarital assets and marital and nonmarital liabilities.

a) Such an interim order shall be entered only upon good cause shown and upon sworn motion establishing specific factual basis for the motion. The motion may be filed by either party and shall demonstrate good cause why the matter should not be deferred until the final hearing.

b) The court shall specifically take into account and give appropriate credit for any partial distribution of marital assets or liabilities in its final allocation of marital assets or liabilities. Further, the court shall make specific findings in any interim order under this section that any partial distribution will not cause inequity or prejudice to either party as to either party's claims for support or attorney's fees.

c) Any interim order partially distributing marital assets or liabilities as provided in this subsection shall be pursuant to and comport with the factors in subsections (1) and (3) as such factors pertain to the assets or liabilities made the subject of the sworn motion.

d) As used in this subsection, the term "good cause" means extraordinary circumstances that require an interim partial distribution.

(6) As used in this section:

a) 1. Marital assets and liabilities" include:

    a. Assets acquired and liabilities incurred during the marriage, individually by either spouse or jointly by them.

    b. The enhancement in value and appreciation of nonmarital assets resulting either from the efforts of either party during the marriage or from the contribution to or expenditure thereon of marital funds or other forms of marital assets, or both.

    c. Interspousal gifts during the marriage.

    d. All vested and nonvested benefits, rights, and funds accrued during the marriage in retirement, pension, profit-sharing, annuity, deferred compensation, and insurance plans and programs.

2. All real property held by the parties as tenants by the entireties, whether acquired prior to or during the marriage, shall be presumed to be a marital asset. If, in any case, a party makes a claim to the contrary, the burden of proof shall be on the party asserting the claim that the subject property, or some portion thereof, is nonmarital.

3. All personal property titled jointly by the parties as tenants by the entireties, whether acquired prior to or during the marriage, shall be

presumed to be a marital asset. In the event a party makes a claim to the contrary, the burden of proof shall be on the party asserting the claim that the subject property, or some portion thereof, is nonmarital.

4. The burden of proof to overcome the gift presumption shall be by clear and convincing evidence.

b) "Nonmarital assets and liabilities" include:
1. Assets acquired and liabilities incurred by either party prior to the marriage, and assets acquired and liabilities incurred in exchange for such assets and liabilities;
2. Assets acquired separately by either party by noninterspousal gift, bequest, devise, or descent, and assets acquired in exchange for such assets;
3. All income derived from nonmarital assets during the marriage unless the income was treated, used, or relied upon by the parties as a marital asset;
4. Assets and liabilities excluded from marital assets and liabilities by valid written agreement of the parties, and assets acquired and liabilities incurred in exchange for such assets and liabilities; and
5. Any liability incurred by forgery or unauthorized signature of one spouse signing the name of the other spouse. Any such liability shall be a nonmarital liability only of the party having committed the forgery or having affixed the unauthorized signature. In determining an award of attorney's fees and costs pursuant to s. 61.16, the court may consider forgery or an unauthorized signature by a party and may make a separate award for attorney's fees and costs occasioned by the forgery or unauthorized signature. This subparagraph does not apply to any forged or unauthorized signature that was subsequently ratified by the other spouse.

(7) The cut-off date for determining assets and liabilities to be identified or classified as marital assets and liabilities is the earliest of the date the parties enter into a valid separation agreement, such other date as may be expressly established by such agreement, or the date of the filing of a petition for dissolution of marriage. The date for determining value of assets and the amount of liabilities identified or classified as marital is the date or dates as the judge determines is just and equitable under the circumstances. Different assets may be valued as of different dates, as, in the judge's discretion, the circumstances require.

(8) All assets acquired and liabilities incurred by either spouse subsequent to the date of the marriage and not specifically established as nonmarital assets or liabilities are presumed to be marital assets and liabilities. Such presumption is overcome by a showing that the assets and liabilities are nonmarital assets and liabilities. The presumption is only for evidentiary purposes in the dissolution

proceeding and does not vest title. Title to disputed assets shall vest only by the judgment of a court. This section does not require the joinder of spouses in the conveyance, transfer, or hypothecation of a spouse's individual property; affect the laws of descent and distribution; or establish community property in this state.

(9) The court may provide for equitable distribution of the marital assets and liabilities without regard to alimony for either party. After the determination of an equitable distribution of the marital assets and liabilities, the court shall consider whether a judgment for alimony shall be made.

(10) To do equity between the parties, the court may, in lieu of or to supplement, facilitate, or effectuate the equitable division of marital assets and liabilities, order a monetary payment in a lump sum or in installments paid over a fixed period of time.

(11) Special equity is abolished. All claims formerly identified as special equity, and all special equity calculations, are abolished and shall be asserted either as a claim for unequal distribution of marital property and resolved by the factors set forth in subsection (1) or as a claim of enhancement in value or appreciation of nonmarital property.

Domestic Relations Law (New York)

Section 236

(...)

3. Agreement of the parties. An agreement by the parties, made before or during the marriage, shall be valid and enforceable in a matrimonial action if such agreement is in writing, subscribed by the parties, and acknowledged or proven in the manner required to entitle a deed to be recorded. Notwithstanding any other provision of law, an acknowledgment of an agreement made before marriage may be executed before any person authorized to solemnize a marriage pursuant to subdivisions one, two and three of section eleven of this chapter. Such an agreement may include
    (1) a contract to make a testamentary provision of any kind, or a waiver of any right to elect against the provisions of a will; (2) provision for the ownership, division or distribution of separate and marital property; (3) provision for the amount and duration of maintenance or other terms and conditions of the marriage relationship, subject to the provisions of section 5–311 of the general obligations law, and provided that such terms were fair and reasonable at the time of the making of the agreement and are not unconscionable at the time of entry of final judgment; and (4) provision for the custody, care, education and maintenance of any child of the parties, subject to the provisions of section two hundred forty of

this article. Nothing in this subdivision shall be deemed to affect the validity of any agreement made prior to the effective date of this subdivision.

(…)

5. Disposition of property in certain matrimonial actions.

   a) Except where the parties have provided in an agreement for the disposition of their property pursuant to subdivision three of this part, the court, in an action wherein all or part of the relief granted is divorce, or the dissolution, annulment or declaration of the nullity of a marriage, and in proceedings to obtain a distribution of marital property following a foreign judgment of divorce, shall determine the respective rights of the parties in their separate or marital property, and shall provide for the disposition thereof in the final judgment.
   b) Separate property shall remain such.
   c) Marital property shall be distributed equitably between the parties, considering the circumstances of the case and of the respective parties.
   d) In determining an equitable disposition of property under paragraph c, the court shall consider:

      (1) the income and property of each party at the time of marriage, and at the time of the commencement of the action;
      (2) the duration of the marriage and the age and health of both parties;
      (3) the need of a custodial parent to occupy or own the marital residence and to use or own its household effects;
      (4) the loss of inheritance and pension rights upon dissolution of the marriage as of the date of dissolution;
      (5) the loss of health insurance benefits upon dissolution of the marriage;
      (6) any award of maintenance under subdivision six of this part;
      (7) any equitable claim to, interest in, or direct or indirect contribution made to the acquisition of such marital property by the party not having title, including joint efforts or expenditures and contributions and services as a spouse, parent, wage earner and homemaker, and to the career or career potential of the other party;
      (8) the liquid or non-liquid character of all marital property;
      (9) the probable future financial circumstances of each party;
      (10) the impossibility or difficulty of evaluating any component asset or any interest in a business, corporation or profession, and the economic desirability of retaining such asset or interest intact and free from any claim or interference by the other party;
      (11) the tax consequences to each party;
      (12) the wasteful dissipation of assets by either spouse;

(13) any transfer or encumbrance made in contemplation of a matrimonial action without fair consideration;

(14) any other factor which the court shall expressly find to be just and proper.

e) In any action in which the court shall determine that an equitable distribution is appropriate but would be impractical or burdensome or where the distribution of an interest in a business, corporation or profession would be contrary to law, the court in lieu of such equitable distribution shall make a distributive award in order to achieve equity between the parties. The court in its discretion, also may make a distributive award to supplement, facilitate or effectuate a distribution of marital property.

f) In addition to the disposition of property as set forth above, the court may make such order regarding the use and occupancy of the marital home and its household effects as provided in section two hundred thirty-four of this chapter, without regard to the form of ownership of such property.

g) In any decision made pursuant to this subdivision, the court shall set forth the factors it considered and the reasons for its decision and such may not be waived by either party or counsel.

h) In any decision made pursuant to this subdivision the court shall, where appropriate, consider the effect of a barrier to remarriage, as defined in subdivision six of section two hundred fifty-three of this article, on the factors enumerated in paragraph d of this subdivision.

Section 170

§ 170. Action for divorce. An action for divorce may be maintained by a husband or wife to procure a judgment divorcing the parties and dissolving the marriage on any of the following grounds:

(1) The cruel and inhuman treatment of the plaintiff by the defendant such that the conduct of the defendant so endangers the physical or mental well being of the plaintiff as renders it unsafe or improper for the plaintiff to cohabit with the defendant.

(2) The abandonment of the plaintiff by the defendant for a period of one or more years.

(3) The confinement of the defendant in prison for a period of three or more consecutive years after the marriage of plaintiff and defendant.

(4) The commission of an act of adultery, provided that adultery for the purposes of articles ten, eleven, and eleven-A of this chapter, is hereby defined as the commission of an act of sexual intercourse, oral sexual conduct or anal sexual

conduct, voluntarily performed by the defendant, with a person other than the plaintiff after the marriage of plaintiff and defendant. Oral sexual conduct and anal sexual conduct include, but are not limited to, sexual conduct as defined in subdivision two of section 130.00 and subdivision three of section 130.20 of the penal law.

(5) The husband and wife have lived apart pursuant to a decree or judgment of separation for a period of one or more years after the granting of such decree or judgment, and satisfactory proof has been submitted by the plaintiff that he or she has substantially performed all the terms and conditions of such decree or judgment.

(6) The husband and wife have lived separate and apart pursuant to a written agreement of separation, subscribed by the parties thereto and acknowledged or proved in the form required to entitle a deed to be recorded, for a period of one or more years after the execution of such agreement and satisfactory proof has been submitted by the plaintiff that he or she has substantially performed all the terms and conditions of such agreement. Such agreement shall be filed in the office of the clerk of the county wherein either party resides. In lieu of filing such agreement, either party to such agreement may file a memorandum of such agreement, which memorandum shall be similarly subscribed and acknowledged or proved as was the agreement of separation and shall contain the following information: (a) the names and addresses of each of the parties, (b) the date of marriage of the parties, (c) the date of the agreement of separation and (d) the date of this subscription and acknowledgment or proof of such agreement of separation.

France

Constitution du 4 octobre 1958

Article 1
La France est une République indivisible, laïque, démocratique et sociale. Elle assure l'égalité devant la loi de tous les citoyens sans distinction d'origine, de race ou de religion. Elle respecte toutes les croyances.

Loi du 9 décembre 1905, Loi concernant la séparation des Églises et de l'État

Article 2
La République ne reconnaît, ne salarie ni ne subventionne aucun culte. En conséquence, à partir du 1er janvier qui suivra la promulgation de la présente loi, seront supprimées des budgets de l'État, des départements et des communes, toutes dépenses relatives à l'exercice des cultes.

Pourront toutefois être inscrites auxdits budgets les dépenses relatives à des services d'aumônerie et destinées à assurer le libre exercice des cultes dans les établissements publics tels que lycées, collèges, écoles, hospices, asiles et prisons.

Les établissements publics du culte sont supprimés, sous réserve des dispositions énoncées à l'article 3.

Code civil français

Article 147
On ne peut contracter un second mariage avant la dissolution du premier.

Article 184
Tout mariage contracté en contravention aux dispositions contenues aux articles 144, 146, 146–1, 147, 161, 162 et 163, peut être attaqué soit par les époux eux-mêmes, soit par tous ceux qui y ont intérêt, soit par le ministère public.

Article 1387
La loi ne régit l'association conjugale quant aux biens, qu'à défaut de conventions spéciales, que les époux peuvent faire comme ils le jugent à propos, pourvu qu'elles ne soient pas contraires aux bonnes moeurs ni aux dispositions qui suivent.

Article 1400
La communauté, qui s'établit à défaut de contrat ou par la simple déclaration qu'on se marie sous le régime de la communauté, est soumise aux règles expliquées dans les trois sections qui suivent.

Article 1401
La communauté se compose activement des acquêts faits par les époux ensemble ou séparément durant le mariage, et provenant tant de leur industrie personnelle que des économies faites sur les fruits et revenus de leurs biens propres.

Article 1497
Les époux peuvent, dans leur contrat de mariage, modifier la communauté légale par toute espèce de conventions non contraires aux articles 1387, 1388 et 1389. Ils peuvent, notamment, convenir: 1° Que la communauté comprendra les meubles et les acquêts; 2° Qu'il sera dérogé aux règles concernant l'administration; 3° Que l'un des époux aura la faculté de prélever certains biens moyennant indemnité; 4° Que l'un des époux aura un préciput; 5° Que les époux auront des parts inégales; 6° Qu'il y aura entre eux communauté universelle.

Les règles de la communauté légale restent applicables en tous les points qui n'ont pas fait l'objet de la convention des parties.

Article 1536

Lorsque les époux ont stipulé dans leur contrat de mariage qu'ils seraient séparés de biens, chacun d'eux conserve l'administration, la jouissance et la libre disposition de ses biens personnels. Chacun d'eux reste seul tenu des dettes nées en sa personne avant ou pendant le mariage, hors le cas de l'article 220.

Article 1569

Quand les époux ont déclaré se marier sous le régime de la participation aux acquêts, chacun d'eux conserve l'administration, la jouissance et la libre disposition de ses biens personnels, sans distinguer entre ceux qui lui appartenaient au jour du mariage ou lui sont advenus depuis par succession ou libéralité et ceux qu'il a acquis pendant le mariage à titre onéreux. Pendant la durée du mariage, ce régime fonctionne comme si les époux étaient mariés sous le régime de la séparation de biens. A la dissolution du régime, chacun des époux a le droit de participer pour moitié en valeur aux acquêts nets constatés dans le patrimoine de l'autre, et mesurés par la double estimation du patrimoine originaire et du patrimoine final. Le droit de participer aux acquêts est incessible tant que le régime matrimonial n'est pas dissous. Si la dissolution survient par la mort d'un époux, ses héritiers ont, sur les acquêts nets faits par l'autre, les mêmes droits que leur auteur.

The Principles and Legal Foundation Governing the Relations between Muslim Religious Practice and Public Authorities

I) Religious associations: Muslims are invited to "set up a single national body to represent the Muslim religion, in the same way as other religions present in France".

II) Mosques: mayors are invited to seek solutions comparable, for example, with those used for the Chantiers du Cardinal association, or to make municipal premises available to Muslim associations as they do to political parties, trade unions and other associations.

III) As regards ministers of religion, this is said to be a question of internal organization of the religion in which the State cannot intervene. However, the text states: "unless good grounds to the contrary exist, they shall be recruited and paid in future by the associations who employ them. It would be desirable for a majority of them to hold French nationality and to have a cultural and religious level appropriate to their duties".

IV) Chaplains must be appointed by "the union of Muslim cultural associations".

V) Private Muslim educational establishments are subject to the same rules as other private educational establishments.

VI) As regards dress codes, the text states that "signs of membership of a religion shall not be displayed, under the circumstances stated in EC case law". As regards dietary rules, the authorities may offer special meals (the text only refers to a possibility; the courts may be required to rule in future on whether this is optional or compulsory). Ritual slaughter must comply with "the conditions imposed by legislation and by animal protection, public health and environmental protection regulations". Here again, the text implies the desire to respect Muslims' dietary rules.

VII) In the case of places of burial, the text states that Muslim plots "have been allowed", which suggests that their legality may be disputable. In the event of doubt as to whether the deceased was a "Muslim", it is up to the religious authority, not the mayor, to give a ruling.

VIII) During religious festivals, "public employees may be granted leave of absence, subject to the exigencies of the service, to take part in the ceremonies celebrated on the occasion of the main festivals of their religion" This provision grants a long-standing claim by the Muslim community. (Basdevant-Gaudemet 1996: 66)

Germany

German Civil Code (BGB)

1363. Community of accrued gains

(1) The spouses live under the property regime of community of accrued gains if they do not by marriage contract agree otherwise.

(2) The property of the husband and the property of the wife do not become the common property of the spouses; the same applies to property that one spouse acquires after marriage. The accrued gains that the spouses acquire in the marriage, however, are equalised if the community of accrued gains ends.

1373. Accrued gains
Accrued gains means the amount by which the final assets of a spouse exceed the initial assets.

1374. Initial assets

(1) Initial assets means the assets that belong to a spouse at the beginning of the property regime after the deduction of the liabilities; the liabilities may be deducted only to the amount of the assets.

(2) Assets which a spouse acquires after the beginning of the property regime as a result of death or with regard to a future right of succession, as gifts or as advancements, are added to the initial assets after the deduction of the liabilities, to the extent that in the circumstances they are not to be seen as income.

1375. Final assets

(1) Final assets means the assets that belong to one spouse at the end of the property regime after the deduction of the liabilities. The liabilities are also deducted, if third parties may be claimed on under section 1390, to the extent that they exceed the amount of the assets.

(2) The final assets of a spouse are increased by the amount by which these assets are reduced as a result of the fact that a spouse, after the beginning of the property regime,

1. made gratuitous dispositions by which he was not fulfilling a moral duty or showing regard for decency,
2. squandered property, or
3. performed acts with the intention of disadvantaging the other spouse.

(3) The amount by which the assets are reduced is not added to the final assets if the reduction was effected at least ten years before the end of the property regime or if the other spouse was in agreement with the gratuitous disposition or the squandering.

1378. Equalisation claim

(1) If the accrued gains of one spouse exceed the accrued gains of the other spouse, the half of the surplus is due to the other spouse as an equalisation claim.
(2) The amount of the equalisation claim is limited by the value of the assets that remain, after deduction of the liabilities, at the end of the property regime.

(3) The equalisation claim arises on the ending of the property regime and from this date on it is inheritable and assignable. An agreement on the equalisation of the accrued gains that the spouses enter into, during proceedings instituted to dissolve the marriage, for the eventuality of the dissolution of the marriage, must be notarially recorded; section 127a also applies to an agreement that is recorded in proceedings on family matters before the court hearing the case. Apart from this, neither spouse may before the end of the property regime bind himself to dispose of the equalisation claim.

(4) The equalisation claim is statute-barred in three years; the period begins on the date on which the spouse discovers that the property regime has ended. However, the claim is statute-barred at the latest thirty years after the property regime ends. If the property regime ends as the result of the death of a spouse, moreover, the provisions that govern the limitation of a claim to a compulsory share apply.

1380. Set-off of advancements

(1) Against the equalisation claim of a spouse is set off what he is given by the other spouse by inter vivos legal transaction with the provision that it is to be set off against the equalisation claim. In case of doubt it is to be assumed that dispositions should be set-off if their value exceeds the value of occasional gifts which are customary in keeping with the standard of living of the spouses.

(2) When the equalisation claim is calculated, the value of the disposition is added to the accrued gains of the spouse who made the disposition. The value is determined according to the date of the disposition.

1381. Refusal of satisfaction for gross inequity

(1) The debtor may refuse to satisfy the equalisation claim to the extent that the equalisation of accrued gains in the circumstances of the case would be grossly inequitable.

(2) Gross inequity may in particular be given if the spouse who made the smaller amount of accrued gains for a long period culpably failed to discharge his financial duties which arise from the marital relationship.

Bibliography

Abdal-Rahim, A.R. 1996. The family and gender laws in Egypt during the Ottoman period, in El Azhary Sonbol, A. (ed.) *Women, the Family, and Divorce Laws in Islamic History*, Syracuse, NY: Syracuse University Press, 96–111.

Abu-Odeh, L. 1992. Post-colonial feminism and the veil: Considering the differences, *New England Law Review*, 26(4), 1527–37.

— 1997. Comparatively speaking: the "honor" of the "East" and the "passion" of the "West." *Utah Law Review*, 1997(2), 287–307.

— 2004. Modernizing Muslim family law: The case of Egypt, *Vanderbilt Journal of Transnational Law*, 37(4), 1043–146.

Abu-Sahlieh, S.A.A. and Bonomi, A. (eds) 1999. *Le Droit musulman de la famille et des successions à l'épreuve des ordres juridiques occidentaux*, Zürich: Schulthess.

Afifi, M. 1996. Reflections on the personal laws of Egyptian Copts, in El Azhary Sonbol, A. (ed.) *Women, the Family and Divorce Laws in Islamic History*, Syracuse, NY: Syracuse University Press, 202–18.

Ahmed, L. 1992. *Women and Gender in Islam*, New Haven and London: Yale University Press.

al-Ashmawi, M.S. 1994. *Islam and the Political Order*, Washington, DC: The Council for Research in Values and Philosophy.

al-Hibri, A.Y. 1997. Islam, law and custom: Redefining Muslim women's rights, *American University Journal of International Law and Policy*, 12(1), 1–44.

— 1999. Islamic and American constitutional law: Borrowing possibilities or a history of borrowing? *University of Pennsylvania Journal of Constitutional Law*, 1(3), 492–527.

— 2000. *Muslim Marriage Contract in American Courts*. Available at: http://www.minaret.org/azizah.htm (accessed 26 October 2009).

— 2005. The nature of Islamic marriage: Sacramental, covenantal, or contractual?, in Witte, Jr., J. and Ellison, E. (eds) *Covenant Marriage in Comparative Perspective*, Grand Rapids, Mich.: W.B. Eerdmans Publishing, 182–216.

al-Hilli, M. 1985. *Sharayi' al-Islam*, Vol. 2, compiled by M.T. Danish-Pashuh, translated by A.A. Yazdi, Tehran: Tehran University Press.

al-Sayyid, S. 1969. *Fiqh al-sunnah*, Beirut: Dār al-Kitāb al-Arabī.

Al-Sharmani, M. 2007. *Recent Reforms in Personal Status Laws and Women's Empowerment: Family Courts in Egypt (American Anthropological Association Annual Meeting Abstracts)*, Berkeley: University of California Press.

Ali, A. 2003. *Islam Rethought: Gender, Sexuality, and Marriage in Islam*. Available at: http://cyber_bangla0.tripod.com/aa/Islam_Rethought.html (accessed 3 November 2009).

Althusser, L. 1971. *Lenin and Philosophy, and Other Essays*, translated by Ben Brewster, London: New Left Books.

Amstutz, M. 2005. In-between worlds: Marleasing and the emergence of interlegality in legal reasoning. *European Law Journal*, 11(6), 766–84.

An-Na'im, A.A. 1990. *Toward an Islamic Reformation: Civil Liberties, Human Rights, and International Law*, Syracuse, N.Y.: Syracuse University Press.

— 2002. *Islamic Family Law in a Changing World: A Global Resource Book*, London and New York: Zed Books.

Arenson, R.J. and Shapiro, I. 1996. Democratic autonomy and religious freedom: a critique of *Wisconsin v. Yoder*, in Shapiro, I. and Hardin, R. (eds) *Political Order*, New York: New York University Press, 365–411.

Badran, Margot. 1995. *Feminists, Islam, and Nation: Gender and the Making of Modern Egypt*, Princeton: Princeton University Press.

Baillie, N.B.E. 1965. *A Digest of Moohammdan Law: Compiled and Translated from Authorities in the Original Arabic*, with an introduction and explanatory notes, Lahore: Premier Book House.

Bader, V. 2009. Legal pluralism and differentiated morality: Shari'a in Ontario?, in Grillo, R. et al. (eds) *Legal Practice and Cultural Diversity*, Surrey, England: Ashgate, 49–72.

Bakht, N. 2004. Family arbitration using sharia law: Examining Ontario's *Arbitration Act* and its impact on women, *Muslim World Journal of Human Rights*, 1(1). Available at: http://www.bepress.com.proxy.bib.uottawa.ca/cgi/viewcontent.cgi?article=1022&context=mwjhr (accessed 3 November 2009).

Bala, N. and Chapman, K. 2002. Separation agreements and contract law: From the trilogy to *Miglin*, in *Child & Spousal Support Revisited*, Toronto: Law Society of Upper Canada, 1–26.

Balkati, S. 1995. *L'Islam de France et laïcité*, Paris: Ligue de l'Enseignement.

Barlas, A. 2002. *"Believing Women" in Islam: Unreading Patriarchal Interpretations of the Qur'an*, 1st edn, Austin: University of Texas Press.

Barry, B. 1999. Statism and nationalism: A cosmopolitan critique, in Shapiro, I. and Brilmayer, L. (eds) *Global Justice*, New York: New York University Press, 12–66.

Basdevant-Gaudemet, B. 1996. Le statut juridique de l'Islam en France, *Revue du Droit Public*, 2, 355–85.

— 2004. Islam in France, in Aluffi Beck-Peccoz, R. and Zincone, G. (eds) *The Legal Treatment of Islamic Minorities in Europe*, Leuven: Peeters, 59–82.

Bencheikh, S. 1998. *Marianne et le Prophète: L'Islam dans la France laïque*, Paris: Grasset.

Benda-Beckmann, F. von. 2002. Who's afraid of legal pluralism? *Journal of Legal Pluralism and Unofficial Law*, 47, 37–82.

Bentham, J. 1970 (1789). *An Introduction to the Principles of Morals and Legislation* (J.H. Burns and H.L.A. Hart (eds)), Oxford: Oxford University Press.

Berman, P.S. 2002. The Globalization of Jurisdiction, *University of Pennsylvania Law Review*, 151(2), 311–546.

— 2005a. Towards a cosmopolitan vision of conflict of laws: Redefining governmental interests in a global era, *University of Pennsylvania Law Review*, 153(6), 1819–82.

— 2005b. From international law to law and globalization, *Columbia Journal of Transnational Law*, 43(2), 485–556.

Bhabha, H.K. 1994. *The Location of Culture*, London and New York: Routledge.

Bhutto, B. 1998. Politics and the Muslim woman, in Kurzman, C. (ed.) *Liberal Islam: A Sourcebook*, Oxford: Oxford University Press, 107–111.

Bix, B. 1998. Bargining in the shadow of love: The enforcement of premarital agreements and how we think about marriage, *William and Mary Law Review*, 40(1), 145–208.

Blanchard, P. et al. 2003. *Le Paris arabe: deux siècles de présence des Orientaux et des Maghrébins*, Paris: La Découverte.

Bosworth, C.E. (ed.) 1991. *The Encyclopaedia of Islam*, new edn, Leiden: Brill.

Boyd, M. 2004. Executive Summary of *Dispute Resolution in Family Law: Protecting Choice, Promoting Inclusion*, Toronto: Government of Ontario. Available at: http://www.attorneygeneral.jus.gov.on.ca/english/about/pubs/boyd/ (accessed 19 October 2009).

Brand, L.A. 1998. *Women, the State and Political Liberalization: Middle Eastern and North African Experiences*, New York: Columbia University Press.

Brierley, J.E.C. 1992. The renewal of Quebec's distinct legal culture: The new Civil Code of Quebec, *University of Toronto Law Journal*, 42(4), 484–503.

Brod, G.F. 1994. Premarital agreements and gender justice, *Yale Journal of Law and Feminism*, 6(2), 229–96.

Bromley, P.M. 1957. *Family Law*, London: Butterworths & Co.

Brown, D. 2004. *A New Introduction to Islam*, Malden, Mass. and Oxford: Blackwell Publishing.

Brubaker, R. 1992. *Citizenship and Nationhood in France and Germany*, Cambridge, Mass. and London: Harvard University Press.

Butler, J. 1990. *Gender Trouble: Feminism and the Subversion of Identity*, London: Routledge.

Carter, S.L. 1991. *Reflections of an Affirmative Action Baby*, New York: Basic Books.

Charrad, M.M. 2001. *States and Women's Rights: The Making of Postcolonial Tunisia, Algeria, and Morocco*, Berkeley: University of California Press.

Chaudhry, Z. 2004. What is our share? A look at women's inheritance in Islamic law, *Azizah Magazine*, 3(3), 14–19.

Cohen, F.S. 1935. Transcendental nonsense and the functional approach, *Columbia Law Review*, 35(6), 809–49.

Cohen, L. 1987. Marriage, divorce and quasi rents; or, I give him the best years of my life, *Journal of Legal Studies*, 16(2), 267–304.

Coleman, D.L. 1996. Individualizing justice through multiculturalism: The liberals' dilemma, *Columbia Law Review*, 96(5), 1093–167.

Cook, W.W. 1927. Scientific method and the law, *American Bar Association Journal*, 13(6), 303–9.

Cossman, B. 1997. Returning the gaze? Comparative law, feminist legal studies and the postcolonial project, *Utah Law Review*, 1997(2), 525–44.

Dane, P. 1980. Religious exemptions under the free exercise clause: A model of competing authorities, *Yale Law Journal*, 90, 365–76.

de la Chapelle, B. 1997. Le phénomène polygame en France, *Revue Française des Affaires Sociales*, 51(2), 145–58.

de Sousa Santos, B. 1987. Law: a map of misreading—toward a postmodern conception of law, *Journal of Law and Society*, 14(3), 279–302.

— 2002. *Toward a New Legal Common Sense: Law, Globalization and Emancipation*, 2nd edn, London: Butterworths LexisNexis.

Déprez, J. 1988. Droit international privé et conflit de civilisations: Aspects méthodologiques. Les relations entre systèmes d'Europe occidentale et systèmes islamiques en matière de statut personnel, *Recueil des Cours de l'Académie de droit international de La Haye*, 1988(4), 200–17.

— 1996. Statut personnel et pratiques familiales des étrangers musulmans en France: aspects de droit international privé, in Foblets, M.-C. (ed.) *Familles – Islam – Europe: Le Droit Confronté au Changement*, Paris: Karthala, 57–123.

Doi, A.R.I. 1984. *Shari'ah: The Islamic Law*, London: Ta Ha Publishers.

Dubler, A.R. 2003. In the shadow of marriage: Single women and the legal construction of the family and the state. *Yale Law Journal*, 112(7), 1641–716.

Dworkin, R. 1984. Liberalism, in Sandel, M. (ed.) *Liberalism and its Critics*, New York: New York University Press, 60–79.

El Alami, D.S. and Hinchcliffe, D. 1996. *Islamic Marriage and Divorce Laws of the Arab World*, London: Kluwer Law International.

El-Husseini, R. 1999. Le droit international privé français et la répudiation islamique, *Revue Critique de Droit International Privé*, 88(3), 427–68.

Ellison, R. 1952. *The Invisible Man*, New York: Random House.

Elwan, O. 1999. Le droit interreligieux égyptien auprès des tribunaux allemands, in von Bar, C. (ed.) *Islamic Law and its Reception by the Courts in the West: Congress from 23 to 24 October 1998 in Osnabrück*, Köln: Heymann, 53–81.

Endut, N. 2000. Malaysia's plural legal system and its impact on women, in Mohamad, M. (ed.) *Muslim Women and Access to Justice: Historical, Legal and Social Experience in Malaysia*, Peneng, Malaysia: Women's Crisis Centre, 19–36.

Esposito, J.L. and DeLong-Bas, N. 2001. *Women in Muslim Family Law*, 2nd edn, Syracuse, NY: Syracuse University Press.

Ewick, P. and Silbey, S. 1998. *The Common Place of Law: Stories from Everyday Life*, Chicago: University of Chicago Press.

Fineman, M. 1983. Implementing equality: Ideology, contradiction and social change: A study of rhetoric and results in the regulation of the consequences of divorce, *Wisconsin Law Review*, 1983(4), 789–886.

Finley, L.M. 1986. Transcending equality theory: A way out of the maternity and the workplace debate, *Columbia Law Review*, 86(6), 1118–82.

Fischer-Lescano, A. and Teubner, G. 2004. Regime-collisions: The vain search for legal unity in the fragmentation of global law, translated by M. Everson, *Michigan Journal of International Law*, 25, 999–1046.

F.K. 2000. Les familles polygames en France mises au pied du mur. –Eclairage. *SDA-Service de Base Français*, 12 January.

Foley, R. 2004. Muslim women's challenges to Islamic law: The case of Malaysia, *International Feminist Journal of Politics*, 6(1), 53–84.

Fournier, P. 2006. In the (Canadian) shadow of Islamic law: Translating mahr as a bargaining endowment, *Osgoode Hall Law Journal*, 44(4), 649–77.

— 2007. La femme musulmane au Canada: Profane ou sacrée? *Canadian Journal of Women and the Law*, 19(2), 227–42.

— 2009. Transit and translation: Islamic legal transplants in North America and Western Europe, *The Journal of Comparative Law*, 4(1), 1–38.

— 2010. Flirting with God in Western secular courts: *Mahr* in the West, *The International Journal of Law, Policy and the Family*, 24(1), 1–28.

Fraser, N. 1997. From redistribution to recognition?: Dilemmas of justice in a "postsocialist" age, in Fraser, F. (ed.) *Justice Interruptus: Critical Reflections on the "Postsocialist" Condition*, London: Routledge, 11–39.

Freeze, C. and Howlett, K. 2005. McGuinty government rules out use of sharia law, *The Globe and Mail*, 12 September, A1.

Fuller, L.L. 1958. Positivism and fidelity to law, *Harvard Law Review*, 71, 630–72.

Fuller, L.L. and Perdue, W.R., Jr. 1936. The reliance interest in contract damages: 2, *Yale Law Journal*, 46, 373–420.

Fyzee, A.A.A. 1974. *Outlines of Muhammadan Law*, 4th edn, Delhi: Oxford University Press.

Galanter, M. 1974. Why the "haves" come out ahead: Speculations on the limits of legal change, *Law and Society Review*, 9(1), 95–160.

Gaudreault-DesBiens, J.-F. 2005. The limits of private justice? The problems of the state recognition of arbitral awards in family and personal status disputes in Ontario, *World Arbitration and Mediation Reporter*, 16(1), 18–31.

Gény, F. 1919. *Méthode d'Interprétation et Sources en Droit Privé Positif: Essai Critique*, 2nd edn, Paris: F. Pichon et Durand-Auzias.

Gillette-Frénoy, I. 1993a. *La Polygamie en France et le Rôle des Femmes*, Paris: Edition G.A.M.S.

— 1993b. La polygamie en France pratiquée par les immigrants d'Afrique Subsaharienne, et le rôle des femmes, *L'Ethnographie*, 89(2), 131–69.

Goldman, D.B. 2003. Historical aspects of globalization and law, in Dauvergne, C. (ed.) *Jurisprudence for an Interconnected Globe*, Burlington, VT: Ashgate, 43–70.

Goody, J. 1990. *The Oriental, the Ancient and the Primitive: Systems of Marriage and the Family in the Pre-industrial Societies of Eurasia*, Cambridge and New York: Cambridge University Press.

Greenberg-Kobrin, M. 1999. Civil Enforceability of Religious Prenuptial Agreements, 32 *Colum, J.L. & Soc. Prob.* 359, 359 & n. 117.

Grey, T.C. 1989. Holmes and legal pragmatism, *Stanford Law Review*, 41(X), 787–870.

Griffiths, J. 1986. What is legal pluralism? *Journal of Legal Pluralism and Unofficial Law*, 24, 1–56.

Guggenheimer, L. 1996. A modest proposal: The feminomics of drafting premarital agreements, *Women's Rights Law Reporter*, 17(2), 147–208.

Gutmann, A. 1993. The challenge of multiculturalism in political ethics, *Philosophy and Public Affairs*, 22(3), 171–206.

Haddad, Y.Y. 1988. Islam and gender: Dilemmas in the changing Arab world, in Haddad, Y.Y. and Esposito, J. (eds) *Islam, Gender and Social Change*, Oxford: Oxford University Press, 3–29.

Hajjar, L. 2004. Religion, state power, and domestic violence in Muslim societies: A framework for comparative analysis, *Law and Social Inquiry*, 29(1), 1.

Hale, R.L. 1923. Coercion and distribution in a supposedly non-coercive state, *Political Science Quarterly*, 38(3), 470–94.

— 1943. Bargaining, duress, and economic liberty, *Columbia Law Review*, 43, 603–42.

Hallaq, W.B. 1997. *A History of Islamic Legal Theories: An Introduction to Sunni Usul al-fiqh*, Cambridge: Cambridge University Press.

Halley, J. 2006. *Split Decisions: How and Why to Take a Break from Feminism*, Princeton, NJ: Princeton University Press.

Hart, H.L.A. 1958. Positivism and the separation of law and morals, *Harvard Law Review*, 71, 593–629.

Hassan, S.Z.S. and Cederroth, S. 1997. *Managing Marital Disputes in Malaysia: Islamic Mediators and Conflict Resolution in the Syariah Courts*, Richmond, Surrey: Curzon.

Hervieu-Léger, D. 1998. The past in the present: Redefining laïcité in multicultural France, in Berger, P. (ed.) *The Limits of Social Cohesion*, London: Westview Press, 38–83.

Hodkinson, K. 1984. *Muslim Family Law: A Source Book*, London: Canberra.

Holmes, O.W. 1920. *Collected Legal Papers*, New York: Harcourt, Brace and Howe.

— 1993. The path of the law (1897), in Fisher, W.W. III et al. (eds) *American Legal Realism*, New York: Oxford University Press, 15–24.

Hoodfar, H. 1996. Circumventing legal limitation: Mahr and marriage negotiation in Egyptian low-income communities, *Shifting Boundaries in Marriage and*

Divorce in Muslim Communities, Women Living Under Muslim Laws, Special dossier no. 1 (1996), 121–42.

— 1997. *Between Marriage and the Market: Intimate Politics and Survival in Cairo*, Berkeley: University of California Press.

Hussain, J. 2004. *Islam: Its Law and Society*, 2nd edn, Sydney: Federation Press.

Johnson, B. 1981. *The Critical Difference: Essays in the Contemporary Rhetoric of Reading*, Baltimore: Johns Hopkins University Press.

Jolls, C. 2000. Accommodation mandates, *Stanford Law Review*, 53(2), 223–306.

Jones-Pauly, C. 2008. Marriage contracts of Muslims in the diaspora: Problems in the recognition of mahr contracts in German law, in Quraishi, A. and Vogel, F.E. (eds) *The Islamic Marriage Contract: Case Studies in Islamic Family Law*, Cambridge, Mass.: Islamic Legal Studies Program, Harvard Law School, 299–330.

— Unpublished. Marriage contracts of Muslims in the diaspora: Problems in the recognition of mahr contracts in German law, unpublished draft manuscript.

Jonker, G. 2000. Berlin between integration and segregation, *Cultural Dynamics*, 12(3), 311–29.

Joppke, C. and Morawska, E. 2003. Integrating immigrants in liberal nation-states: Policies and practices, in Joppke, C. and Morawska, E. (eds) *Toward Assimilation and Citizenship: Immigrants in Liberal Nation-States*, London: Palgrave Macmillan, 1–36.

Jutras, D. 2001. The legal dimensions of everyday life, *Canadian Journal of Law and Society*, 16(1), 45–66.

Kahan, L.S. 1984. Note, Jewish Divorce and Secular Courts: The Promise of Avitzur, 73 *Geo. L.J.* 193, 216–19.

Kahn, P. 1999. *The Cultural Study of Law*, Chicago: University of Chicago Press.

Kalscheur, G.A. 2004. John Paul II, John Courtney Murray, and the relationship between civil law and moral law: A constructive proposal for contemporary American pluralism, *Journal of Catholic Social Thought*, 1(2), 231–75.

Kamali, M.H. 1991. *Principles of Islamic Jurisprudence*, revised edn, Cambridge: Islamic Texts Society.

Kastoryano, R. 1990. Muslim migrants in France and Germany: Law and policy in family and group identity, in Mallat, C. and Connors, J. (eds) *Islamic Family Law*, London: Graham & Trotman, 167–80.

Kelek, N. c2005. *Die fremde Braut: ein Bericht aus dem Inneren des türkischen Lebens Deutschland*, Köln: Kiepenheuer & Witsch.

Kennedy, D. 1976. Form and substance in private law adjudication, *Harvard Law Review*, 89(8), 1685–778.

— 1982. Distributive and paternalist motives in contract and tort law, with special reference to compulsory terms and unequal bargaining power, *Maryland Law Review*, 41(4), 563–658.

— 1986. Toward a critical phenomenology of judging, *Journal of Legal Education*, 36(4), 518–62.

— 1992. Sexual abuse, sexy dressing, and the eroticization of domination, *New England Law Review*, 26(4), 1309–94.

— 1997. *A Critique of Adjudication: Fin de Siècle*, Cambridge, Mass.: Harvard University Press.

— 2000. From the will theory to the principle of private autonomy: Lon Fuller's consideration and form, 100 *Columbia L. Rev.* 94–175.

— 2003. Two globalizations of law and legal thought: 1850–1869, *Suffolk University Law Review*, 36(3), 631–80.

— 2005. A left phenomenological critique of the Hart/Kelsen theory of legal interpretation, in Cáceres, E. et al. (eds) *Problemas Contemporaneos de la Filosofia Del Derecho*, México: Universidad Nacional Autónoma de México, 371–83.

Klassen, W. 1991. Religion and the nation: An ambiguous alliance, *University of New Brunswick Law Journal*, 40(1), 87–99.

Kleinhans, M.-M. and Macdonald, R.A. 1997. What is a critical legal pluralism? *Canadian Journal of Law and Society*, 12(2), 25–46.

Kymlicka, W. 1995. *Multicultural Citizenship: A Liberal Theory of Minority Rights*, Oxford: Oxford University Press.

Labidi, L. 2001. From sexual submission to voluntary commitment: The transformation of family ties in contemporary Tunisia, in Hopkins, N.S. (ed.) *The New Arab Family* (Cairo Papers in Social Science, vol. 24), 117–39.

Layish, A. 1978. Contributions of the modernists to the secularization of Islamic law, *Middle Eastern Studies*, 14(3), 263–77.

Lefebvre, H. 1991. *The Production of Space*, translated by D. Nicholson-Smith, Oxford: Blackwell.

Legrand, P. 1996. How to compare now? *Legal Studies*, 16(2), 232–42.

— 1997. The impossibility of "legal transplants", *Maastricht Journal of European and Comparative Law*, 4(1), 111–24.

— 1999a. John Henry Merryman and comparative legal studies: A dialogue, *American Journal of Comparative Law*, 47(1), 3–66.

— 1999b. *Fragments on Law as Culture*, Deventer: Tjeenk Willink.

Legrand, P. and Munday, R. (eds) 2002. *Comparative Legal Studies: Traditions and Transitions*, Cambridge: Cambridge University Press.

Leruth, M.F. 1998. The Neorepublican Discourse on French National Identity, *French Politics and Society*, 16(4), 49–60.

Llewellyn, K. 1930. A realistic jurisprudence—the next step, *Columbia Law Review*, 30(4), 431–65.

Lombardi, C.B. 1998. Islamic law as a source of constitutional law in Egypt: The constitutionalization of the sharia in a modern Arab state, *Columbia Journal of Transnational Law*, 37(1), 81–124.

Low, S.M. and Lawrence-Zúñiga, D. (eds) 2003. *The Anthropology of Space and Place: Locating Culture*, Malden, Mass.: Blackwell.

Lund, T. 2006. Some interesting medieval dower cases, *University of Toledo Law Review*, 37(3), 659–704.

McCauliff, C.M.A. 1992. The medieval origin of the doctrine of estates in land: Substantive property law, family considerations, and the interests of women, *Tulane Law Review*, 66(4), 919–1014.

Macdonald, R.A. 1986. Pour la reconnaissance d'une normativité implicite et "inférentielle," *Sociologie et Sociétés*, 18(1), 47–58.

— 1996. Les vieilles gardes: hypothèses sur l'émergence des normes, l'internormativité et le désordre à travers une typologie des institutions normatives, in Belley, J.G. (ed.) *Le Droit Soluble: Contributions Quebecoises à l'Etude l'Internormativité*, Paris: Librerie Générale de Droit et de Jurisprudence, 233–72.

— 2004. The acoustics of accountability: Towards well-tempered tribunals, in Sajo, A. (ed.) *Judicial Integrity*, Boston: Nijhoff, 141–81.

— 2005. Kaleidoscopic federalism, in Gaudreault-DesBiens, J.F. and Gélinas, F. (eds) *The States and Moods of Federalism: Governance, Identity and Methodology*, Montreal: Yvon Blais, 261–83.

— 2007. Here, there … and everywhere: Theorizing Jacques Vanderlinden; theorizing legal pluralism, in Kasirer, N. (ed.) *Étudier et Enseigner le Droit: Hier, Aujourd'hui et Demain – Études Offertes à Jacques Vanderlinden*, Montreal: Yvon Blais, 381–413.

— unpublished. *Pluralistic Human Rights; Universal Human Wrongs*.

Macedo, S. 1998. Transformative constitutionalism and the case of religion: Defending the moderate hegemony of liberalism, *Political Theory*, 26(1), 56–80.

Maghniyyah, M.J. 1995. *The Five Schools of Islamic Law*, 1st edn, Qum, Iran: Anssariyan.

Manji, I. 2004. *The Trouble with Islam: A Muslim's Call for Reform in her Faith*, New York: St. Martin's Press.

Marshall, L.C. 1985. The religion clauses and compelled religious divorces: A study in marital and constitutional separations, *Northwestern University Law Review*, 80(1), 204–58.

Marx, K. 1978. On the Jewish question, in Tucker, R.C. (ed.) *The Marx-Engels Reader*, New York: Norton, 26–52.

Mashhour, A. 2005. Islamic law and gender equality—could there be a common ground?: A study of divorce and polygamy in sharia law and contemporary legislation in Tunisia and Egypt, *Human Rights Quarterly*, 27(2), 562–96.

Mattei, U.A. 1994a. Efficiency in legal transplants: An essay in comparative law and economics, *International Review of Law and Economics*, 14(4), 3–19.

Mehdi, R. 2005. Facing the enigma: Talaq-e-tafweez a need of Muslim women in Nordic perspective, *International Journal of the Sociology of Law*, 33(3), 133–47.

Melissaris, E. 2004. The more the merrier? A new take on legal pluralism, *Social and Legal Studies*, 13(1), 57–79.

Mernissi, F. 1998. A feminist interpretation of women's rights in Islam, in Kurzman, C. (ed.) *Liberal Islam: A Sourcebook*, Oxford: Oxford University Press, 112–26.

Merry, S.E. 1986. Everyday understandings of the law in working-class America, *American Ethnologist*, 13(2), 253–70.

— 1988. Legal pluralism: A literature review, *Law & Society Review*, 22(5), 869–96.

Mill, J.S. 1859. *On Liberty*, London: J.W. Parker.

Minow, M.L. 1997. *Not Only For Myself: Identity, Politics and Law*, New York: The New Press.

— 2000. About women, about culture: About them, about us, *Daedalus*, 129(4), 125–45.

Mir-Hosseini, Z. 1993. *Marriage on Trial: A Study of Islamic Family Law: Iran and Morocco Compared*, London: I.B. Tauris & Co.

— 2000. *Marriage on Trial: A Study of Islamic Family Law: Iran and Morocco Compared*, revised edn, London: I.B. Tauris & Co.

Mnookin, R. and Kornhauser, L. 1979. Bargaining in the shadow of the law: The case of divorce, *Yale Law Journal*, 88(5), 950–97.

Monateri, P.G. 1998a. "Everybody's talking": The future of comparative law, *Hastings International and Comparative Law Review*, 21(4), 825–46.

— 1998b. The "weak" law: Contaminations and Legal cultures, in *Italian National Reports for the XVth International Congress of Comparative Law, Bristol 1998*, Milano: Guiffre Editore.

— 2000. A quest for the multicultural origins of the "Western legal tradition", *Hastings Law Journal*, 51(3), 479–556.

Morse, A., Jr. and Sayeh, L. 1995. Tunisia: Marriage, divorce and foreign recognition, *Family Law Quarterly*, 29(3), 701–20.

Muir-Watt, H. 2000. La fonction subversive du droit comparé, *Revue Internationale de Droit Comparé*, 52(3), 503–27.

Mundy, M. 1988. The family, inheritance and Islam: A re-examination of the sociology of fara'id law, in al-Azmeh, A. (ed.) *Islamic Law in its Social and Historical Context*, London: Routledge, 1–123.

Nasir, J.J. 1994. *The Status of Women Under Islamic Law and Under Modern Islamic Legislation*, London: Graham & Trotman.

— 2002. *The Islamic Law of Personal Status*, 3rd edn, The Hague and New York: Kluwer Law International.

Nichols, J.A. 2007. Multi-tiered marriage: Ideas and influences from New York and Louisiana to the international community, *Vanderbilt Journal of Transnational Law*, 40, 135–96.

Nussbaum, M.C. 1999. *Sex and Social Justice*, Oxford: Oxford University Press.

— 2000. *Women and Human Development: The Capabilities Approach*, Cambridge: Cambridge University Press.

Okin, S.M. 1998. Feminism and multiculturalism: Some tensions, *Ethics*, 108(4), 661–84.

— 1999. Is multiculturalism bad for women? in Cohen, J., Howard, M. and Nussbaum, M.C. (eds) *Is Multiculturalism Bad for Women?: Susan Moller Okin with Respondents*, Princeton: Princeton University Press, 7–26.

Oppermann, B. 2006. The impact of legal pluralism on women's status: An examination of marriage laws in Egypt, South Africa, and the United States, *Hastings Women's Law Journal*, 17(1), 65–92.

Pallesmaa, J. 1996. *The Eyes of the Skin*, London: Academy Editions.

Pearl, D. and Menski, W. 1998. *Muslim Family Law*, 3rd edn, London: Sweet & Maxwell.

Peletz, M.G. 2002. *Islamic Modern: Religious Courts and Cultural Politics in Malaysia*, Princeton: Princeton University Press.

Pineau, J. 1992. La philosophie générale du nouveau Code civil du Québec, *Canadian Bar Review*, 71(3), 423–44.

Poirier, D. and Boudreau, M. 1992. Formal versus real equality in separation agreements in New Brunswick, *Canadian Journal of Family Law*, 10(2), 239–56.

Porras, I.M. 1995. On terrorism: Reflections on violence and the outlaw, in Danielsen, D. and Engle, K. (eds) *After Identity: A Reader in Law and Culture*, New York and London: Routledge, 294–313.

Pound, R. 1909. Liberty of contract, *Yale Law Journal*, 18(7), 454–87.

— 1910. Law in books and law in action, *American Law Review*, 44(1), 12–36.

— 1954. The role of the will in law, *Harvard Law Review*, 68(1), 1–19.

Powers, D.S. 1986. *Studies in Qur'an and Hadith: The Formation of the Islamic Law of Inheritance*, Berkeley: University of California Press.

Pratt Ewing, K. 2000. Legislating religious freedom: Muslim challenges to the relationship between "church" and "state" in Germany and France, *Daedalus*, 129(4), 31–54.

Rahim, A. 1911. *The Principles of Muhammadan Jurisprudence: According to the Hanafi, Maliki, Shafi'i and Hanbali Schools*, Lahore: P.L.D Publishers.

Rapoport, Y. 2000. Matrimonial gifts in early Islamic Egypt, *Islamic Law and Society*, 7(1), 1–36.

Reisman, M. 1999. *Law in Brief Encounters*, New Haven: Yale University Press.

Riles, A. (ed.). 2001. *Rethinking the Masters of Comparative Law*, Oxford: Hart Publishing.

Robbers, G. 2000. The legal status of Islam in Germany, in S. Ferrari and Bradney, A. (eds) *Islam and European Legal Systems*, Aldershot: Ashgate Dartmouth, 147–54.

Rohe, M. 2003. Islamic law in German courts, *Hawwa: Journal of Women in the Middle East and the Islamic World*, 1(1), 46–59.

— 2004a. The legal treatment of Muslims in Germany, in Aluffi Beck-Peccoz, R. and Zincone, G. (eds) *The Legal Treatment of Islamic Minorities in Europe*, Leuven: Peeters, 83–108.

— 2004b. The formation of a European shari'a, in Malik, J. (ed.) *Muslims in Europe: From the Margin to the Centre*, Munster: Lit Verlag, 161–84.

Rude-Antoine, E. 1990. *Le Mariage Maghrébin en France*, Paris: Éditions Karthala.

— 1992. *L'Immigration Face Aux Lois de la République*, Paris: Editions Karthala.

— 1997. *Des Vies et des Familles. Les Immigrés, la Loi et la Coutume*, Paris: Editions Odile Jacob.

Ruxton, F.H. 1916. *Maliki Law: A Summary from the French Translation of Mukhtasar Sidi Khalil*, London: Luzac.

Ryder, B. 2008. The Canadian conception of equal religious citizenship, in Moon, R. (ed.) *Law and Religious Pluralism in Canada*, Vancouver: UBC Press, 87–109.

Sacco, R. 1991. Legal formants: A dynamic approach to comparative law, *American Journal of Comparative Law*, 39(1), 1–34.

Safran, W. 1991. State, nation, national identity, and citizenship: France as a test case, *International Political Science Review*, 12(2), 219–38.

Saïd, E.W. 1978. *Orientalism*, New York: Vintage Books.

Samiuddin, A. and Khanam, R. (eds). 2002. *Muslim Feminism and Feminist Movement (South-East Asia)*, Delhi: Global Vision Publishing House.

Savigny, F.C. von. 1975 (1831). *Of the Vocation of Our Age for Legislation and Jurisprudence*, translated by A. Hayward, New York: Arno Press.

Schacht, J. 1982. *Introduction to Islamic Law*, Oxford: Clarendon Press.

Schleifer, A. 1985. The legal aspects of marriage according to Hanafi Fiqh, *The Islamic Quarterly*, 39(4), 193–219.

Schneider, E. 1986a. Describing and changing: Women's self-defense work and the problem of expert testimony on battering, *Women's Rights Law Reporter*, 9(3/4), 195–222.

— 1986b. The dialectic of rights and politics: Perspectives from the women's movement, *New York University Law Review*, 61(4), 589–653.

Schultz, M.M. 1982. Contractual ordering of marriage: A new model for state policy, *California Law Review*, 70(2), 204–334.

Séguin, R. 2005. Quebec squashes idea of Islamic tribunals, *The Globe and Mail*, 27 May, A1.

Shaffer, M. and Rogerson, C. 2003. Contracting spousal support: Thinking through *Miglin*, *Canadian Family Law Quarterly*, 21(1), 49–101.

Shah, P. 2009. Transforming to accommodate? Reflections on the shari'a debate in Britain, in Grillo, R. et al. (eds) *Legal Practice and Cultural Diversity*, Surrey, England: Ashgate, 73–91.

Shalakany, A. 2001a. Between identity and redistribution: Sanhuri, genealogy and the will to Islamise, *Islamic Law and Society*, 8(2), 201–44.

— 2001b. The origins of comparative law in the Arab world, or how sometimes losing your *asalah* can be good for you, in Riles, A. (ed.) *Rethinking the Masters of Comparative Law*, Oxford: Hart Publishing, 152–89.

Siegel, R.B. 1994. Home as work: The first woman's rights claims concerning wives' household labor, *Yale Law Journal*, 103(5), 1073–218.

Singerman, D. 1995. *Avenues of Participation: Family, Politics, and Networks in Urban Quarters of Cairo*, Princeton: Princeton University Press.

Smith, S.D. 2004. The pluralist predicament: contemporary theorizing in the law of religious freedom, *Legal Theory*, 10(2), 51–76.

Stake, J.E. 1992. Mandatory planning for divorce, *Vanderbilt Law Review*, 45(2), 397–454.

Stark, B. 2005. *International Family Law*, Aldershot: Ashgate.

Swisher, P.N. 1979. Divorce planning in antenuptial agreements: Toward a new objectivity, *University of Richmond Law Review*, 13(2), 175–96.

Taguieff, P.-A. 1995. L'Identité Nationale: Un Débat Français. Regards Sur l'Actualité, no. 209–210, Paris: La Documentation Français, 13–28.

Tamanaha, B.Z. 1993. The folly of the "social scientific" concept of legal pluralism, *Journal of Law and Society*, 20(2), 192–217.

— 1995. An analytical map of social scientific approaches to the concept of law, *Oxford Journal of Legal Studies*, 15(3), 501–35.

— 2000. A non-essentialist version of legal pluralism, *Journal of Law and Society*, 27(2), 296–321.

Taussig, M. 1993. *Mimesis and Alterity*, New York: Routledge.

Taylor, C. 1994. The politics of recognition, in Gutmann, A. (ed.) *Multiculturalism: Examining the Politics of Recognition*, Princeton: Princeton University Press, 25–73.

Teubner, G. 1997. Breaking frames: The global interplay of legal and social systems, *American Journal of Comparative Law*, 45(1), 149–69.

Trebilcock, M.J. and Keshvani, R. 1991. The role of private ordering in family law: A law and economics perspective, *University of Toronto Law Journal*, 41(4), 533–90.

Tucker, J.E. 1985. *Women in Nineteenth-century Egypt*, Cambridge: Cambridge University Press.

Turpin, D. 1994. La réforme de la condition des étrangers par les lois des 24 août et 30 décembre 1993, et par la loi du 25 novembre 1993, *Revue Critique de Droit International Privé*, Jan–Mar, 1–61.

Tushnet, M. 1996. Defending the indeterminacy thesis, *Quinnipiac Law Review*, 16(3), 339–56.

Tussman, J. and tenBrock, J. 1949. The equal protection of the laws, *California Law Review*, 37(3), 341–81.

Van Praagh, S. 1992. Stories in law school: An essay on language, participation, and the power of legal education, *Columbia Journal of Gender and Law*, 2(1), 111–44.

— 1996. The chutzpah of chasidism, *Canadian Journal of Law and Society*, 11(2), 193–216.

— 2008. View from the *succah*: Religion and neighbourly relations, in Moon, R. (ed.) *Law and Religious Pluralism in Canada*, Vancouver: UBC Press, 21–40.

Venkatraman, B.A. 1995. Islamic states and the United Nations Convention on the elimination of all forms of discrimination against women: Are the *shari'a* and the convention compatible? *American University Law Review*, 44(5), 1949–2028.

Vocking, H. 1993. Organisations as attempts at integration of Muslims in Germany, in Speelman, G. et al. (eds) *Muslims and Christians in Europe: Breaking New Ground—Essays in Honour of Jan Slomp*, Kampen: Kok, 100–11.

Von Jhering, R. 1951. In the heaven of legal concepts: A fantasy (1884) (selections), in Cohen, M.R. and Cohen, F.S. (eds) *Readings in Jurisprudence and Legal Philosophy*, Boston: Little, Brown and Company, 678–89.

Wani, M.A. 1987. *Maintenance Rights of Muslim Women: Principles, Precedents and Trends*, New Delhi: Genuine Publications.

— 1995. *The Islamic Law on Maintenance of Women, Children, Parents and Other Relatives: Classical Principles and Modern Legislations from India and Muslim Countries*, Kashmir: Upright Study Home.

— 1996. *The Islamic Institution of Mahr: A Study of its Philosophy, Working and Related Legislations in the Contemporary World*, 1st edn, Kashmir: Upright Study Home.

Watson, A. 1974. *Legal Transplants: An Approach to Comparative Law*, Edinburgh: Scottish Academic Press, Edinburgh.

— 1993. *Legal Transplants*, 2nd edn, Atlanta: University of Georgia Press.

— 1995. From legal transplants to legal formats, *American Journal of Comparative Law*, 43(3), 469–76.

— 1996. Aspects of reception of law, *American Journal of Comparative Law*, 44(2), 335–52.

— 2000. *Legal Transplants Again: Ius Commune Lectures on European Private Law*, Maastricht: Research School Ius Commune, Maastricht.

Wax, A.L. 1998. Bargaining in the shadow the market: Is there a future for egalitarian marriage? *Virginia Law Review*, 84(4), 509–672.

Welchman, L. 2007. *Women and Muslim Family Laws in Arab States: A Comparative Overview of Textual Development and Advocacy*, Amsterdam: Amsterdam University Press.

Zahra, M.A. 1955. Family law, in Khadduri, M. and Liebesny, H.J. (eds) *Law in the Middle East*, Washington: Middle East Institute, 132–78.

Index